Looting and Rape in Wartime

PENNSYLVANIA STUDIES IN HUMAN RIGHTS

Bert B. Lockwood, Jr., Series Editor

A complete list of books in the series is available from the publisher.

LOOTING AND
RAPE IN WARTIME

LAW AND CHANGE IN

INTERNATIONAL RELATIONS

TUBA INAL

PENN

UNIVERSITY OF PENNSYLVANIA PRESS

PHILADELPHIA

Published by
University of Pennsylvania Press
Philadelphia, Pennsylvania 19104-4112
www.upenn.edu/pennpress

Printed in the United States of America on acid-free paper
10 9 8 7 6 5 4 3 2 1

Library of Congress Cataloging-in-Publication Data
Inal, Tuba.
    Looting and rape in wartime : law and change in international relations / Tuba Inal—1st ed.
        p.   cm.—(Pennsylvania studies in human rights)
    Includes bibliographical references and index.
    ISBN: 978-0-8122-4476-2 (hardcover : alk. paper)
    1. Rape as a weapon of war. 2. Pillage. 3. War crimes. 4. Women—Crimes against
5. Women (International law). 6. International relations. I. Title. II. Series: Pennsylvania studies in human rights.
KZ7162.I53   2013
341.4'83   2012038309

To my parents

Contents

Chapter 1

Prohibition Regimes

One of the important questions in international relations theory is "Why and how does change happen (if it happens at all)?" This question is especially critical in the central form of international relations, which is the conduct of war. According to the mainstream theories of international relations, particularly realism, in an anarchical world where states (the main actors in international relations) are primarily concerned about survival, war, as the ultimate resort of states, is one area where we should be deeply pessimistic about change. Why, then, do states make laws binding themselves to change the ways they conduct war? And how is it that a practice long considered perfectly normal in war comes to be perceived as abnormal and becomes the subject of an international prohibition?

This book explores when and why states prohibited two closely associated practices in war—namely, pillage and rape. Given that women had historically been considered the property of men,[1] why did the international laws that regulated pillage of property not include "pillage" of women—that is, why did the regulations against rape develop almost a hundred years later than the ones against pillage? Although rape and loot continued to go hand in hand for centuries,[2] why were both eventually prohibited and why was one prohibited before the other?

Feminist international relations scholars have long argued that gender ideologies and the marginalization of women within political institutions are at the root of the perpetuation of certain structures in international relations—whether it is the lack of change or the direction of change.[3] The historical discrepancy between the handling of rape and pillage by international law, therefore, brings out a second question. How can this historical discrepancy help us understand the impact of gender on change in international relations?

By explaining specific questions about the development of the prohibition regimes against pillage and rape in war, this book addresses two related theoretical issues: how change happens in international relations and the role of gender as a category in this process of change.

For a prohibition regime to emerge, certain material factors, ideational factors, and agents must be at work. While material factors alone cannot explain the regime changes, they need to be taken into consideration since states do make calculations (regarding the material costs and benefits of any action) when they create and sign on to international laws. In this respect, the costs and benefits of continuing or discontinuing certain practices in war should be examined. Two types of ideational factors also need consideration. The first is the ideas about the practice (including the normative context with core norms and the normative shocks); the second is the belief, on the part of states, in the preventability of that particular practice. The agents (the norm entrepreneurs both within and outside the state apparatus) who were active in the promotion and creation of these prohibition regimes constitute the third focal point of this study. In this story of regime emergence, gender—both as a socially constructed ideology and as a barrier to exclude women from institutions and processes like international lawmaking—appears as the key to solve the puzzle of why the prohibition regime against rape emerged almost a hundred years later than the regime against pillage.

Regimes and Prohibition Regimes

What is a regime? What is a prohibition regime? And how do we know whether a regime and a prohibition regime exist? Furthermore, why and how do regimes in general and prohibition regimes in particular emerge and develop?

What Is a Regime? What Is a Prohibition Regime?

A regime is "sets of implicit or explicit principles, norms, rules, and decision-making procedures around which actors' expectations converge in a given area of international relations."[4] The major theoretical concern of this book is how a certain principle or behavior becomes the norm and rule, that is, how actors' expectations about following certain principles and behaving in certain ways converge at a certain point in time. The focus will be on a particular kind of regime, a prohibition regime:

> Global prohibition regimes are made up of a certain kind of norms, which prohibit, both in international law and in the domestic criminal laws of states, the involvement of state and non-state actors in particular activities. . . . These norms strictly circumscribe the conditions under which states can participate in and authorize these activities and proscribe all involvement by non-state actors. Those who refuse or fail to conform are labeled deviants and condemned not just by states but by most communities and individuals as well.[5]

States and people come to consider particular activities "deviant" as the regime emerges and they seek to suppress them. Therefore, prohibition regimes exist where "the substance of these [prohibitory] norms and processes by which they are enforced are institutionalized."[6] These regimes are like "municipal criminal laws" that ban activities rather than regulating them, and they seek to protect state and individual interests by providing order, security, and justice. By deterring and punishing the "deviant" activities through force (criminal justice or military measures), these regimes also "give force and symbolic representation to the moral values, beliefs and prejudices of those who make the laws."[7]

The cases I discuss fit into these definitions of global prohibition regimes. Pillage (or looting, plunder, sacking, "appropriation of property") in war is the first case. Defined as the forceful acquisition, seizure, or destruction of property of the inhabitants of a town or place by the soldiers of an invading army without proper compensation to the owners, pillage was a normal part of war for centuries. To name just a few examples, the Visigoths pillaged Rome in 409 and the Vandals pillaged the city in 455; the Crusaders pillaged Belgrade and many villages and towns in Asia Minor in 1096, Jerusalem in 1099, and Constantinople and the Greek islands in 1204; the Napoleonic armies looted Italian towns in 1805–6, and in return the Russian army looted the French countryside. These lootings included destruction and plunder of food, gold, silver, art treasures, holy relics (as in the case of Constantinople), literary classics, and all kinds of transportation resources, such as horses. Here is how a local historian described the pillage of the French countryside:

> They wanted the ruin, the devastation, the desolation and the destruction to complete their demented task of pillage. They shattered doors

and windows, panes of glass, hacked down paneling . . . ripped up tiles, burnt barns and haystacks, destroyed shrines, vineyards, broke up implements and tools, and threw into the gutter the phials and glass jars of the pharmacists.[8]

Eventually, pillage became undesirable and deviant, and the norm against pillage prohibited the involvement of states and their armies in the practice, with an aim of granting more order and security to people involved in a military invasion.[9] The prohibition against pillage also clearly reflected the moral values and beliefs of the time, such as the liberal values of progress, civilized behavior, and the sanctity of private property.

Various legal bodies and texts have defined rape in different ways. For the purposes of this book, the definition adopted by the International Criminal Tribunal for Rwanda (ICTR) is used: "a physical invasion of a sexual nature, committed on a person under circumstances which are coercive."[10] Throughout history, it is almost impossible to find a war where rape did not happen. To give just a few historical examples, Crusaders raped women as they marched to Constantinople in 1096 and 1204; German troops raped Belgian women in World War I; Russian troops raped German women and Japanese troops raped Chinese women in World War II; Pakistani soldiers raped Bangladeshi women in 1971; and American soldiers raped Vietnamese women during the Vietnam War. Rape, too, came to be regarded as deviant and undesirable and eventually was prohibited. The regime that ultimately banned rape in war should be considered a prohibition regime because it banned rather than regulated the activity.

How Do We Know a Prohibition Regime When We See One?

Although we define regimes as "sets of implicit or explicit principles, norms, rules and decision-making procedures,"[11] it is hard to detect the existence of implicit regimes, especially in the security realm where military necessity or security interests may render them invisible. Therefore, I am interested in explicit regimes, in particular, legalized regimes. Here, following Abbott and Snidal, legalization means "legally binding obligations that are precise and that delegate authority for interpreting and implementing the law."[12] Subjecting a clause of an international legal document to "the legalization test for international regimes" put forward by Abbott et al. can help us determine whether the clause can be considered a prohibition against an activity.[13]

This kind of formal understanding of law attracts some level of criticism.[14] Martha Finnemore and Stephen J. Toope, for instance, criticize formal approaches to legalization by saying that they ignore customary international law as well as interstitial law.[15] Some of their criticisms should be taken very seriously, and the main focus of this book is an attempt to answer some of the very important questions they raise against this framework (e.g., is legalization a dependent variable or an independent one? If legalization is a phenomenon to be explained, what other factors might explain it, and how important are they?).[16] A less formal approach, however, will not explain some very important issues raised by Finnemore and Toope's framework, and my investigation resides at the heart of these issues: Why are some parts of the customary and interstitial laws legalized and some left out? Why are states willing to formally codify some parts of customary laws and not others? More specifically (and to repeat the initial question in this context), given that women had historically been considered the property of their husbands (or fathers) and given that both pillage and rape had long been prohibited by customary law,[17] why did states choose to codify pillage as a violation of international law yet neglect rape for almost a century after that codification? Therefore, I approach the subject of regime change from a legalistic point of view, associating normative changes with positive legal changes that followed them. I use the definition of legalization put forward by Abbott et al. in a special issue of the journal *International Organization* called *Legalization and World Politics* and their distinction between "hard legalization" and "soft legalization." The "hardness" of a prohibition regime's legalization establishes its existence.

Abbott et al. define legalization in terms of the characteristics of rules and procedures of institutional forms and laws. In order to determine the level of legalization, they look at its three components: obligation, precision, and delegation. *Obligation* means whether states are "bound by a rule or commitment in the sense that their behavior thereunder is subject to scrutiny under the general rules, procedures, and discourse of international law, and often of domestic law as well." It can range from an expressly nonlegal norm on the lower end to a binding rule (*jus cogens*) on the higher end.[18] *Precision* is the degree to which the rules unambiguously define the conduct they require, authorize, or prescribe (or prohibit). Therefore, the rules of a regime may be vague or highly elaborated and precise. *Delegation* occurs when the regime grants third parties authority to implement, interpret, and apply the rules. A high form of delegation is when there is an international court, organization or a mechanism for domestic application as opposed to leaving it to diplomacy.[19]

Abbott et al. use a scale in which each of the components of legalization may rank high, moderate, or low.[20] They also use certain indicators in order to place certain regimes on these scales.[21] Based on this theoretical framework, a prohibition regime is defined as a particular category of norms prohibiting a particular activity by state and non-state actors through an international legal document that is legally binding, precise, and that possibly delegates authority for interpretation and implementation. Therefore, in order to determine when a prohibition regime is created, it is necessary to look for a high degree of obligation and precision, combined with at least a low degree of delegation.

The Cases

Using Abbott et al.'s approach through tests of obligation, precision, and delegation to detect the codification of the prohibitions of these two practices in war, and examining four documents of international law to trace the codifications, establish almost a 100-year gap between the prohibitions of pillage and rape (see Table 1). The international legal documents under consideration are the Hague Conventions of 1899 and 1907, as the first pieces of codified laws of land warfare; the Geneva Conventions of 1949, which were written after World War II in order to ensure better protection of civilians in war; the Additional Protocols to the Geneva Conventions (1949), accepted in 1977 to adapt the laws of war to new military technologies and types of war; and the Rome Statute of 1998, establishing the International Criminal Court (ICC) in order to judge the most serious international crimes.

Table 1. Emergence of Prohibition Regimes for Pillage and Rape in War

		Obligation	Precision	Delegation
Pillage	The Hague (1907)	High	High	Moderate-low
	Geneva (1949)	High	High	High
Rape	The Hague (1907)	N/A	N/A	N/A
	Geneva (1949)	Low	Moderate-low	Low
	Geneva (1977)	Moderate	High	Low
	Rome Statute (1998)	High	High	High

Why and How Does a Regime Develop?

"How and when international political orders [including international regimes] are created, maintained, changed and abandoned"[22] is one of the important questions of international relations theory. When we look at the literature explaining international regimes, we see three groups of approaches: power-based approaches such as realism, interest-based approaches such as neoliberal institutionalism, and knowledge-based approaches such as constructivism.[23] Since *power-based approaches* consider regimes as products of the distribution of power in the international system or the tools of the powerful states, therefore showing little causal significance, they are unable to explain why they emerge without the involvement of powerful state interests (in the realist sense) or why they change and die without corresponding changes in the distribution of power.[24] While a brief exploration of possible powerful state interests or changes in the distribution of power behind the creation of these two prohibition regimes is warranted, it is necessary to concentrate on the other two groups of approaches.

Interest-based approaches look at regimes in terms of "logic of consequentiality."[25] In other words, they see regimes emerging as a result of the recognition of mutual interests by the states. According to this approach, states are self-interested, goal-seeking actors with rationally ordered preferences ensuring maximum utility, which are stable over time. When there is a collective action problem that prevents states from achieving their objectives in the most efficient way, regimes develop to facilitate coordination and cooperation under interdependence. Therefore, regimes are consequentially formed for achieving common interests, and change happens when interests change. As Goldstein et al. put it for the issue of creation of international law, "Law [is] deeply embedded in politics: affected by political interests, power, and institutions."[26] In this approach, what leads to regime development and legalization are not the norms underlying the process but the interests and strategic choices of actors. Although some of the theorists of these approaches acknowledge the importance of ideas in triggering the formation of regimes,[27] they do so only when they cannot explain the emergence of a regime through material interests; they fail to elucidate "why some ideas and not others find their way into policy."[28]

Knowledge-based approaches, however, look at regimes in terms of "logic of appropriateness."[29] In this approach, state interests are not exogenous, but are derived from ideas and constructed through social interaction.[30] The sources of regimes are the intersubjective relationships between states and the international system constituting state identities, which instruct appropriate behavior in a given situation. Knowledge-based approaches assert that the ideas that instruct and form regimes come from states, non-state actors (both nongovernmental and intergovernmental organizations),[31] or historical contingencies,[32] and that these ideas trigger change.

So how exactly does a prohibition regime emerge? According to Nadelmann, although international regimes usually reflect the interest structures of their members, moral and emotional factors play a role in their creation as well. This is especially true in the case of prohibition regimes, which, Nadelmann contends, "like criminal laws, tend to involve moral and emotional considerations more so than most other laws and regimes."[33] He emphasizes the role of "moral proselytism" and how the desire to reconstruct the world in one's own image on the part of both states and non-state actors plays an important role in international politics.[34] In order to find out whether that is the case, we must determine how state interests, as opposed to ideas and emotions, play into the creation of a prohibition regime.

Both interest-based and knowledge-based approaches are necessary to explain the emergence of prohibition regimes in particular and change in general. Attempts to reconcile interest-based and knowledge-based approaches[35] were criticized by scholars who said that the sharp differences in the ontological assumptions of these two approaches make them incompatible.[36] According to knowledge-based approaches, since state behavior (including regime formation) is a product of social structures constructing rules, norms, and social identities, interest-based ontology—with its assumptions of a presupposed rationality and state interests pursued by this rationality—cannot be reconciled with their sociological ontology. These scholars argue that the divide between the knowledge-based ideas of states as role-players (acting on the basis of the logic of appropriateness) and interest-based ideas of states as utility-maximizers (acting on the basis of the logic of consequentiality) does not allow for a synthesis.

I agree that it is not possible to synthesize these two approaches; however, we can use both of them to explain different facets of a phenomenon in international relations. It is analytically useful to assume that states are rational actors and that they try to maximize their utility—presupposing that their utility or interest is defined by the norms, rules, ideas, and their identities, and that utility maximization is a role they are assigned to play by their identity of being a nation-state at a certain point in history. The process (or social construction) through which these identities (and hence interests) are defined brings about state behavior and historical outcomes or change.

This book seeks to explain the process of social construction that led to the creation of certain norms and laws and prevented the creation of others. Understanding the source of change, whether it be "humanitarian sentiments, ideas of chivalry and honor [or] points of agreement as to military convenience,"[37] requires an understanding of what I call the "core norms" or principles defining the "normative context" of a particular historical period and "normative shocks," which develop contingently. I also underline the role of the non-state actors or "norm entrepreneurs" both in the transformation of the normative context and in the transformation of potential events into normative shocks. Last, I argue that it is necessary to analyze the cost-benefit structures of the state actors that are not independent of the normative context.

For the purposes of this book, core norms are defined as beliefs and visions about one's self (person, social group, or state) and the characteristics that define that self, which become sources of behavioral norms about the appropriate behavior for that self, given these characteristics.[38] They are constitutive, creating actors with a particular identity and set of interests, hence becoming foundations for regulative norms like prohibition regimes.[39] Accordingly, "normative context" becomes the environment in which these core norms exist as a web of intersubjective meanings shared by groups of people or states. In order to help explain regime change, I use the concept of normative shocks.[40] In the context of prohibition regimes, normative shocks are tragic situations or events that shock the public conscience into focusing on particular activities or institutions and change the core norms, taking people out of the existing normative context and into another one.[41]

Although the concept of normative shock comes from the knowledge-based approaches—with their emphasis on how shocking events or crises change the way international actors see the world, hence their identities and the norms about appropriate behavior for these new identities—it is possible to find the idea of shock in interest-based approaches to international relations, too. For example, Oran Young, in his institutional bargaining model, underlines the importance of exogenous shocks in helping regime formation when actors obstruct the process as they maneuver for positional advantages and they lose track of the common interests. He argues that exogenous shocks such as the Chernobyl accident (1986) or the discovery of the ozone hole over Antarctica (1985) give the necessary boost to solve these collective action problems and they lead to the creation of the regimes by capturing and gal-vanizing attention.[42] An example from the economic realm is the emergence of the Keynesian paradigm after the Great Depression (1929), an economic catastrophe that led to the great departure from orthodoxy all around the world.[43]

The concept of normative shock that I am using, however, is different from the shock in these approaches in two related respects. First of all, nor-mative shocks are not solely related to material state interests and therefore are not always directly felt by the states. It is easier for states to create norms and laws related to their material interests as long as they agree among them-selves, that is, solve the collective action problem. Oran Young emphasizes that under these circumstances external shocking events are only necessary in order to put an issue on the international agenda and help states reach compromise among themselves. Yet what happens when the issue is not hurt-ing any material state interests, or when the creation of an international re-gime does not have an immediate impact on them? It appears that, for norms and laws related to human security, the processes, as well as the actors playing any role in these processes, are different. Actors and events that will create (non-material) state interests must be present; sometimes they will even cre-ate those state interests, despite competing material interests (such as in the case of land mines or some of the environmental norms).

The second difference regarding my conception of normative shocks, then, is that they are not exogenous. Most of the time, events that may be-come normative shocks happen without anybody recognizing them. Jeffrey Legro addresses this issue in his critique of the concept of an exogenous shock as an indeterminate explanation because it does not explain why similarly shocking events lead to different outcomes.[44] Mass rapes in Belgium in World War I, in Nanking and Germany during World War II, and in Bangladesh during its independence war (1971), to give just a few examples, had little to no effect on state behavior in creating a norm and law against rape. Even the more recent mass rapes in the former Yugoslavia were not as traumatic as Chernobyl as a slap in the face of states. Only after women's movements de-veloped a normative context in which violence against women is considered a human rights problem could occurrences of mass rape become shocking for the world.

World War II is another example where norm evolution processes re-quired a shock to bring people out of an existing normative framework and into another one. The exogenous shocks that World War II generated affected both international and domestic political systems, which "prove[d] that politics [and war] must be conducted differently or thought about differently."[45] As we see in Berger's analysis, for instance, the highly militaristic political-military cultures of Germany and Japan; thus their foreign policies were radically reshaped as a result of the material and spiritual blow of their defeat in the war.[46] The impact of the war was not something these states could overlook, and the exogenous shock directly led to change.

In the international arena, the impact of the shock of World War II reveals itself in the emergence (and universalization) of strong international human rights norms, institutions, and laws. One important development was the recognition of the flaws in the Hague Regulations (1907) regarding deportations from occupied territories. Theodor Meron says that because the international community believed deportation of civilians was not practiced on a large scale at the beginning of the twentieth century, the Hague Regulations failed to mention it explicitly. The shock of "Nazi Germany's resort to the large scale deportation of civilians for slave labor and extermination during the Second World War," however, "led the drafters to restate in Article 49 of the Fourth Geneva Convention an absolute prohibition [against such deportations]."[47] Yet why did the deportations that happened in nineteenth-century Europe go unrecognized and fail to trigger the norm and law change that revealed itself in the Hague Conventions?[48] The answer to this question deserves another research project, but the very fact that we can ask such a question shows the invisibility of human rights shocks in the absence of a proper normative context created through the agitation of some actors, and shows the intricate connection between the normative context and normative shocks.

As a result, the question posed by Kowert and Legro, "what counts as a shock, how shocking must shocks be and what will we say about the shocks that reinforce rather than change existing collective beliefs,"[49] can be answered by distinguishing between types of regimes. In the case of normative shocks, we need to recognize as well the importance of norm entrepreneurs (and experts or epistemic communities[50] in some issue areas). When we look at the two prohibition regimes against rape and pillage, the shockingness of the shock and (more frequently) the direction of the development of new norms and policies are determined by these entrepreneurs and experts to a large extent.[51]

The norm creation process—and the emergence, creation, or detection of a shock—is part of this study. Once the shock happens, norm entrepreneurs and experts provide the alternative policy prescriptions that derive from or build on their previous work, and whose emergence on the political agenda is made possible by the shock. The role these people play is crucial for creating the image of the shock in the human rights area, since human rights issues typically are invisible and disregarded—as opposed to, for instance, economic shocks, which are more objective and directly felt.[52] Whereas preparing the basis for the demand for policy change and the alternative (the mechanism or legal prescription in the case of prohibition regimes) and using these for the desired end once the shock occurs is common to all issue areas, when obvious state interests are not involved, for example in human rights issues, there is much more work to be done by the activists in making the shock a shock. In contrast, exogenous shocks make themselves felt with less need for external promotion. This means a normative shock will not be a shock without the part played by the norm entrepreneurs. But at the same time, norm entrepreneurs cannot influence the norm evolution process without an event that has the potential to become a shock.

On the issue of norm "prominence," Ann Florini also argues that contingency (like shock) plays a major role.[53] Crises are sources of political change, but in the end they are a matter of interpretation. Ideas and interpretations transform disastrous events into crises or shocks, but interpreters lack material in the absence of disastrous events. It is also important to understand why certain interpretations and ideas triumph over others,[54] which brings us back to the normative context and core norms. As Legro's analysis of change in international relations reveals, the effects of shocks depend on preexisting structures, so it is necessary to understand the interaction between events (shocks), collective ideas (normative context and core norms), and calculating agents (norm entrepreneurs) if we are to understand change.[55]

In the process of campaigning for a new norm and creating a normative shock, norm entrepreneurs use different tactics depending on the problem they are tackling. Regarding human rights issues, where shocks are often not obvious until some people make them so, one tactic is to associate the new issue with existing norms. "No norm exists in a vacuum," according to Florini; the new norm has to fit coherently with other prevailing norms.[56] Especially in the human rights area, these should be the core norms for a successful campaign because they are more immune to political contention. The successful campaign against the Atlantic slave trade, for instance, could not sustain itself on the basis of the prevailing norm of economic efficiency. It could gain impetus only when it was grounded on the core norms of the Enlightenment's promise of the natural rights of man.[57]

The fit between a new norm and existing core norms must be strongly emphasized to make the case: when the existing norm is already in international law, norm entrepreneurs must convince the audience that the emerging norm is a logical extension of that law or a necessary change to it if the existing law will fulfill its function at all.[58] Price describes this combination of an already existing framework on which the new norm can be built and the efforts of the norm entrepreneurs to use it appropriately as "grafting," or "the mix of genealogical heritage and conscious manipulation involved in such normative rooting and branching."[59]

In discussing the prohibition of pillage and rape in war, I will analyze the three cases: (1) creation of the prohibition regime against pillage, (2) noncreation of a prohibition regime against rape, and (3) creation of the prohibition regime against rape under four levels of normative context: core norms, normative shocks, norm entrepreneurs, and cost-benefit structures.[60]

The normative context that led to the creation of the prohibition of pillage in the nineteenth century consisted of three core norms related to Europeans' self-image —progress, civilization, and sanctity of private property. Political theorists had introduced and propagated these ideas starting in the eighteenth century; yet, the major actors who used them to call for a change in the conduct of war were the jurists and publicists of the nineteenth century.[61] The normative shock, in the case of pillage, came with the Revolutionary and Napoleonic Wars of the late eighteenth and early nineteenth centuries. Since these wars brought large-scale pillage back to Europe after a century of relative reduction of the practice, they provided the basis for its prohibition later in the nineteenth century.

Looking at the normative context of the nineteenth century with respect to women's status and the understanding of rape, we can expect that rape would not be prohibited as a violent outrage upon women. Women were considered the sexual property of men, and rape was unacceptable to the extent that it violated the property rights of gentlemen who "owned" the rape victims. Class was an important factor in making the wives and daughters of the propertied class off-limits while relegating the rape of lower-class women to a non-issue. Also noteworthy was the paradoxical implications of the word *rape* for the nineteenth-century European women who sought legal redress for the crime. As we will see in the case of England, if rape victims said they were raped and described the ordeal, they would be considered unrespectable. Since rape was a crime only when committed against a respectable woman, it became virtually impossible to prosecute and convict rapists.[62]

The absence of women from the law-making process at the Hague Conferences is significant, too.[63] Although nineteenth-century feminists were very much aware of the oppression of women by the rape laws in their countries, as well as by the crime itself and its societal consequences for the victims, their ideas and work did not take the form of transnational advocacy and did not reach The Hague. The fact that there were no women delegates at the conferences undoubtedly contributed to the issue's dereliction. Feminists have long argued that the state (and especially the military) are gendered institutions, and the absence of women from these institutions leads to the marginalization of women's issues within them.[64] According to feminist international relations scholars, one of the important facets of the marginalization of women in international relations is the use of myths that help to perpetuate war and exclude women from citizenship due to their exclusion from "armed civic virtue." Men as the proprietors of this armed civic virtue are valued and recognized as agents due to their contribution to the defense of sovereignty and security; they are the sovereign and warrior citizens, the defenders of the sovereign state and of the victimized, dependent, and weak citizens, that is, women. Women, on the other hand, are associated with peace, not seen as contributors to the protection of the sovereign state as warriors. As a result, women have traditionally become invisible, their voices have been marginalized, and they are unable to affect international relations due to their exclusion from positions of power—especially from war departments, foreign ministries, and international negotiations.[65]

Given that the number of women in a particular state institution directly correlates with the appearance and promotion of women's perspectives and interests on that institution's agenda,[66] it is not surprising that rape was excluded from the international legal documents written by male-dominated conferences. Access to institutions is a key component in influencing policy,[67] and the lack of access to the process of international lawmaking through state or non-state channels blocked women's agenda significantly.

Accordingly, once women became active participants in these international conferences, the prohibition of rape began to enter international law. We will see that the presence of women's issues in the final texts is directly linked to women's physical presence as active conference participants (see Table 2).

As a result of the prevailing normative context, which was not women-friendly, and the absence of actors to push for changes in that normative context in the international arena, a normative shock could not happen. In terms

Table 2. Participation of Women in Diplomatic Conferences

	Total number of delegates	Number of women delegates[a]	Percentage of women delegates	Number of women's organizations
Hague Peace Conferences 1899, 1907[b]	405	0	0	1[d]
Geneva Diplomatic Conference 1949	205	12	5.8	2[e]
Geneva Diplomatic Conferences 1974, 1975, 1976, 1977[c]	1,435	88	6.1	10
Rome Conference 1998	1,400	267	19	200-300

(a) Excludes administrative secretaries and administrative staff, but includes advisers.
(b) Total number of delegates in both conferences.
(c) The Additional Protocols to the Geneva Conventions of 1949 were prepared by these four conferences; number of delegates listed is the total for all four.
(d) ICW was not an official participant at the 1907 Conference, but submitted a petition.
(e) The International Alliance of Women and the World's Young Women's Christian Association were not official participants of the conference, although they communicated their demands to the ICRC beforehand.

of its pervasiveness in European wars, rape was not different from pillage. For instance, in 1898 a British author wrote about the Napoleonic Wars as disasters with far-reaching and horrible consequences from which the world had not yet been able to recuperate, among which he counts "slaughter, plunder, pestilence, agony, rape and ruin."[68] Among these disastrous events, only rape proved not shocking enough for the Europeans to address. The question still remains why rape did not enter into international law sooner, at least as a property crime. The normative context was conducive for such a framing in the law, so why were women not "property enough"? The second element of the ideational factors—that is, the ideas about the preventability of a practice—provides an answer. But in order to understand why this idea is important we must first look at the cost-benefit calculations that states make when they are considering international commitments.

International relations scholars approach the question of why states make international laws and why they make them the way they do from different perspectives. As with the regime theories (power-based, interest-based and knowledge-based), some scholars argue that states value international laws only as a potential tool to use against weaker states as it becomes convenient. This realist perspective asserts that in the anarchic world order, with no government above the states to enforce rules, states make these laws so that they can use them to further their national interests in the never-ending global struggle for power.[69] If states know that they can ignore and violate these laws when the laws contradict their interests, however, why do they negotiate these treaties so meticulously? Are they being extremely careful about every word in every article of a treaty in order to make sure that international law reflects their interests as much as possible and ensure relative gains against their enemies? If states have no intention of complying with the laws, knowing that in the end all comes down to who has more material power, why lose time, energy, and resources on something that is politically trivial?

In fact, when we look at the negotiations of these international treaties, a very different picture appears. The powerful states who, according to realists, determine the rules of the game seem to struggle the most to protect their power positions, and they do not always get their way, especially with humanitarian law. Rather, the evidence supports the traditional legal views of international law, where weaker states demand more legalization to protect themselves against the powerful.[70]

I do not argue that the power of a state does not mean anything, or that ideas like the nineteenth-century liberal euphoria in the case of the Hague Conference swept humanitarianism into all states. At The Hague in 1899, the meticulous negotiations that lasted six weeks demonstrate that some states, specifically Britain, tried to impair the project of codification. Britain's role is especially noteworthy—as the world's preeminent state, it had utmost power to both draw on and violate rules. So why did it try to prevent this codification of international law? General J. C. Ardagh, the British delegate, proposed that the conference accept the Brussels Declaration (1874) as a general basis for instruction on the laws and customs of war to be given to troops, without any pledge to accept all the articles as voted by the majority. For Britain, he said, having "full liberty to accept or modify the articles is of supreme importance."[71] Despite this intense opposition, the rules were codified, and Britain ultimately signed and ratified the convention.

Ultimately, realism cannot explain why states purposely excluded rape from the Hague Conventions (and, for the most part, from the subsequent

Geneva Conventions) when these agreements included prohibitions against other similar practices.

Neoliberals (the scholars of interest-based approaches) argue that since international law helps make cooperation under anarchy possible by furthering common interests and reducing uncertainty, states negotiate to make sure that international law will indeed serve these interests. In this respect, clear legal obligations on state parties, mechanisms for enforcement through reciprocity, and management through institutions are key factors that get the attention of states in international lawmaking.[72]

Constructivists (knowledge-based theorists) emphasize the centrality of norms and shared understandings of appropriate behavior that induce lawmaking and compliance, which means states do not want to make commitments they believe they cannot comply with.[73] Noncompliance has costs that states do not want to bear unnecessarily. Having a reputation as a legitimate, well-behaved member of the international society is important for states, and they do not want this reputation to be hurt by becoming "the spoilsport" or "the outlaw" who disrespects the most fundamental rules of international society.[74] One of the most important of these rules is *pacta sunt servanda* (pacts must be obeyed), whose existence leads to "distaste for breaking the law" on the part of all states.[75] Various documents of international law show signs of this thinking. In the words of the president of the Brussels Conference (1874), Russian delegate Baron Jomini, "It would be a wrong to the contracting parties to imagine that they could have the intention of not abiding by their agreement." Along the same lines, General den Beer Poortugael, the Dutch delegate at the Hague Peace Conference (1899), declared that "there is no better watchman than the nation's honor." He said that, since "Honor is like an isle with a steep and landless shore. When once it has been lost, it cannot be regained anymore," forfeiting an oath or an accepted agreement is unthinkable for nations, as with individuals unless they are willing to sacrifice their honor.[76]

The debates over the prohibition of pillage and many other topics in the international conferences I look at partly support the neoliberal argument. States usually strive to clarify obligations and enforcement mechanisms because "clear legal standards reinforce reciprocal enforcement by clarifying what acts constitute violations and which do not."[77] For example, during the first Hague Conference in 1899, recognizing that some states wanted to make some laws vague to be able to escape the violator status at times, neutral states demanded more clarification.[78] Complaining about the lack of precise articles on the rights and obligations of the neutral states, Mr. Eyschen, the delegate from Luxemburg, summarized the situation: "even if success in formulating precise rules were not always attained, it would be useful at all events to have it stated by the Conference that there is a controversy on certain points. In these cases pretensions would be less and conduct more restrained."[79]

Hard bargaining and desire for clarification in lawmaking, however, do not happen over every topic, and they do not happen solely for the purpose of preventing defection by other parties. States also demand clarification for knowing/making known exactly what they are committing themselves to. The desire to clarify the laws changes according to the perceived degree of difficulty of compliance on their part because they do not want to be accused of violation easily. When they believe it is impossible to comply, they do not commit and they do not want clarification stipulating any precise obligation. When they believe it is possible to comply, they strive to make the law very clear and detailed. As Abbott and Snidal's analysis demonstrates, when "preferences and capacities" of states are divergent, soft laws with less precision and limited delegation become more attractive to them.[80]

When we look at the long and hard process of writing these international laws, we see meticulous bargaining and outlining because states want the laws to work. We see careful negotiations over murky exceptions and constraints like "military necessity" inserted into the laws of war because states want valid justifications when rules are violated.[81] Therefore, we should expect them to avoid commitments on subjects that they believe are out of their hands, especially ones that cannot be justified by "military necessity."

As we will see in Chapters 2 and 4, the states in The Hague left the issue of the prohibition of rape vague on purpose, and the states decisively excluded rape from grave breaches[82] in the Geneva Conventions (1949). The debates in both The Hague and Geneva substantiate my expectations that states want to commit to a treaty because it serves (or does not conflict with) their perceived material interests and/or because they think it is the appropriate thing to do given their identities as members of the international society. They make these commitments only if they also believe that they can fulfill their obligations (to a reasonable degree), and they want more details and clarity over what constitutes obedience and violation for these commitments.

Pillage, like other practices that were prohibited, fits these requirements. The changes in the structure of armies and wars since the eighteenth century had already made pillage costly and undesirable for states. It broke the discipline of the army and compromised the relations between the army and the civilian population in their own countryside and in the occupied territories. It also lost its function of financing wars, since the modern state had already found taxation as the new source. Prohibiting pillage, therefore, would serve their interests, even though a multilateral treaty to do it was not necessary because the primary impetus for change came from their own pillage practices rather than their rival's. Prohibition through a multilateral treaty, however, would not hurt any state, either.

Pillage was also becoming more and more abhorrent in the eyes of the European public, who gave increasing weight to eighteenth-century ideas about the sanctity of private property, being civilized, and the progress toward higher forms of civilization. The Napoleonic Wars especially reminded European states how their identity was defined within these terms by demonstrating what kind of state behavior they did not want in Europe anymore.

Last but not least, states believed that they could prevent pillage. Conscripted armies of the nineteenth century were not like the mercenaries of the previous centuries, who joined the army primarily for booty; nineteenth-century armies were fighting for the nation, and as long as they were fed and clothed properly and kept under strict discipline in military camps, they could be prevented from pillaging.

Rape was surely as costly as pillage in terms of damaging army discipline and breeding hostility among the civilian population; in fact, that is precisely why army codes going back to the fourteenth century prohibited rape and pillage.[83] It was also a repulsive act for "civilized" Europeans. Even in the seventeenth century, Grotius wrote that rape was not an acceptable practice for "civilized" nations. Domestic rape cases in the late eighteenth and nineteenth centuries show that people did not even want to talk about rape in the context of the new prudery of the time. Toward the end of the nineteenth century, with the influence of evolutionary theory, people began to think of rapists as primitive organisms who ranked lower on the evolutionary scale. That is why aggressor states usually do not admit to rape, and victimized states use rape as a propaganda tool to show the savageness of the enemy.[84]

When it came to beliefs about its preventability, however, rape was drastically different from pillage. Historically, rape was considered a crime of passion that got out of control.[85] This was also the prevailing sentiment in the nineteenth century (as well as most of the twentieth century). Rape was seen solely as a sexual act, rather than an aggressive and violent manifestation of sexuality.[86]

With the growing influence of psychoanalysis at the beginning of the twentieth century, theories considering rape as a mental problem started to develop. Rapists were thought to have "character disorders" that made it impossible for them to control their impulses.[87] The "drive reduction" or "instinct" model using psychoanalysis explained male behavior of rape as an effect of inherent urges beyond immediate control.[88] This model argued that since male sexuality innately contains aggression due to the "primitive necessity of pursuit and penetration, whilst the female recognizes this and submits,"[89] rape happens when a mentally challenged man happens to be unable to control these urges. "Sexual offenders were often good citizens in all but this one respect,"[90] and "one of the best combat soldiers I have known"[91] were typical descriptions for rapists, which excused the behavior of the perpetrator.

The attitude toward rape in war is particularly revealing in terms of demonstrating the idea of inevitability. What some scholars called a "sexual deprivation theory" of military rape seems to have been pervasive in the minds of the military and the statesmen, as well as the general public, throughout much of history. According to this theory, because military personnel do not have many sexual opportunities, they satisfy their sexual impulses through rape.[92] Soldiers "revved up by war" and "needy" may get "briefly out of control" and, according to this mentality, it is "normal" to see rape as an unpleasant yet inevitable byproduct of war.[93] The fact that rape in war has been ubiquitous further allowed the military and statesmen to render it inevitable.[94]

This gendered ideology of rape as "inevitable," especially in war, had historically produced the use of brothels by militaries to "curb" the need for sex, and hence rape. Since rape is a discipline spoiler, states want to prevent it, yet decide they need to provide a sexual outlet for soldiers. Besides the desire to prevent the spread of venereal diseases, this "institutionalized rape" through the use of brothels serves the purpose of preventing something unpleasant (or the "indistinguishable part of a poisonous wartime stew called 'lootpillageandrape'") by providing something routine.[95]

Providing soldiers with prostitutes is not always possible either, due to the logistics of war or a domestic constituency's attitude toward prostitution, as we saw in the case of World War II and the United States army. And prostitution usually has not been able to prevent rape in war, as we see in the case of "comfort women"[96] and the Japanese army in World War II. Given the widespread beliefs about rape's inevitability, it is not surprising that states long avoided legal commitments to prevent rape in war.

A seeming contradiction surrounding states' reluctance to develop a prohibition regime against rape emerges from a look at military manuals and army codes. For instance, Richard II's laws in the fourteenth century and the Lieber Code in the nineteenth century prohibited rape in war and stipulated the death penalty for its perpetrators. States develop military codes to provide guidelines for soldiers in accomplishing specific tasks and, ultimately, victory in war. Soldiers who violate the codes may be court-martialed and punished because they hurt the mission or damage army discipline. Or the state may choose not to pursue the case; it is completely up to the state because the code belongs solely to the state. There is no direct humanitarian cause, commitment, or case at stake. Hence, states can put everything necessary for the accomplishment of military objectives into these codes without considering whether they will be able to enforce them. If they can, it will serve them; if they cannot, nothing happens. These examples demonstrate the significance of the difference between international commitments and domestic ones. States' army codes are not internationally binding. A state is free to enforce them or not and there is no international audience to question their enforcement.

It is clear that rape can be damaging to army discipline as well as to the relationship with civilian populations, so a state may want to include a prohibition against it in its army code. The code may prevent at least some incidences of rape (especially when the penalty is death), although states may still believe that rape is inevitable in war. If so many rapes happen that punishing all the perpetrators would be impossible without hurting the war effort, a state may choose not to do so. If states commit to an international law prohibiting rape, however, it becomes another story. Expectations as to the enforcement of international prohibition arise among the other members of the international society, and refraining from punishing the perpetrators will be considered violating the law or not fulfilling legal obligations, which seriously damages a state's reputation.

Chapter Overview

Prohibition Regime Against Pillage

I begin my investigation into the reasons for a difference in the development of prohibition regimes against pillage and rape in Chapter 2, by studying the Hague Conventions of 1899 and 1907 (in particular 1907 because of the additional measures it adds in terms of delegation), which established the prohibition regime against pillage. Considering the Hague Regulations in terms of the degree of obligation they bring for the state parties, we should place them at the high end of the obligation spectrum. Indeed, the whole Section III of the Convention with Respect to the Laws and Customs of War on Land (Hague II) is about the prohibitions and regulations regarding enemy's property.[97] Three different articles of Hague II formally prohibit pillage. Feilchenfeld interprets the existence of the word "formally" in Article 47 as an indicator of the "absolute character of the rule." He also says that the obligation for the occupying force created by the same article is to "both prevent and to punish pillaging" as well as "to restore pillaged property and to indemnify the owner."[98] The articles also very clearly require state parties to observe these prohibitions by issuing instructions to their armed forces in conformity with the Hague Regulations.[99] Louis Renault, a prominent international law professor, one of the dominant figures at the Hague Conference of 1907 as well as one of the winners of the Nobel Peace Prize in 1907, emphasized this point further in his Nobel lecture in 1908. He said that the inclusion, on the suggestion of the German delegation,[100] of a new article in the Hague Convention of 1907 (Article 3), making a violator state party subject to penalties and responsible for all acts committed by the members of its armed forces, gave rise to international liability and removed all doubts about the compulsory character of the statute.[101] Therefore, applying the indicators of obligation framed by Abbott et al.,[102] the Hague Conventions have "unconditional obligation-language and other indicia of intent to be legally bound," which indicate the highest degrees of obligation.

As with obligation, the precision of the Hague Regulations with regard to pillage is very high. Besides two explicit mentions that "pillage is prohibited," Section III of the Convention defines in detail what kinds of properties can and cannot be confiscated and how other matters of property should be managed in an occupied territory (for example, taxes, dues, tolls, cash, funds, destruction by bombardment, requisitions, contributions, public property, forests, agricultural works, railways, land telegrams, telephones, steamers, ships, arms, real property, property of communes, religious and charitable institutions, arts and science, historical monuments). Moreover, the belligerent state's "responsibility for acts committed by the members of its armed forces is clearly defined,"[103] which brings additional precision in terms of accountability. These provisions qualify as "determinate rules: only narrow issues of interpretation" on the indicators of precision table of Abbott et al.,[104] which put them at the highest end of the precision scale.

The Hague Conventions do not provide a clear mechanism of delegation for the violation of the Regulations and any disputes related to them,[105] although there are some important provisions that can be interpreted as an obligation on states to prosecute violators: both the 1899 and 1907 regulations require the violation of those prohibitions to "be made the subject of proceedings."[106] The 1907 regulations have an additional article that states, "A belligerent party which violates the provisions of the said Regulations shall, if the case demands, be liable to pay compensation. It shall be responsible for all acts committed by persons forming part of its armed forces." Graber interprets this change from the 1899 document as a recognition of the fact that violation of these rules gives rise to international liability.[107] Therefore, looking at the indicators of delegation put forward by Abbott et al.,[108] the structure of the regulation of pillage and private property in the Hague Conventions can be called moderate/low on the delegation scale. They require "conciliation and mediation" at the least and "nonbinding arbitration" at most in terms of dispute resolution and "coordination standards" in terms of rule making and implementation.

When we look at the Geneva Conventions' (1949) handling of pillage, we see that while obligation and precision continue to be high, the moderate delegation of the Hague Conventions is strengthened. The Geneva Conventions continue to impose a high degree of obligation on state parties to observe the prohibition against pillage by both repeating the fact that it is prohibited and including "appropriation of property" (along with other war crimes) in the category of grave breaches.[109] Precision is also high for pillage because Article 33 openly says, "Pillage is prohibited."[110]

The Geneva Conventions provide a system of delegation by requiring domestic legislation and prosecution for violations in the case of grave breaches. Because pillage is included in the grave breaches as "appropriation of property," it is therefore subject to delegation since "Each High Contracting Party shall be under the obligation to search for persons alleged to have committed, or to have ordered to be committed, such grave breaches, and shall bring such persons, regardless of their nationality, before its own courts. It may also, if it prefers, and in accordance with the provisions of its own legislation, hand such persons over for trial to another High Contracting Party concerned, provided such High Contracting Party has made out a prima facie case."[111] Applying Abbott et al.'s indicators of delegation to determine the level of delegation, it is safe to conclude that this provision brings about "binding internal policies-legitimation of decentralized enforcement" at the very least and even "binding regulations with consent or opt-out,"[112] which leads to the conclusion that delegation becomes high in this case.

As a result, the lower criterion that I use for analyzing the development of a prohibition regime—that is, one regarding high obligation and precision along with some degree of delegation—takes the Hague Conventions (1899, 1907) as the point of creation for the prohibition regime against pillage. A higher criterion, requiring a higher degree of delegation, would pick out the Geneva Conventions (1949).

Prohibition Regime Against Rape

Searching for the exact moment when the prohibition regime against rape was created is a harder task because of the resistance of lawmakers to recognize it as a wrong in itself. In order to establish the exact timeline through which the prohibition regimes develop, I look at four basic documents of the international law of war: the Hague Conventions (1899, 1907), the Geneva Conventions (1949), the Additional Protocols to the Geneva Conventions of 1949 (1977), and the Rome Statute (1998).

Chapter 3 starts the review by examining the Hague Conventions, which made no effort to create a prohibition against rape as they did against pillage. Since the Hague Regulations do not mention rape, it is not possible to derive any formal obligation, let alone a binding one, for states to prevent rape in war. Even if we consider "family honors and rights" mentioned in Article 46 as indirectly referring to rape,[113] this article does not demand a commitment to prevention. Nor does it provide a rule as a basis for scrutiny, since it uses a language of "respect" rather than prohibition (unlike the other practices outlawed in the Regulations).[114] This provision could be regarded as a "recommendation" at best, requiring very low obligation even if we presume that it indirectly referred to rape.

The most important problem with the Hague Regulations with respect to rape is a lack of precision. What does "family honors and rights" mean? What do they include? How will they be respected? What kind of action would be considered a violation of them? "Respect for family honors and rights" could be considered as a "standard only meaningful with reference to specific situations"[115] if we assume that it implicitly includes rape. However, given the failure of the provision to even mention rape, it is "impossible to determine whether conduct applies," and we must put the article at the lowest end of the precision degrees. These are extremely vague concepts that permit states to ignore their violations easily. As we will see, the vagueness of the concept "family honors and rights" may have contributed to the disregard for rape at the Nuremberg and (to a large extent) the Tokyo Trials that prosecuted German and Japanese political and military leaders after World War II.

Since it is questionable whether rape is prohibited by the Hague Regulations, delegation definitely does not exist in this case. Therefore, we can exclude the Hague Conventions (1899, 1907) from the legal timeline prohibiting rape in war.

Given that the basic puzzle of why the prohibitions against pillage and rape did not occur simultaneously with the Hague Conventions, where one was prohibited and the other not, Chapter 3 concentrates on how and why the Hague Conventions excluded rape and in what kind of normative context this could happen. I also examine the situation of the women's movement in the nineteenth century and women's attitude toward rape, as well as their lack of effect on the international law creation process. An overview of nineteenth-century Europe's property, marriage, and rape laws—with special attention to France (which has a civil law tradition) and Britain (which has a common law tradition)—are especially helpful in our understanding of the normative context, in which women were treated as property by the laws, but at the same time "not property enough" to be granted the protections that it received. I conclude the chapter with reflections on the idea of "the inevitability of rape" in nineteenth-century European society.

Chapter 4 studies the continued non-prohibition of rape by the Geneva Conventions and the Additional Protocols. While the first international legal document to mention rape as an unacceptable practice in war was the Geneva Conventions, there are still some problems about the degree of obligation the Conventions impose on states to prevent rape in war. First of all, Article 27 says, "Women shall be especially protected against any attack on their honor, in particular against rape, enforced prostitution, or any form of indecent assault." Therefore, it is possible to conclude that the provisions are protective but not prohibitive,[116] as opposed to other practices, like pillage, for which an open prohibition is stated.[117] This discrimination against rape in the text gives the sense that rape is not necessarily something state parties are under a legal obligation to prevent, but rather that it is a distasteful practice everybody must try to avoid, that is, a recommendation and guideline.[118] When it comes to rape, therefore, the Geneva Conventions are at the lower end of the obligation scale.

In terms of precision, Article 27 of the Geneva Conventions IV (1949) can be an example of a rule with a degree of precision that has "broad areas of discretion"[119] leading to moderate/low precision. Nevertheless, they constituted a step forward, since for the first time in history an international legal document mentioned the word *rape* as a subject of international humanitarian law.[120] Despite the fact that Article 27 specifically states the practice that must be avoided and that requires "protection against," what Article 27 means by "protection" is unclear. It also does not explain what constitutes rape or any kind of sexual assault.

With regard to its provisions on the enforcement of grave breaches, the Geneva Conventions is a case of hard legalization (in terms of delegation), since it brings obligation on the states to bring perpetrators before domestic courts or hand them over for trial by other parties.[121] Hence, there is a "binding third party (court)" or "domestic court jurisdiction" requirement leading to a high degree of delegation.[122] We cannot, however, apply the same delegation measure for the Geneva Conventions when it comes to rape because rape is not included among the grave breaches.[123] As a result, the Geneva Conventions (1949) cannot be regarded as the point at which the prohibition regime against rape was created, since it does not fulfill obligation and delegation. I do, however, recognize the Geneva Conventions as a step forward in the creation of this prohibition regime because it mentions the word *rape*.

The two Additional Protocols changed the status of rape slightly in terms of obligation and precision, although there was no change in delegation because the list of grave breaches continued to exclude rape. The Second Protocol on the Protection of Victims of Non-International Armed Conflicts adopted a language of prohibition instead of protection, which is different from both the original Geneva Conventions and the First Protocol on the Protection of Victims of International Armed Conflicts.[124] This change increased the degree of obligation, at least in the law for non-international armed conflicts. Additionally, the original article in the 1949 Conventions, defining rape as an attack on women's honor, was changed, which signals a change in the way women are viewed—that is, from less than property to human beings who deserve protection from violence. Despite these developments, because of the continuing problems of obligation and delegation, it is not possible to derive a prohibition regime against rape from the Additional Protocols.

Chapter 5 focuses on one of the "hardest" (in Abbott and Snidal's terms) international laws in force today, the Rome Statute of the International Criminal Court (1998). Article 8 defining war crimes explicitly mentions rape, sexual slavery, enforced prostitution, forced pregnancy, enforced sterilization, or any other form of sexual violence as grave breaches of the Geneva

Conventions.[125] The Rome Statute is also different from the Geneva Conventions in that state parties are responsible not only for the investigation and prosecution of grave breaches, but for all crimes under the jurisdiction of the ICC. Article 86 says: "States Parties shall, in accordance with the provisions of this Statute, cooperate fully with the Court in its investigation and prosecution of crimes within the jurisdiction of the Court." States are obligated to prevent the crimes mentioned in the Statute and prosecute the violators or hand them in for prosecution to the ICC. Besides, rape is clearly among these crimes within the Court's jurisdiction. It is an "unconditional obligation [with] language and other indicia of intent to be legally bound."[126]

Because the Rome Statute—in both Article 7 concerning crimes against humanity and Article 8 on war crimes—includes not only rape but also other forms of sexual violence as grave breaches of the Geneva Conventions, we can measure its precision on the highest end, as the articles fit into "determinate rules-only narrow issues of interpretation" in the indicators of precision.[127]Additionally, the ICC, as a court with "binding third party decisions," has jurisdiction over all the crimes mentioned in the Rome Statute, meaning it also has the highest degree of delegation.[128] Therefore, with high degrees of obligation, precision, and delegation, the Rome Statute created a strong prohibition regime against rape in war.

Chapter 5 concentrates on how this change in law happened both materially (through the drafting changes) and normatively (through the work of women's organizations), and analyzes the role of the conflicts in the former Yugoslavia and Rwanda in this process.

The Prohibition of Pillage in War

The practice of pillage was essential in medieval feuds, became a weapon of European warfare by 1500, and continued to be a regular part of any war through the early eighteenth century.[1] It had had two legitimate functions: hurting the enemy and maintaining one's own army when in charge of the enemy's countryside.[2] Even Grotius, known as the father of the laws of war with his important work, *The Rights of War and Peace* (1625), considered normal the destruction and plunder of enemy's property.[3] He wrote:

> Cicero, in the third of his Offices, declares, It is not against the Law of Nature to spoil or plunder him whom it is lawful to kill. No wonder then if the Law of Nations allows to spoil and waste an Enemy's Lands and Goods, since it permits him to be killed. Polybius tells us in the fifth of his History, by the Right of War it is lawful to take away, or destroy, the Forts, Havens, Cities, Men, Ships, Fruits of the Earth, and such like Things of an Enemy. And we read in Livy, There are certain Rights of War, which, as we may do, so we may suffer, as the burning of Corn, the pulling down of Houses, the taking away of Men and Cattle. We may find in History, almost in every Page, the dismal Calamities of War, whole Cities destroyed, or their Walls thrown down to the Ground, Lands ravaged, and every Thing set on fire. And we may observe, these Things are lawful to be done, even to those that surrender themselves.[4]

Interestingly, the idea that rape in war is unacceptable started to emerge well before the idea that pillage is unacceptable. In the seventeenth century, for instance, although there was a close connection between women and booty (since looting was permissible, so was rape), attempts to forbid rape for one's own soldiers were already appearing in the writings of jurists.[5] Grotius said:

> The Ravishing of Women is sometimes permitted in War, and some-times not. They that permit it, respect only the Injury done to the Body of an Enemy, which by the Law of Arms they think should be subject to all Acts of Hostility. But others, with more Reason, look not to that Injury alone, but also to the Act of Brutality, which being nei-ther necessary for the Security of those who commit it, nor proper for the Punishment of those against whom it is committed, should be as much punished in War as in Peace; and this last is the Law of Nations, if not all, yet of the most civilized.[6]

Ultimately, pillage appeared in the Hague Conventions (1899, 1907), the first international legal documents that codified the laws of land warfare and obligations of an occupying power on occupied territories, as a banned prac-tice. In the post-World War II period, its prohibition was restated as a war crime by various international legal documents, such as the Geneva Conven-tions (1949), the Additional Protocols to the Geneva Conventions (1977), the Rome Statute for the International Criminal Court (1998), the Charter of the Military Tribunal at Nuremberg (1945), the Statute of the International Criminal Tribunal for the Former Yugoslavia (1993), and the Statute of the International Criminal Tribunal for Rwanda (1994).[7]

Historical Background

The Lieber Code (1863)

The Lieber Code (1863) was the foundation for the laws of land warfare that were first codified in the Hague Conventions. It was the first attempt to gather new or modern ideas about acceptable and unacceptable practices in war into a code. Issued to the Union troops during the American Civil War, it was written by Francis Lieber, a German American jurist who was both person-ally and professionally involved in the Civil War. He knew the horrors of war not only as a veteran of the Napoleonic Wars, but also as a father whose three sons were soldiers in the Civil War, fighting on both sides. In 1861 he left

South Carolina College, where he had been in the muted minority because of his strong anti-slavery opinions, and enthusiastically joined the North, where he wanted to be not just a professor but also a publicist influencing government policy.[8]

Lieber immediately set about solving the government's problem of exchanging prisoners of war without recognizing the Confederacy. After the death of one of his sons in the Civil War in 1862, he had become determined to push his interpretation of the laws of war on the Union army. He proposed the establishment of a committee to draw up the code on the conduct of war for the Union armies, and pressed for it against resistance from the government. Lieber was aided by his connection with Henry Halleck, general-in-chief of the Union armies (1862–1864) and an expert on the "science of war" and international law and his persistence paid off when he was asked to prepare the code.[9] In 1862, at the request of U.S. secretary of war Edwin Stanton, Lieber was appointed as the only civilian member of a board that would "propose amendments or changes in the Rules and Articles of War and a code of regulations for the government of Armies in the field as authorized by the laws and usages of War."[10]

Though Lieber wrote the code for use in a civil war, it was retained by American troops during the Spanish-American War (1898) and then republished in 1914 by the United States War Department for use in international wars. A German version of the Lieber Code was used by the German troops during the Franco-Prussian War of 1870.[11] The fact that Lieber had fought in the Prussian Army against Napoleon and was very much influenced by that experience is particularly relevant.[12] Indeed, both Lieber's published and unpublished materials show his deep concern about the horrors of war. For example, he collected newspaper clippings and notes on matters such as Confederate attempts for starting an epidemic, using exploding rifle balls, or booby-trapping surrendered positions.[13] According to Freidel, Lieber was an emotional scholar, easily wrapped up in his enthusiasm for his strongly held beliefs. But most of the time he was calm enough to work within the delicate political processes as a respected and authoritative professor.[14]

Lieber was a firm believer in private property, and the Lieber Code clearly reflected his "stanch defense of property rights" (which did not include slavery).[15] The most significant articles of the Lieber Code in terms of the protection of property and the prohibition of pillage are Articles, 22, 37, 38, 44, 47, and 72:

Article 22:

Nevertheless, as civilization has advanced during the last centuries, so has likewise steadily advanced, especially in war on land, the distinction between the private individual belonging to a hostile country and the hostile country itself, with its men in arms. The principle has been more and more acknowledged that the unarmed citizen is to be spared in person, property, and honor as much as the exigencies of war will admit.

Article 37:

The United States acknowledge and protect, in hostile countries occupied by them, religion and morality; strictly private property; the persons of the inhabitants, especially those of women: and the sacredness of domestic relations. Offenses to the contrary shall be rigorously punished.

This rule does not interfere with the right of the victorious invader to tax the people or their property, to levy forced loans, to billet soldiers, or to appropriate property, especially houses, lands, boats or ships, and churches, for temporary and military uses.

Article 38:

Private property, unless forfeited by crimes or by offenses of the owner, can be seized only by way of military necessity, for the support or other benefit of the army or of the United States.

If the owner has not fled, the commanding officer will cause receipts to be given, which may serve the spoliated owner to obtain indemnity.

Article 44:

All wanton violence committed against persons in the invaded country, all destruction of property not commanded by the authorized officer, all robbery, all pillage or sacking, even after taking a place by main force, all rape, wounding, maiming, or killing of such inhabitants, are prohibited under the penalty of death, or such other severe punishment as may seem adequate for the gravity of the offense.

A soldier, officer or private, in the act of committing such violence, and disobeying a superior ordering him to abstain from it, may be lawfully killed on the spot by such superior.

Article 47:

Crimes punishable by all penal codes, such as arson, murder, maiming, assaults, highway robbery, theft, burglary, fraud, forgery, and rape, if committed by an American soldier in a hostile country against its inhabitants, are not only punishable as at home, but in all cases in which death is not inflicted the severer punishment shall be preferred.

Article 72:

Money and other valuables on the person of a prisoner, such as watches or jewelry, as well as extra clothing, are regarded by the American Army as the private property of the prisoner, and the appropriation of such valuables or money is considered dishonorable, and is prohibited.

Nevertheless, if "large" sums are found upon the persons of prisoners, or in their possession, they shall be taken from them, and the surplus, after providing for their own support, appropriated for the use of the army, under the direction of the commander, unless otherwise ordered by the government. Nor can prisoners claim, as private property, large sums found and captured in their train, although they have been placed in the private luggage of the prisoners.

It is important to note that the Lieber Code prohibits both rape and pillage explicitly in Articles 44 and 47. Since it was not international law, but an army code written for managing the U.S. army's conduct in the American Civil War, I do not include it in my chronology of law development. It is interesting to note, however, that Lieber did not fail to include rape in his code—in contrast to his colleagues in Europe. I will address some possible explanations for this variation in Chapter 4, when I discuss Additional Protocol II (1977), which was also written for civil wars.

The Brussels Conference (1874)

The Lieber Code is usually considered to have launched the "golden decade of restraints on warfare,"[16] as it inspired the first attempt to codify international law of war, the Brussels Declaration (1874). Russian delegate Baron Jomini, presiding at the Brussels Conference, said that the declaration was written with the regulations of President Lincoln for making the sufferings of war milder (the Lieber Code) in mind.[17] The draft convention was prepared with the backing of D. A. Miliutin, the Russian defense minister who was close to Tsar Alexandre II, and by Friedrich Martens (F. F. Martens), who called the Brussels Conference "a natural development of the Lieber Code."[18] The Brussels Declaration was intended to establish universal rules of warfare, including regulations for treatment of prisoners of war and noncombatants.

The author of the draft code, Martens, was a Russian scholar of international law and a diplomat. He was one of the most prominent professors from the Russian academia, which had very active international law programs. He was also part of the Russian delegations to all the international conferences between 1868 and 1909, including all Red Cross Conferences, the Brussels Conference, and the Hague Conferences, during which time he served at the Russian Ministry of Foreign Affairs. He was a firm believer in individual rights, and he situated the individual at the center of international law. He "considered protection of the rights, interests and property of a human being to be the substance of the entire system of international relations and regarded respect for human rights as a yardstick of the degree of civilization of states and international relations."[19] The centrality of private property in the draft convention he prepared may be traced to his dissertation topic on the law of private ownership during war ("On the Law of Private Property in Time of War"); its publication in 1869 and subsequent translations made him well-known in Europe at the time.[20] Martens also believed that the true international legal consciousness resulted from changes in the development of the individual. He argued that more developed or "civilized" international laws are for more civilized states, while natural law norms are for states with lower levels of civilization. In his inaugural lecture (1871), Martens proclaimed: "International law will only stand on a firm foundation, when the natural and historical laws of the development of peoples have been elucidated. . . . International treaties which conform to the conditions of the cultural development of peoples do not contain the embryo of their inevitable violation and elimination."[21]

Reviewing Martens's ideas, we can easily understand why he might have included the protection of private property in the draft and omitted Lieber's prohibition of rape, which did not "conform to the conditions of the cultural development of [the] people" in Europe at the time. He was one of the publicists who used Grotius's method of introducing "specific customs which [are] imbued with . . . conservative political ideologies" into the language of the laws of war. [22] The language of the drafts he prepared, therefore, would not have contained any progressive elements of his time.

While Martens was a firm believer in the power of international law, he was not part of the antiwar movement that was growing rapidly in the late nineteenth century (125 peace associations in 1895 in Europe, excluding Russia). Martens found these peace associations' goal of the abolition of war utopian and considered the establishment of clearly defined and accepted laws of war the only solution for the horrors of war.[23]

In 1874, at the initiative of Russia, Martens's draft was submitted to the Brussels Conference. Most European countries did not welcome the idea of writing down the laws of war in the form of a convention.[24] England, in particular, resisted the idea. Ultimately, England agreed to participate only on condition that "there would be no discussion of the relations between belligerents in general, no attempt to state new principles, and the conference would limit discussion strictly to the Russian code and would refrain from considering points of maritime law."[25] The text itself was not objectionable to most state parties, especially the powerful ones, but they opposed the idea of restricting war by international law. Their opposition came in spite of the fact that the laws were rearticulating already existing principles of international law and in keeping with "the legal awareness and humanism" on the rise among the European public.[26]

In its language around pillage, the Brussels Declaration was very strong. Article 39 said, "Pillage is formally forbidden." Article 18 also stated, "A town taken by assault should not be given over to pillage by the victorious troops." Besides the other articles dealing with the protection of private property (Articles 6, 38, 40), this double prohibition of pillage is interesting given that a proposal to delete one of them was rejected without debate.[27]

One thing that is noteworthy about the handling of pillage by the Brussels Conference is that the original draft prepared by Russia mentioned pillage only in Section I (The Rights of the Belligerent Parties with Regard to Each Other) and Chapter IV (Sieges and Bombardments),[28] not in Section II (The Rights of the Belligerent Parties with Regard to Private Persons), although this section did contain articles stipulating protection of private property. Article 51 of the original draft (Article 39 in the final text) said: "The troops must respect private property in the occupied country and not destroy it without urgent need."[29] This article was modified into "Booty must be formally prohibited"[30] by the commission in the new draft prepared by Baron Jomini, the Russian delegate. The Swiss delegate, Mr. Hammer, proposed substituting "booty" with "pillage" and "must be" with "is."[31] Baron Baude, the French delegate, wanted to add "fire and pillage" into the article, which was opposed by the German delegate, who said that fire implies destruction so its place is elsewhere.[32] Ultimately, the commission gave Article 51 (Article 39 in the final text) its final form: "Pillage is formally prohibited."

The issue was revisited later in the conference, since Mr. Lanza, the Italian delegate, regretted the change of wording. Other delegates responded by saying that there are spoils allowed on the battlefield (for example, horses, ammunition, or guns) and that the commission only intended to prohibit the spoils taken at the expense of private property. General Leer, the other Russian delegate, added that it is precisely the forbidden booty that is called pillage. Lanza demanded that these explanations be inserted into the protocol.[33] This debate reveals the attempts to clarify the fact that property can be justifiably confiscated by occupying powers as long as it is for meeting "military necessity" and not for looting private property at the discretion of the soldiers. The state parties wanted to make it very clear that while pillage of private property would be prohibited, necessities for the occupying army could be confiscated.

We can find similar efforts to clarify the prohibition of pillage during the discussion of the other article on the subject. When Article 17 of the draft code (Article 18 in the final document), "A city taken by assault should not be given over for pillage by the victorious troops," was being considered, the Swiss delegate said that the expression "city" must be interpreted in the sense of the previous paragraphs, where it is a matter of "cities, villages or agglomerations of houses." The president of the conference, Baron Jomini (Russia), responded that this interpretation was not suspicious and the Swiss delegate should reproduce his observation during the general reading.[34] In one of the later meetings, Mr. Lambermont (Belgium) demanded a change of wording in the article: Instead of "should not be given," he proposed "cannot be given."[35] Baron Jomini responded that "should" (*doit*) is more peremptory, implying a formal obligation, so it was to be used in the article.

In the end, the conference failed to produce a final document that was acceptable to all the state parties. One remarkable point about this failure was that while jurists initially feared that the dominance of military men on the commissions would make negotiations harder (because military men would resist the reduction of their powers), it was the diplomats who blocked the success of the conference.[36] The draft was ultimately adopted as a declaration instead of becoming a law. States found the idea of restricting war through international law unacceptable, even though the document itself was not objectionable to most.[37] In addition to Britain—as the only great power lacking a large standing army leading the opposition to making the document international law, small states resisted the idea as well. They thought codification of the law of war would make them easy prey, believing that established laws of war would make people too comfortable and stifle the need for resistance against occupying powers.[38] Later during the Hague Conference, the Belgian delegate, Auguste Beernaert, would explain Belgium's opposition to the Brussels draft by stating:

> by undertaking to restrict war to States only, the citizens remaining to a certain extent only mere spectators, would not the risk be run of reducing the factors of resistance by weakening the powerful mainspring of patriotism?. . . . [T]elling the citizens not to mingle in the struggles in which the fate of their country is at stake [will be] encouraging that baneful indifference. . . . Small countries especially need to fill out their factors of defense by availing themselves of all their resources.[39]

With the backing of France and Britain, small states also found the document too favorable for occupying forces (they called it the "Code of Conquest"). The draft gave advantage to large aggressor states by granting legal combatant status only to professional soldiers and not to civilians who take up arms to fight against occupying powers.[40]

Even though the Brussels Declaration never became law, "it is alleged that the moral force of the project was so great that belligerents after 1874 observed its rules although it was criticized for its vagueness. The Institute of International Law . . . . reached the conclusion that the code contained the essential rules of the laws of war which were recognized by all civilized states."[41] Interestingly enough, it was also considered "more humane" and more respectful of the rights of noncombatants than the Lieber Code.[42]

Martens was not disheartened by the failure of the Brussels Conference.

He continued to defend his views in the press, publish popular books on laws of war, advise governments about international disputes,[43] and act as a member of many law societies and institutions in Europe, including the Institute of International Law. His work would ultimately bear its fruit in The Hague.

The Hague Peace Conferences (1899, 1907)

In 1899, Russian tsar Nicolas II called an international peace conference in The Hague. It was not difficult to convene, because the tsar and other European statesmen were nervous about the over-militarization in Europe. New weapons were being invented every year, and European powers were competing to acquire the new technologies before their rivals. This arms race was becoming too heavy to bear for everyone. Russia was particularly concerned, because its industry was unable to meet the demands of this arms race.[44] In order to draw attention to their concerns, the Russians even presented a letter to the conference, proposing to fix the amount of effective military and naval forces and budgets, among other things.[45]

Although the focus of the conference was peace, a section called The Laws and Customs of War on Land (the Hague Regulations) was added. The conference turned the Brussels Declaration into a legal convention with some modifications. This would not be a smooth process. In fact, before the conference began, the states, including Russia, had voiced concerns about disarmament, which prompted officials in the Russian Ministry of Foreign Affairs to consider withdrawing the invitation for the conference. But Friedrich Martens had other plans. He had already prepared the program, and he turned the conference into a peace conference, an important part of which would be a convention on the laws and customs of war.[46] Delegates from Germany, Austria-Hungary, Belgium, China, Denmark, Spain, the United States of America, the United States of Mexico, France, Great Britain and Ireland, Greece, Italy, Japan, Luxemburg, Montenegro, Netherlands, Persia, Portugal, Romania, Russia, Serbia, Siam, Sweden and Norway, Switzerland, Turkey, and Bulgaria gathered at The Hague.

As was the case at the Brussels Conference, the process of codifying the laws and customs of war would not be an easy task this time. At the very beginning of the debates on the laws of war on land, the British delegate read a statement:

Without seeking to know the motives to which may be attributed the non-adoption of the Brussels Declaration, it is permissible to suppose that the same difficulties may arise at the conclusion of our labors at The Hague. In order to brush them aside and to escape the unfruitful results of the Brussels Conference . . . we would better accept the Declaration only as a general basis for instructions to our troops on the laws and customs of war, without any pledge to accept all the articles as voted by the majority. . . . [Governments will thus retain] full liberty to accept or modify the articles.[47]

Unsurprisingly, Martens took on the question directly:

The object of the Imperial Government has steadily been the same, namely, to see that the Declaration of Brussels, revised in so far as this Conference may deem it necessary, shall stand as a solid basis for the instructions in case of war which the Governments shall issue to their armies on land. Without doubt, to the end that this basis may be firmly established, it is necessary to have a treaty engagement similar to that of the Declaration of St. Petersburg in 1868. It would be necessary that the signatory and acceding Powers should declare in a solemn article that they have reached an understanding as to uniform rules, to be carried over into such instructions. This is the only way of obtaining an obligation binding on the signatory Powers. It is well understood that the Declaration of Brussels will have no binding force except for the contracting or acceding States. . . . [This document will be a] mutual insurance association against the abuse of force in time of war.[48]

With Martens's help as the chairman of the subcommission that prepared the section on the laws and customs of war, the states could reach a unanimous agreement on a text.[49]

Ultimately, all powers that participated in the Hague Conference in 1899 signed and ratified the convention (except China and Switzerland, both of which waited until 1907). Only France, England, and Russia, however, inserted the convention into their military manuals.[50] The 1907 modifications to the convention, meanwhile, required the state parties to issue instructions to their armies according to the convention.

The Main Actors

In the nineteenth century, the main actors in international politics were states, the great powers in particular. Individual publicists or jurists, however, were not only effective in terms of initiating and preparing draft codes for international consideration (as we see in the cases of Lieber and Martens), but also in terms of pushing their governments to participate in the efforts to establish the codes through international conferences. They used their positions as respectable legal authorities "to advance their own formulations on the legal agenda of war."[51] On the subject of the Brussels Conference for instance, French minister Baron Baude complained: "It appeared obvious to me that we could not decline the invitation to participate in the project's deliberations, especially on a subject which current publicists have kept, without cease, in the public eye."[52]

After the failure of the Brussels Conference, these jurists continued their work under the umbrella of the Institute of International Law, under the wing of another important publicist, Johann Caspar Bluntschli. Together they produced drafts of a potential code, including the Oxford Manual (1880). Their efforts notwithstanding, state opposition to the codification of the laws of war continued. In fact, Bluntschli, the chief promoter of the Oxford Manual, was publicly humiliated by his own government when the Prussian Ministry of War replied to his proposal with a harsh critique: "the expression 'civilized warfare' used by Bluntschli, seems hardly intelligible; for war destroys this very equilibrium. . . . Absolute military action in time of war is an indispensible condition of military success."[53]

By the late nineteenth century, the internationalization (at least in the Western world) of ideas and organizations, as well as a "consciousness of oneness" began to develop.[54] Peace societies were flourishing all over Europe (and included women's peace organizations), international lawyers were organizing across borders, and the increased role of the press helped to raise public awareness about international events.[55] Although nongovernmental participation in the Hague Conference was nowhere near that of nongovernmental organizations (NGOs) in contemporary international conferences (in both scale and influence), these organizations—alongside very interested media— were present at The Hague in 1899. Besides the Institute of International Law, there were peace groups, peace institutes, and pro-free-trade organizations.[56] Most government delegations were not prepared to receive the lobbying efforts of these organizations and the public was excluded from the Conference, but that did not stop these actors' efforts.[57] For instance, one of the prominent women in the peace movement, the recipient of the 1905 Nobel Peace Prize, a noblewoman and a writer from Austria, Bertha von Suttner, opened a salon at The Hague during the conference where diplomats and peace activists could meet.[58] International law experts within the government delegations, including Martens (Russian delegate), Tobias Michael Carel Asser (Dutch delegate, 1911 Nobel Peace Prize winner), Louis Renault (French delegate, 1907 Nobel Peace Prize winner), Voislave Veljkovitch (Serbian delegate), Chevalier Descamps (Belgian delegate), Nagao Ariga (Japanese delegate), Heinrich Lammasch (Austria-Hungary's delegate), and Philipp Zorn (German delegate) turned out to be very influential actors. For example, when the work of the conference faced the possibility of collapsing because of two opposing views over the meaning of combatants and noncombatants (in the Convention on the Laws and Customs of War on Land), it was Martens's proposal, which came to be known as the Martens Clause, that solved the deadlock.[59]

In the end, the fact that the conference failed to produce disarmament and instead revised and codified the laws of war was disappointing to most of the peace activists. The growing women's movement would also eventually complain that the conference ignored women, but the outbreak of World War I would curtail their efforts and temporarily silence their issues.

The Law

The Hague Conventions of 1899 and 1907 are the legal documents that created the prohibition regime against pillage (in particular 1907 because of the additional measures it includes in terms of delegation). In Section III of the Hague Regulations, three articles prohibit pillage. In order to assess the obligation the regime imposed on the state parties, three aspects should be considered. First, Article 47, the second article that prohibits pillage, adopts a language of absolute prohibition by saying, "Pillage is formally prohibited." This absolute prohibition requires states to prevent and punish violators and compensate victims.[60] Second, the state parties are obligated to issue instructions to their armed forces in conformity with the Hague Regulations to ensure compliance.[61] Third, Article 3 of the 1907 text establishes international liability for violator states. These articles make the Hague Conventions' degree of obligation high with respect to its regime regulating pillage.

The articles of the Hague Conventions related to the prohibition of pillage, being very determinate rules both in defining the act prohibited and in the accountability this brings, rank at the highest end of the precision scale. What exactly is prohibited and the responsibilities of states with respect to prohibited acts are defined in exact terms in the pillage regime.

The Hague Conventions contain two articles that can be interpreted as requiring "conciliation and mediation" at least and "nonbinding arbitration" at most in terms of dispute resolution and "coordination standards" in terms of rulemaking and implementation, which put them at the moderate/low end of the delegation spectrum. First, Article 56 of both the 1899 and 1907 Regulations calls for violation of the Conventions' prohibitions to "be made the subject of proceedings." Second, Article 3 of the 1907 Regulations imposes responsibility on each state party for the violations committed by its armed forces in the form of liability to pay compensation.[62]

The Normative Context and the Normative Shock

While jurists were writing about the necessity to prohibit rape, and while most armies' codes in Europe prohibited rape by the seventeenth century,[63] both jurists and army codes allowed pillage (though with restrictions that would help keep the military discipline). What happened in the eighteenth and nineteenth centuries that reversed this trend, leading to the establishment of the first international law of war providing a clear prohibition of pillage and a clear nonprohibition of rape? Did pillage lose its functionality as a military practice while rape did not, or did something else happen?

I will address these questions in three steps. The first step looks at the early to mid- eighteenth century, when the structure of war and its costs and benefits had changed. Additionally, the ideological basis of the norm change for pillage developed through the creation of the normative context, with the core norms of the sanctity of private property, necessity to be civilized, and progress toward higher forms of civilization. The second step addresses the late eighteenth and early nineteenth centuries, when a normative shock in Europe made states consider a need to prohibit pillage. The third step came in the late nineteenth century, when pillage was prohibited.

The Eighteenth Century: The Decline of Pillage

Until the eighteenth century, pillage was a weapon, and its result, booty, had two purposes: compensation for the wrong that had caused the war (which was basically a feud between princes, extending to their subjects and their properties), and incentive for soldiers (i.e., mercenaries).[64] Three developments in the eighteenth century changed the cost-benefit balance regarding pillage. The evolution of the modern state eliminated the private interest in taking booty, standing professional armies with strict discipline were established, and the development of large-scale business made it possible for the state to fund wars through taxation instead of pillage.[65] In addition, undisciplined armies pillaging and deserting were hurting the ambitions of the modern states and their absolutist monarchs who wanted complete control over their territories. These developments meant pillage became costly by upsetting the discipline of the professional armies, while its benefits to the state became insignificant.[66]

These changes alone cannot explain the emergence of a global prohibition regime, since the change in costs and benefits was related more to the behavior of one's own army than to that of rival armies, usually a big part of the reason behind the endeavors to develop prohibition regimes. Moreover, almost all governments resist regulation of their conduct through international rules (particularly in the security realm), even if a regulation may have great benefits. In fact, we find states regulating their own armies' plundering for the sake of discipline as early as 1393, when the Swiss Confederates forbade looting by their own soldiers before complete victory—that is, until the commanding officer gave permission.[67] The same principle was applied over and over again by various armies in order to maintain discipline.[68] During the sixteenth and seventeenth centuries, many military laws also prohibited fights among soldiers for booty in order to ensure discipline and efficiency.[69]

These regulations, which deemed unrestricted looting normal but attempted to control its harmful effects on military objectives, eventually gave way to another type of regulation in Europe: curbing pillage to improve relations between the soldiers and the civilian population.[70] This kind of regulation originated with the purpose of protecting the warlords' own subjects, since mercenary soldiers were treating the subjects of their own lord's land the same way as the subjects of the enemy, essentially looting everyone as they passed along on the way to the war. Then, mostly in the seventeenth century, came the rules forbidding soldiers from looting the enemy population for personal benefit, but allowing the army to collect property for the state in the form of contributions (or requisitions).[71]

By the early eighteenth century, pillage was becoming more and more of a burden on armies. The modern state—with its professional standing army, strong controlling bureaucracy, and taxing power—did not need out-of-control soldiers running around for booty instead of making sure a battle was completely won, nor did it need them deserting after looting for fear of punishment (which became a big problem in the eighteenth century).[72] Looting not only caused loss of discipline, but also led civilians to become bitter toward invading armies, which did not help war efforts. For example, Redlich points out that because of looting "the French Revolutionary and Napoleonic armies . . . lost all sympathy of the non-French bourgeoisie, which in many places had originally welcomed the invading troops as emancipators."[73]

Clearly, the changes in the cost-benefit structure of pillage influenced how it was regarded and regulated—but only with regard to one's own army. Attempts to condemn and prohibit the practice on a larger scale, such as through mutual treaties or even through the writings of jurists were absent.[74] As a result, we do not see any attempts to eliminate it, except to the extent that it upset military discipline.

What Is Special About the Eighteenth Century?

The European wars during the early and mid-eighteenth century were limited in both purpose and scope. They were different from the devastating systemic wars involving most European powers during the seventeenth century, such as the Thirty Years' War (1618–1648), and during the late eighteenth and early nineteenth centuries, such as the French Revolutionary Wars (1792–1802).[75] Since the Peace of Westphalia (1648) "removed moral content from war" by giving sovereignty to each state, and thus the right to make war (*competence de guerre*), states' focus shifted from the problem of starting the war (*jus ad bellum*) to the problem of determining and following "the laws and usages of war" (*jus in bello*).[76] Facing these issues in the eighteenth century, therefore, the king of Prussia, Frederick the Great, and the empress of the Holy Roman Empire, Maria Theresa, established a clear set of rules for the art of war based on the existing customs in Europe.[77] Some important features of this art were sound money and regular taxes, which gave way to only exceptional use of levies or pillage; magazines of food, clothing, and munitions; regular pay and long training for the soldiers; and a "by the book" approach and avoidance of recklessness.[78] That military academies and military journals grew and soldiers were properly trained helped eighteenth-century armies with their prescribed codes prepared by the central bureaucracy in the process of stabilization and control of the forces.[79]

This century also witnessed major ideological changes.[80] First, liberal ideas gained greater influence across Europe; they included an emerging idea of the sanctity of private property[81] and a new self-definition of Europe as a group of "civilized" nations with a certain definition of civilization "progressing" toward higher forms of civilization. These changes increasingly helped Europeans perceive pillage as an unpleasant practice.[82] The second major ideological change was the reconceptualization of war as a contest between states rather than individuals.[83] In the context of these core norms or principles (such as the sanctity of property and being civilized and liberal, as well as the idea of wars being fought between states, which necessitated the protection of individuals in war), a new norm, namely one against pillage in war, began to emerge. Pillage came to be seen as an exception, an infamous institution, by the early nineteenth century.[84]

LIBERALISM, PRIVATE PROPERTY, "PROGRESS" AND "CIVILIZATION"

Economic Liberalism and Private Property. The eighteenth century, commonly called the Age of Enlightenment, marked the development of some very powerful new ideas in Europe, which would affect the social, political, and economic reorganization of the world. Though not unchallenged, most of these ideas grew from the general framework of liberalism. Thus, in order to understand the significance of "private property," "progress," and "civilization" in the context of the eighteenth century, it is necessary to understand liberalism. Starting in the sixteenth century the colonization of new lands had created new wealth, which then provided a foundation for the eventual rise of industrial capitalism and led to the emergence of new wealthy classes. These developments were followed by the popularization of revolutionary ideas about human possibility (belief in reason, progress, and perfectibility promulgated by philosophers like Descartes, Bayle, Spinoza, Bacon, and Locke in the seventeenth century and Montesquieu, Turgot, Condorcet, Voltaire, Hume, Smith, Bentham, Mendelssohn, and Kant in the eighteenth). As a result of these economic, political, and intellectual developments, the old institutions in Europe—absolutist monarchies, landed aristocracy, and mercantilist economies—started to break down.

The new classes were influenced by the new ideas, which declared that for the sake of progress, political, economic, and social restraints on human reason must be lifted. They wanted their share of political and economic power. Liberalism, founded on the principle of individual liberty in both the political and economic senses, was born out of these conditions. While the growing idea of personal liberty led to the rise of popular participation and government in the political sense, it also led to the rise of laissez-faire capital-ism (with its most important components, free trade and private property) in the economic sense. The new powerful classes, primarily the middle classes, wanted minimum government, which would not interfere with their free en-terprise and trade, but would ensure the enforcement of business contracts and the protection of their private property. According to eighteenth-century thinkers, economic progress brought about political progress, the progress of government toward "more comprehensive and civilized systems of policy" where "government and property. . . . arrived at that stability and perfection."[85]

Adam Smith's theories prepared the basis of the comprehensive form of this new perspective on economics. With his book *An Inquiry into the Na-ture and Causes of the Wealth of Nations*, published in 1776, Smith made the case for laissez-faire economics, arguing that if people are left to themselves, without interference from the government, the best economic outcomes for everyone will result, thanks to the market forces (or "the invisible hand," as he calls it), where every person's self-interest automatically serves every other's.[86] For example, when people are allowed to accumulate as much property as they can, they will work more and save more, which, in turn, will contribute to the progress and well-being of everyone by adding to overall production.[87] According to this argument, progress was a side effect of the rise of prop-erty, and this progress or civilization benefited even the poor by contributing to humankind's "liberation from the limitations of our primitive nature."[88] Though Smith did not spend much time justifying private property (this pro-cess had been going on for over a century, although on the basis of a differ-ent philosophical claim, private property as a natural right rather than as a contributor to progress), he certainly talked about "the sacred and inviolable rights of private property" in the context of eighteenth-century capitalism as an integral part of his theory.[89] Smith's approach not only reflects the status private property had gained by that time. It also strengthened the case for private property for subsequent generations, who saw it as the source of eco-nomic efficiency and development.[90]

Some Enlightenment scholars criticized private property, but their work reflected the status it had gained by the eighteenth century and the notion that it contributed to the "progress" of Europe. For instance, Jean-Jacques Rousseau, one of the most influential theorists of the time, harshly criticized the idea of private property by saying that modern civilization's progress owes its existence partly to private property, yet it comes with a price: it brought about misery and slavery.[91] It is no wonder, then, that eighteenth-century

Europe, in its euphoria over the progress of its civilization, would consider private property to be one of the main building blocks of its existence and treat it as such.

Progress and Civilization. What did eighteenth- and nineteenth-century Europeans mean by "progress"? Rather than a general understanding of "forward movement or advances in technology,"[92] they thought of it as "the course of things since the beginning—in spite of possible minor deviations and the occasional occurrence of backwaters in the stream of history—[which] has been characterized by a gradual progressive increase, or a wider diffusion, of goodness, or happiness, or enlightenment, or of all of these,"[93] as the idea that "civilization has moved, is moving, and will move in a desirable direction."[94] They had a "belief in the essential goodness and self-sufficiency of man and faith in the power of science to banish suffering and bring about the 'evanescence of evil.' "[95]

Although a "doctrine of progress" was already beginning to emerge in the seventeenth century, it was in the eighteenth century that Western Europe started to believe that perfection or human perfectibility (on earth), thanks to the human reason and will, could be attained.[96] During this century, progress "became synonymous with the perfection or betterment or improvement of mankind."[97] French philosophers like the marquis de Condorcet, for instance, believed that France was approaching an "idyllic felicity" with the perfect constitution, and once other nations adopted the same principles of government, the millennium would arrive.[98] In England, although the idea of progress was not as popular as it was in France, it found its place in the writings of many theorists such as Adam Smith, whose *An Inquiry into the Nature and Causes of the Wealth of Nations* explains how human society historically progressed in the economic sense and predicts "an indefinite augmentation of wealth and well-being."[99]

The idea of the "blessed law of progress" would be further reinforced by the Industrial Revolution: "a nation which travels sixty miles an hour must be five times as civilized as one which travels only twelve."[100] According to nineteenth-century scholars, progress had been going on since the beginning of history but we became aware of it only in the seventeenth and eighteenth centuries, particularly with the Enlightenment,[101] after which point it became "the most characteristic and pervasive theme in modern Western thought."[102]

RECONCEPTUALIZATION OF WAR

Starting in the seventeenth century and gaining momentum in the eighteenth, a reconceptualization of war happened. Whereas war had been considered a feud between kings or princes, a new idea—that war was a military action between states—developed as the state was taking on an identity of its own.[103] Though the seeds of the idea started with Grotius, who said, "plundering doth not so much hurt the State, or the King"[104] (rather than just saying that it does not hurt the king, as Redlich points out[105]), it was developed by the eighteenth-century writers on international law. They contended that war occurs between states, not between individual kings and their subjects, and that the citizens of enemy states—along with their private property—should remain subject to law.[106] Abandoning the medieval idea that everything that hurts the enemy is permissible in war, jurists started to emphasize the illegitimacy of the use of unnecessary force that injures the enemy yet does not ensure victory to end the war.[107] The idea that booty belonged to the sovereign and not to soldiers emerged and led to the abandonment of looting in favor of contributions (or requisitions)[108]("collections of money and other fungible things for supporting an army, exacted from the subjects of the enemy") and foraging (forcibly collecting provisions and fodder for troops).[109] As a result, pillage became an infamous institution; when it happened, such as in East Prussia in 1757 or in Poland in 1760, it was viewed with contempt. Eighteenth-century armies widely enforced the old principle "no booty without permission," and looting was punished severely, rather than paying lip service to it as the earlier generations had done: "As late as 1806, on the eve of the Battle of Jena, Prussian troops, still animated by eighteenth-century military tradition, froze and went hungry rather than loot the nearby villages."[110]

Early Nineteenth Century: Revival of Pillage

With the Revolutionary and Napoleonic Wars (which started in the late eighteenth century), the early nineteenth century witnessed the revival of pillage,[111] which came as a normative shock for the "civilized" Europe:

> the light-fingered General Bonaparte, his delinquent young subordinate generals, and his insatiable soldiers together established an unshakable reputation as in every way the most rapacious pillagers in that league of high-grade pillagers that is normally known to historians as "the French Army." By doing so, they subtly but decisively changed the basic ground-rules of the whole game, and determined

how it would continue to be played throughout the remainder of the "Napoleonic" period.[112]

Looted gold, silver, tapestries, books, and artworks were sent to Paris. The French army fed itself through pillage whenever it could get away with it.[113]

The French Revolutionary armies and Napoleon ignored the rules of warfare that had started to emerge in the eighteenth century, particularly regarding pillage. They practiced a "slash and burn philosophy" and bypassed conventional methods of warfare.[114] For instance, after the Battle of Friedland in 1807, Napoleon reviewed and rewarded his soldiers in front of Russian Emperor Alexander to embarrass him; they talked about the ways they killed the Russians, captured a flag and cannon, and drove Russian troops into the water to perish.[115] For the Allied troops, it was "disagreeable and disgusting" to follow the French army because along the road "lay corpses or dying men; the prisoners taken had death stamped on their faces; in short it was impossible to think, without horror, of sleeping on the same spot, perhaps on the same straw, as this fever-stricken army, which had moreover infected the inhabitants on their route and consumed all the provisions."[116]

According to Redlich, there were five main reasons for the revival of pillage in the nineteenth century.[117] The first was connected to the fact that the purpose and scope of wars changed dramatically: they were no longer the wars of the sovereigns of the ancien régime fought by small professional and mercenary forces for territorial and economic advantage; rather they were wars of a "nation in arms" fought for a high moral purpose by the whole nation.[118] That meant conscription. These conscripted armies were not as good as the professional armies of the eighteenth century in terms of discipline. Hence, although conscription ultimately contributed to the elimination of pillage because it eliminated the need for booty as bait for enlistment, it temporarily worsened the situation.[119] Second, the Napoleonic Wars lasted a long time, and food scarcities further damaged discipline. French armies were underfed and underclothed, leading them to "live off the land."[120] The fact that domestic French resources were insufficient to pay for the hundreds of thousands of soldiers made it almost necessary to feed the army from conquered lands and to conquer more lands to maintain a balanced budget and order.[121] Third, the French began to maintain their troops from the capital and income of the captured lands, as in the seventeenth century, instead of provisioning them out of magazines.[122] Napoleon had decreed that half the soldiers' pay would be given in coin rather than paper money, which could only be financed by increased contributions from occupied areas.[123] The fact that French soldiers were paid only after they returned home aggravated the situation. And last, instead of military camps that could be easily controlled, soldiers were quartered in towns and villages, where looting was readily available.

Although Napoleon's official policy rejected the practice of pillaging, he in fact allowed it. He wrote to his brother Joseph, when he became king of Naples:

> The security of your dominion depends on how you behave in the conquered province. Burn down a dozen places which are not willing to submit themselves. Of course, not until you have first looted them; my soldiers must not be allowed to go away with their hands empty.[124]

Napoleon not only allowed pillage but provoked his soldiers to loot as well:

> Soldiers! You are naked and underfed. The government owes you much, but it can give you nothing. Your patience and the courage you display among these bare rocks, are admirable; but they bring you no glory and shed no brilliance upon you. I want to lead you into the most fertile plains in the world. Rich provinces and great cities will fall under your power: there you will find honor, glory and riches. Soldiers of the "It-alie," will you fail to show courage or constancy?[125]

Griffith interprets this speech to the Armée d'Italie as "one of the most brazen and bare-faced incitements to pillage that has ever been issued in the whole history of warfare." "The ragged and starving soldiers" were expected to be more interested in riches than in honor and glory, and in the end, they turned out to be just that.[126]

By succumbing to the temptation of pillaging, the French army sacrificed its military security, its moral rectitude, and its revolutionary virtue, and with its barbarity it "set the international standard for pillaging. . . . [driving] forward a notable degradation in the professionalism of warfare and the valuation of life."[127] As a result, all European armies looted in the Napoleonic Wars.[128] A Prussian officer, Baron Karl Von Muffling, describes this situation in his memoirs. When the Allies took possession of Vitry in 1814, "The troops were billeted and fed by their hosts, as the season was still too rough to bivouac regularly, and live by requisition on the villages, which, at the same time would have made pillaging unavoidable."[129] Because of the mode of warfare, after laborious marches and as soon as they arrived at a bivouac, the Russian and Prussian troops started looting the villages to obtain provisions. They ended up taking from the inhabitants all they had—and practiced some cruelties along the way, despite the personal efforts of the field marshal and generals. "Houses were pulled down for the soldiers to cook and warm themselves. Thus a whole village often disappeared in a night. This could not be helped; but such situations make soldiers hard-hearted and cruel."[130]

The discipline in both armies (Prussian and Russian) also suffered from the pillaging during the Napoleonic Wars.[131] Even after the fall of Paris, the situation was grave. The French in the country, incited by Bonapartist officers, started to attack Allied convoys for booty, so that Allies had to use escorts.[132] It was a "regress" in a world of "progress," from the eighteenth century, when not only ideas about the progress of European civilization became very popular but also practical rules about the conduct of warfare started to take root, to the Revolutionary Wars, where barbarity and insecurity returned.

This untenable situation led to the next important period in Europe's history, when "codifying and creating law to govern international relations" through international conferences began with the Congress of Vienna in 1815 and culminated with the Hague Conferences.[133] "An enthusiasm of humanity"—coming from the Enlightenment but shocked by what it had seen during the Revolutionary Wars—would lead to the improvement of international law.[134] Pillage, "which by 1500 was taken as a matter of course, by 1815 became a practice to be condemned and eliminated."[135] Between the Napoleonic Wars and the writing of the Hague Regulations, the practices of the European nations would steadily develop toward the ideal of protecting private property in war.[136]

The Difference Between Eighteenth- and Nineteenth-Century Warfare

The wars of the eighteenth century were fought by small professional armies with the purpose of defeating the other side at the smallest cost in life and money. In this way, civilian lives and property were spared not only on moral grounds but also because attacking them did not help this kind of war effort. Spending limited military resources on such militarily unnecessary attacks was unsound. The Revolutionary and Napoleonic Wars, however, changed this model of warfare. The new style of war incorporated the whole nation, including civilians. Additionally, the invention of new technologies made war ever more destructive.[137] Indeed, "Napoleon utilized the powers of the nation at his disposal to their utmost to carry on war 'without slackening for a moment until the enemy was prostrated.' "[138] Europe's first response to this massive destructiveness, starting with the Congress of Vienna (1815) and the Concert of Europe,[139] was to search for political or diplomatic ways to prevent war. After this system began to fail with the Crimean War (1854), where the great powers appeared on both sides of the conflict, the focus shifted toward strengthening the laws of war.

Late Nineteenth Century: Prohibition of Pillage

Beginning with the talks on private property in the Congress of Vienna,[140] states made various attempts throughout the nineteenth century to codify the laws of war, which included developing a prohibition regime against pillage (Lieber Code [1863], Brussels Conference [1874], Oxford Code [1880], and Geffcken Code [1894]). These efforts culminated in the Hague Conferences (1899 and 1907),[141] which declared that "The pillage of a town or place, even when taken by assault, is prohibited. Private property cannot be confiscated. Pillage is formally prohibited."[142]

According to Graber, the changes in the landmark codes and the military manuals, as well as the publicists' works between 1863 and 1914, were driven by "the need for a law which would give the maximum protection from the rigors of war to the population of occupied regions without hindering the military objectives of the occupant."[143] The emphasis was on military necessity in the Lieber Code and on humanitarianism in the Brussels Declaration. The Hague Regulations were in between.[144] The laws that were favorable to the occupant by promoting order in the occupied regions were accepted by the states more easily.[145]

The Hague Conventions were "a late codification of a body of law adopted in an atmosphere of nineteenth-century liberalism, shaped by the basic philosophy of that era."[146] For instance, the memoirs of Andrew White, American delegate to the 1899 Hague Peace Conference, provide an idea of the attitude toward private property at the time. White was instructed by his government to secure the immunity of private property at sea in time of war as "a long desired improvement in international law."[147] The subject could not be handled by the second committee due to Russian opposition, some of the other powers in Europe supported the American proposal, and their comments provide insight on the debate. Mr. Van Karnebeek, for instance, the Dutch delegate, said although his country's interests required the retention of the present system, he supported the idea of the protection of private property at sea as "a question of right" and "the proper development of international law."[148] According to his memoirs, Andrew White spent even the intervals during the conference working on the subject, with the expectation that even if private property at sea could not be secured at The Hague, his efforts "must at least pave the way for its admission by a future international conference."[149]

The debates during the Hague Conferences over the protection of private property, including the prohibition of pillage, are also significant in terms of understanding the mindset of the day. The original draft convention said, "Family honor and rights, and the lives and property of persons, as well as their religious convictions, and their practice, must be respected. Private property cannot be confiscated." Mr. Odier, the Swiss delegate, thought this did not provide sufficient protection for private property, so he proposed modifying the article to mention private property twice. This proposal was accepted, and the new version of the article read: "Family honor and rights, the lives of persons, and private property, as well as religious convictions and practice must be respected. Private property cannot be confiscated."[150] During the second conference in 1907, Austria-Hungary proposed to modify Article 46 this way: "Family honor and rights, the lives of persons, religious convictions and practice, as well as in principle private property, must be respected."[151] This restriction regarding the protection of private property was unacceptable to the other delegates. Upon the objection of the president of the conference, Mr. Beernaert (Belgium), saying that the addition of the words "in principle" seemed to "express a reversal of the ideas admitted in 1899," Major General Baron Giesl von Gieslingen (Austria-Hungary) withdrew the amendment.[152]

Articles of the Hague Conventions dealing with prohibition of pillage—Articles 28 and 47—are taken directly from the Brussels Declaration (1874), although the wording of Article 28 is somewhat different from Article 18 of the Brussels Declaration. The adoption of these articles was fairly straightforward, without much debate. According to Graber, "the subject of pillage receives less detailed attention in this period than in previous ones, apparently on the assumption that pillage is universally condemned and recognized as illegal so that the point no longer needs stressing," although what is considered pillage changed a lot.[153] Even when there was disagreement on the exceptions to the sanctity of private property during war, there was absolute agreement that they should not take the form of pillage.[154]

The ideas and principles about "civilization" and "civilized behavior" continued to grow in the nineteenth century. In fact, the belief in progress was virtually unchallenged during most of the nineteenth century.[155] With the growing influence of Darwinism, the idea that humanity advances continuously toward higher forms of being, gained strength. The doctrine of "that which is strongest on the whole must therefore be good, and the ideas which come to prevail must therefore be true"[156] strengthened already existing ideas about human civilization (starting with the European civilization) and its objectives toward perfection.

> The nineteenth-century historian was so loath to admit retrogression that he liked to fancy the river of progress flowing underground all through the Dark Ages, and endowed the German barbarians who overthrew Mediterranean civilization with all the manly virtues. If a nation, or a religion, or a school of art dies, the historian explains why it was not worthy to live. In political science . . . on the theory of progress, what is "coming" must be right.[157]

According to Inge, until World War I people believed that "civilized man had become much more humane, much more sensitive to the sufferings of others, and so more just, more self-controlled, and less brutal in his pleasures and in his resentments."[158]

Even armies, which typically resist any change that may be at odds with the security concerns of the state, reformed themselves along the lines of the new morality that was emerging out of these ideas about progress and civilization. For example, Victorian England saw a shift from efforts to have soldiers who are "mindless brutes" able to survive and obey under vicious discipline. Instead, "moral discipline," in accord with the new morality of the rest of the society, became the objective, in order to have men with moral welfare.[159]

Therefore, writing up international laws limiting and prohibiting barbaric practices of war was very much considered part of the new and enlightened civilization. The publicists of the nineteenth century believed these ideas about civilization, too. In the words of Lieber, "The fundamental idea of all international law is the idea that all civilized nations of our race form a family of nations." Thus, the Europeans (or Westerners in general) were civilized enough to meet the standards of an international law and preserve international peace.[160] In describing his code, he wrote, "I think [the code] . . . will do honor to our country. . . . It is a contribution by the United States to the stock of common civilization."[161]

Similarly, when the state delegates to the Hague Peace Conference came together before the tomb of Hugo Grotius on July 4, 1899, at the initiation of the United States delegation in celebration of the 123rd anniversary of American independence, they described this forefather of international law as "one of whom all civilized lands are justly proud"[162] and who brought the feelings of mercy and humanity (in war) into the modern world.[163] According to Andrew White, the U.S. delegate, the nations paying tribute to Grotius were not only the nations whom Grotius knew to be civilized, but also the nations Grotius had thought were barbarous yet had since become civilized (as can be understood from their presence at the Peace Conference).[164] Since Grotius's day "the progress of reason in theory and of mercy in practice has been constant on both sides of the Atlantic"[165] along with the "diminishing of bad faith in time of peace and cruelty in time of war."[166] According to White, what was special about Grotius was that he wrote his theory of international law at an immoral time (the time of Machiavellian politics),[167] as opposed to the present time, which took inspiration from people like him to progress toward morality.[168] Grotius not only wrote on what international law was during his (immoral) time, but also about what it ought to be, so that nations would be instigated by "That Power in the Universe not ourselves, which makes for Righteousness."[169] While Western civilization on both sides of the Atlantic progressed toward a more moral, righteous, or "liberal and humane"[170] existence through "the permanent law of civilized nations"[171] thanks to the insights of people such as Grotius, the Peace Conference, gathered to end the horrors of war, was a sign that the rest of the world was approaching that point as well. White wrote that he seemed to hear Grotius from his tomb, encouraging the delegates to

> Go on with your mighty work. . . . Guard well the treasures of civilization with which each of you is entrusted. . . . Go on with the work of strengthening peace and humanizing war: give greater scope and strength to provisions which will make war less cruel: perfect those laws of war which diminish the unmerited sufferings of populations.[172]

The idea of "civilization" was very important for the delegates, and they thought that the work of the conference was merely the reflection of the already achieved standards of the civilized peoples. This mindset appears in the very text of the Hague Regulations as well:

> Until a more complete code of the laws of war has been issued, the High Contracting Parties deem it expedient to declare that in cases not included in the Regulations adopted by them, the inhabitants and

the belligerents remain under the protection and rule of the principles of the law of nations, as they result from the usages established among civilized peoples, from the laws of humanity, and the dictates of the public conscience.[173]

These ideas about civilization and being civilized continued to gain power during the late nineteenth century and led to the development of norms against what is perceived to be "uncivilized" (including disrespect for private property, shown particularly by a barbaric practice like pillage) or brutal conduct in war. Those ways of conducting war were ultimately embodied in prohibition regimes, laws or rules in the later part of the nineteenth century, climaxing with the Hague Conventions.[174]

The Geneva Conventions (1949)

Although a prohibition regime against pillage was created by the Hague Conventions, it was further developed and reinforced with the later conventions. When we look at the handling of pillage in the 1949 Geneva Conventions, we see that while obligation and precision continue to be high, the moderate delegation of The Hague is strengthened. The Conventions continue to bring a high degree of obligation on the state parties to observe the prohibition against pillage by both repeating the fact that it is prohibited and including "appropriation of property" in the list of grave breaches, along with other war crimes such as

> willful killing, torture or inhuman treatment, including biological experiments, willfully causing great suffering or serious injury to body or health, unlawful deportation or transfer or unlawful confinement of a protected person, compelling a protected person to serve in the forces of a hostile Power, or willfully depriving a protected person of the rights of fair and regular trial, taking of hostages.[175]

Precision is also high when it comes to pillage, since Article 33 openly says, "Pillage is prohibited."[176]

The Geneva Conventions system of delegation is high in the case of grave breaches ("binding internal policies-legitimation of decentralized enforcement" or "binding regulations with consent or opt-out"[177]), and it encompasses pillage, which is included in the grave breaches as "appropriation of property."

The Draft Convention (IV), prepared by the International Committee of the Red Cross (ICRC) and submitted to the conference in 1949, did not prohibit pillage. The only article that mentioned pillage was Article 13 of the Draft (Article 16 in the final text), which said:

> As far as military considerations allow, each Party to the conflict shall facilitate the measures taken to search for the killed and wounded, to assist the shipwrecked and other persons exposed to grave danger, and to protect them against pillage and ill-treatment.

This article was not changed in the final text, although it cannot be interpreted as prohibiting pillage by the occupying forces since it is about search, care, and protection of civilians in general.

The other important article regarding the protection of private property was Article 30 (Article 33 in the final text), which did not mention pillage:

> No protected person may be punished for an offence he or she has not personally committed. Collective penalties are prohibited.
>
> Measures of reprisal against protected persons and their property are prohibited. Any destruction of personal or real property which is not made absolutely necessary by military operations, is prohibited, as are likewise all measures of intimidation or terrorism.[178]

This Article ended up being divided into two articles in the final text, with some additions to the first part. Article 33 says:

> No protected person may be punished for an offence he or she has not personally committed. Collective penalties and likewise all measures of intimidation or of terrorism are prohibited.
>
> Pillage is prohibited.
>
> Reprisals against protected persons and their property are prohibited.

The second part became a new article, Article 53:

> Any destruction by the Occupying Power of real or personal property belonging individually or collectively to private persons, or to the

State, or to other public authorities, or to social or cooperative organizations, is prohibited, except where such destruction is rendered
absolutely necessary by military operations.

Pillage entered Article 33, and destruction of property became a new
article during one of the committee meetings in which the delegates were
debating another matter, collective penalties. When Article 30 of the Draft
Convention (IV) (Article 33 in the final text), on the issues of collective
penalties and reprisals against protected persons and their property, was
being discussed, the Italian delegate, Mr. Maresca, said that the provision of
Article 30 prohibiting such acts in the future was as important as that introduced by Article 47 of the Hague Convention prohibiting pillage. The article
had the same moral force as the Preamble of the Draft Convention forbidding torture. Brigadier Page, the British delegate, took the opportunity of
this mention of pillage and said that "since reference had most opportunely
been made to Article 47 of the Hague Convention forbidding pillage," he
thought Article 30 should be supplemented by a prohibition of pillage. The
Indian delegate, Mr. Haksar demanded an exact definition of public and
private property, while the Chinese delegate, Mr. Wu opposed the place-
ment of the destruction of property under the title of reprisals because that
would minimize the crime. Wu said they should either omit the destruction
of property from the Geneva Conventions, since it was already covered by
international law through the Hague Conventions, or write it into a separate
article.[179]
Later, after a long and heated discussion over whether protection of private property should be extended to state and collective property (which was
proposed by the Soviet Union), Articles 30 and 53 took their final form. The
United Kingdom proposal to add prohibition of pillage was accepted, but
the committee dropped the word "formally," which appears in Article 47 of
the Hague Conventions IV, because they did not want to weaken other prohibitions by adding adverbs to some of them.[180] Likewise, the Italian delegate's
proposal to add "systematic" before "destruction" in Article 53 was rejected
on the grounds that this "might by implication appear to authorize destruction which was not systematic."[181] The wording of Article 130 of the Draft
Convention (Article 147 in the final text) regarding grave breaches was also
carefully drawn with respect to property. The Italian and Danish delegates
suggested the addition of the words "and seizure" after "destruction" of property, to ensure that all forms of violation of property would be included in

grave breaches. Upon the proposal of the Australian and British delegates, the word "appropriation" was used instead.[182]

We should note that the delegates were very sensitive about avoiding implications that any pillage or destruction of property could be excusable, yet they had no such concern about Article 27 dealing with rape. It is also remarkable that the states carefully reformulated and inserted the prohibition of pillage and destruction of property into the Geneva Conventions even though it already existed in international law. The Report of Committee III to the Plenary Assembly makes it clear that they wanted to reemphasize these prohibitions, which were violated during World War II, by including them in the Geneva Conventions.[183] Why was reemphasizing something that already existed in international law more important than emphasizing something (rape) that was not in international law, but had occurred as part of World War II's atrocities? This question will be addressed in Chapter 4, after looking at the Hague Conventions' lack of interest in prohibiting rape.

Chapter 3

The (Non) Prohibition of Rape in War:
The Hague Conventions

The known history of rape in war goes back to Biblical times.[1] And "the prevalence of rapes committed during modern warfare has kept pace, if not exceeded, the sexual violence of ancient conflicts."[2] Yet, by the twentieth century, rape continued to be as invisible as before. Soldiers who perceived women as inferior sexual objects to be dominated committed opportunistic rapes, and, according to Susan Brownmiller, who in her 1975 book wrote the groundbreaking and silence-breaking chapter on rape in war, armies often used rape as a weapon due to its effectiveness in demoralizing the enemy and giving morale to soldiers by symbolically proving the victory of the victorious side.[3] As Brownmiller puts it, "rape by a conquering soldier destroys all illusions of power and property for men of the defeated side. The body of a raped woman becomes a ceremonial battlefield, a parade ground for the victor's trooping of the colors. The act that is played out upon her is a message passed between men."[4] According to time and context, it served different purposes and different people interpreted both rape itself and its purposes or functions in different ways.[5] But one thing stayed constant: it has been invisible to law.

According to Bassiouni and McCormick, "For the most part, rape, along with pillage, has been viewed as an 'inevitable' aspect of war."[6] In that case, if some combination of strategic material interests and ideational changes culminating in a normative shock led to the creation of the regime against pillage, can we find a similar combination leading to the prohibition of rape?

We do not see any change in the cost-benefit balance for allowing or encouraging rape at any point in history, at least on a large scale. The continued reality of women's oppression determined the social meanings such as the association of women with honor as the property of men. Societies interpreted attacks on women as an attack on the honor of the men who "own" the women, as well as an attack on the community (composed of the men as the public sphere) until 1977, when, at least in international law, women gained "personal dignity."[7] For centuries, then, the physical pain of women has been translated into a social pain through the meanings attached to rape, which has been useful in winning wars at basically no cost.

Due to this understanding of the violation of women's bodies as the violation of men's and community's honor, the men and community who "owned" the women felt collective humiliation as a result of rape. That is why, for instance, when *A Woman in Berlin*, the diary of a woman who experienced and witnessed the mass rapes of German women during the Soviet occupation of 1945, was published in Germany in 1959, some Germans were very upset that these stories were being told, and accused the author of "besmirching the honor of German women."[8] What they meant was besmirching the honor of Germans. According to them, women should not have told their stories of personal pain and violation because what was hurt was German honor; the raped women symbolized the raped country and people.[9] As a result of this widespread social perspective on rape, it can be, and has been, used as a powerful weapon to deeply hurt the enemy.

As far as ideational changes are concerned, we do not find a significant change in the perception of rape from medieval times to the nineteenth century. Since rape was considered an aggressive manifestation of sexuality, people thought that rape in war was normal because it was a combination of two normal things: aggression (normal in war) and sexuality. Rape is not shocking in a normative context where the prevailing assumptions include the uncontrollability of male lust, women as the object of that male lust, and rape as its expression.[10]

Why did the notion of being civilized or liberal, which were the driving ideational forces behind the prohibition regime against pillage, not lead simultaneously to a prohibition against rape? Why were women "property enough" to be raped, but not "property enough" to be protected? Why did states not consider the practice of raping women in war at least as uncivilized and barbaric as pillage? How did the normative context normalizing rape take this shape, how was it perpetuated, how did it influence the situation of women during and after wars, and how did it eventually change enough to lead to international legal change?

The Law

As discussed in Chapter 1, the Hague Conventions (1899, 1907) contain no obligation for state parties to prevent rape by their armed forces. The document does not even mention rape and the closest it does come to discussing rape—Article 46, requiring respect for "family honors and rights"—does not even stipulate prevention. The language of "respect" rather than prohibition leads to very low obligation, even if we presume that "family honor and rights" indirectly referred to rape.

The precision element in the Hague Regulations is very problematic when it comes to rape. The text does not explain what "family honors," "family rights," or "respect" for them entail. Even asking whether or not they include rape is a stretch, because laws need to be clear and the imprecision in this case does not warrant such derivation.[11]

Since obligation and precision are highly problematic in the Hague Conventions with respect to rape, delegation does not exist either. Even if prosecutions happen for violations of the convention, the likelihood that they will include charges for rape is almost nonexistent, given that it is not clear if states had a responsibility to prevent rape. Therefore, we cannot consider the Conventions as the legal documents that created the prohibition regime against rape.

To understand why the Hague Conventions exclude rape from the prohibitions, it is necessary to go back to the Brussels Declaration of 1874, since the drafters of the Conventions copied most of the articles regarding the laws of war from it. The vagueness of "family honors and rights" in Article 46 of the Hague Regulations originated in Brussels. It is also necessary to look at the Lieber Code since it is the source of the Brussels Declaration.

Lieber Code (1863)

It is particularly interesting that the Hague Regulations exclude rape from its prohibitions since they rely heavily on the Lieber Code (1863),[12] which explicitly mentions rape among the list of prohibited acts during war. One peculiarity of the Lieber Code was that, although the publicists of Lieber's time devoted far more space and specificity to the protection of private property than the protection of personal rights, the Lieber Code has eight articles about the protection of personal rights and property rights: four on personal rights, three on both personal and property rights, and one on property rights only.[13] The Code states that

All wanton violence committed against persons in the invaded country, all destruction of property not commanded by the authorized officer, all robbery, all pillage or sacking, even after taking a place by main
force, all rape, wounding, maiming, or killing of such inhabitants, are
prohibited under the penalty of death, or such other severe punishment as may seem adequate for the gravity of the offense. (Section II,
Article 44)

Crimes punishable by all penal codes, such as arson, murder, maiming, assaults, highway robbery, theft, burglary, fraud, forgery, and
rape, if committed by an American soldier in a hostile country against
its inhabitants, are not only punishable as at home, but in all cases in
which death is not inflicted the severer punishment shall be preferred.
(Section II, Article 47)

Brussels Declaration (1874)

By the mid-nineteenth century the conduct of war was still based on customary law, and the only codified international law of war was the Geneva Convention for the Amelioration of the Condition of the Wounded in Armies in
the Field (1864). The war of 1870–1871 between France and Germany became a stage for major differences in military practices, leading to reprisals
because of uncertainties regarding the laws of war. Inspired by the proposal of
the International Committee of the Red Cross (ICRC) about a convention to
govern the conduct of belligerents, Russian tsar Alexander II called the Brussels Conference with the intent of codifying the laws and customs of war.[14]
Friedrich Martens, a Russian scholar of international law and a diplomat influenced by Lieber, prepared the draft convention.[15]

The original draft of the Brussels Declaration (Article 50) said, "The religious convictions, the honor, the life, and the property of pacific populations
should be respected by the enemy army."[16] They later added the protection of
"family rights" to the draft, on the proposal of the Italian delegate Mr. Lanza.
The German delegate Mr. Voigts-Rhetz proposed to delete "honor" from the
article, because the word was employed under similar conditions in another
chapter and it would be suitable to do the same here. His proposal was defeated.[17] The commission declared that by maintaining the word "honor," its
intention is to establish the obligation to respect the honor of the families.[18]

The discussion of the honor issue concludes with this remark, but the
discussion on the parts of the article dealing with private property continues.

Mr. Lanza said that in the first Russian draft, one article formulated a restriction on the absolute respect for private property, and he demanded that the exception be restored in order not to restrict, in the event of need, the occupation of a house, a field, or other property. Mr. Lambermont, the Belgian delegate, responded by saying that the article posed the principle of the respect of private property generally; the restrictions were dealt with in the article handling requisitions and other permitted and prohibited means of war.[19] As a result, the delegates modified Article 50 (Article 38 in the final text) to "The religious convictions, honor and family rights, life and property of the population must be respected." Later it was changed again to "The honor and family rights, life and property of individuals, as well as their religious convictions and exercise of their worship must be respected." On the proposal of the French delegate, Mr. Baude, "Private property cannot be confiscated" was also added.[20]

As we can see from these debates, the delegates discussed the matter of family honor very briefly—what it included or excluded, how it needed to be addressed or explained, whether there was any need for amendments—but none of these items became major issues in the debate, and delegates did not mention rape or women even once. In contrast to this situation, the discussion on private property and pillage was very detailed, and most delegates paid great attention to the framing of the prohibitions regarding them.

The Hague Conventions (1899, 1907)

The Hague Regulations originated from the Lieber Code[21] and incorporated all the prohibitions of the Lieber Code—including pillage and other prohibitions protecting private property, but excluded the prohibition against rape. The delegates at The Hague were aware of this exclusion. The Belgian delegate, Beernaert, complained that the phrase "family honor and rights" in Article 46 (Article 38 of the Draft Convention) was too vague.[22] During the conference, however, when Beernaert made his comment, a long debate on Article 46 started, which (interestingly) resulted in a clearer prohibition of any appropriation of private property and no change in terms of the prohibition of rape. General den Beer Poortugael, the delegate from the Netherlands, said, "it is neither necessary nor possible to define more in detail the sense of this article, the purport of which is evident."[23] Then Colonel Gross von Schwarzhoff, the German delegate, wanted to add a further restriction to the article: "as far as military necessities permit."[24] His proposal was unacceptable to the other delegates because, they argued, the whole point of writing this convention was to protect the people against military necessities. Chevalier Descamps, a second Belgian delegate, said that "it is impossible to admit the destruction of human rights as a legal thesis although recourse is occasionally had thereto if necessary," which means even though military necessity sometimes overrides human rights in practice, Descamps is against accepting this kind of override in theory as part of a legal convention. Mr. Rolin, the delegate from Siam, adamantly opposed the amendment by saying it is wrong to weaken the principles by giving them a doubtful declaration. He said Article 38 is about the general principle of respect for honor, lives of individuals, and private property. The restrictions regarding military necessity existed in the other articles (regarding requisitions for confiscation of property under military necessity, for instance).

As a result of these objections, the amendment was withdrawn, although Colonel von Schwarzhoff said he would withdraw it with the condition that it was thoroughly established that Chevalier Descamps's declaration was the exact interpretation of the article.[25] He wanted to declare that, even though everybody would be accepting that, in principle human rights cannot be violated, when a state can prove that violating parts of this article was absolutely necessary from a military point of view, that situation should be acceptable to all. One can interpret this reasoning as a statement for the position that if violations of a particular prohibition can potentially be justified with military necessity, states may be willing to take on legal obligations that may be difficult to implement at times. The extension of this logic to the cases of pillage and rape would be that, while the acquisition of private property can be justified on the basis of the basic needs of soldiers (and even compensated later), the rape of women (especially "honorable" women of "honorable" gentlemen) cannot be justified in the same way. This makes it all the more important to avoid any clear obligation of its prevention for states.

What is also interesting is what happened after this debate. While delegates were discussing this "military necessity" proposal, everybody forgot about Beernaert's suggestion to clarify "family honors and rights"; however, they did realize that the draft article did not protect private property sufficiently. It said, "Family honor and rights, and the lives and property of persons, as well as their religious convictions, and their practice, must be respected. Private property cannot be confiscated." Mr. Odier, the Swiss delegate, thought this did not provide sufficient protection for private property, so he proposed a change from "property of persons" into "private property whether belonging to individuals or corporations." Mr. Beernaert suggested another formula so that all private property, regardless of whom it belongs to, would come under the protection of the article. His proposal was adopted and the delegates modified the article to read, "Family honor and rights, the lives of persons, and private property, as well as religious convictions and practice must be respected. Private property cannot be confiscated."[26] On the one hand, we might surmise that the delegates thought "family honor and rights" was sufficiently clear in terms of the object of protection it indicated, while "property of persons" was not clear enough. One the other hand, we might assume they did not think it was clear. But as Graber puts it, the vague terms used in describing some of the practices—such as the protection of "honor" or "family rights"—aimed to make acceptance of them easier, "since these terms are broad enough to permit a multitude of interpretations to suit individual opinions."[27] As Mr. Beernaert put it during a hot debate on another issue,

> however great our willingness may be, I am afraid that if we wish to regulate everything and to decide everything conventionally, we shall meet the same difficulties as before [that is, in Brussels]. In my opinion there are certain points which cannot be the subject of a convention and which it would be better to leave, as at present, under the governance of that tacit and common law which arises from the principles of the law of nations.[28]

If that is indeed the case, why did the delegates need the rules referring to protection of women to be vague and open to interpretation? What made debating the subject so impossible?

One possibility is that the Europeans of the nineteenth century—with their emphasis on decency, finesse, manners, and propriety—did not want to spell out the word *rape*, particularly in a diplomatic document. From the mid-eighteenth century onward, as a result of the rise of the idea of delicacy, or prudery, sexuality in any form offended and embarrassed people: "the first new generation of the nineteenth century [was] more strait-laced, inhibited, and conventional than its parents, so that sons discussed their fathers' wild oats, and daughters worried about their mothers' loose sexual behavior."[29]

Perhaps another reason was that the language of diplomacy in the nineteenth century was French, and the French word for *rape*, *le viol*, is a vulgar word enunciating an animalistic violent act that civilized people of that age would not engage in or even talk about.[30] Given the language used in Article

46 versus the other articles prohibiting other acts, however, it is not realistic to put all the burden of the absence of a prohibition against rape in the Hague Conventions on this prudish sensibility. If the delegates really wanted to prohibit rape, one would expect at least the language of prohibition and some mention of women in the article. They could have said "Violation of women is prohibited" (in French, "La violation de femmes est interdite") or "Outrages upon women are prohibited" ("Les indignations sur les femmes sont interdites") or even "Women should be protected" ("Les femmes devraient être protégées"). It still would not qualify as a prohibition regime, but at least it would show that the reason they could not mention rape was their own propriety. Besides, Francis Lieber was a nineteenth-century European, yet he did not refrain from including rape in his code, and with a precise prohibition as well.

Additionally, other debates during the conference illustrate the fact that the states were very much aware of the impact of clarity versus vagueness of law in terms of creating an obligatory prohibition. They tried to exclude measures when they believed they could not comply with them. In cases where they could not exclude these measures, states tried to make the provisions as vague as possible to make them less obligatory.

An interesting example happened during a plenary meeting (in the 1899 Conference), when General Sir John Ardagh, the British delegate, brought up the question of dumdum bullets, although an article prohibiting their use had already been accepted by the conference three weeks before. The accepted article states:

> The use of the bullets which expand or flatten easily in the human body, such as exploding bullets, bullets with hard jackets whose jacket does not entirely cover the core or has incisions in it, should be prohibited.

General Ardagh said:

> It seems to me that the use of these words describing technical details of construction will result in making the prohibition a little too general and absolute. It would not seem to admit of the exception which I would desire to provide for, that is, the present or future construction of some projectile with shock sufficient to stop the stricken soldier and put him immediately *hors de combat*, thus fulfilling the

indispensable conditions of warfare without, on the other hand, causing useless suffering.[31]

He then went on to explain in detail how types of bullets used in war work,
how many millimeters they are, which ones cause more suffering, which ones
penetrate the body, and which ones do not "work" at all—sometimes by citing
published results of experiments with these bullets. He said in order to provide their soldiers with sufficient protection, the British government wanted
to "reserve entire liberty to introduce modifications" in the construction of
projectiles, given that they will not cause useless aggravation of suffering. He
also argued that wars between civilized nations and wars against savages are
different. Civilized nations' soldiers are incapacitated easily with small projectiles while savages, such as Indians, continue to advance even after being
shot several times and will eventually cut off your head since they do not
abide by the laws of war. Therefore, the English wanted to use more capable
bullets against "savage races."[32] To use these bullets, they needed the law to be
vague, with less detail about the construction and functions of the projectiles,
so that when British forces used them against the "savage races," they would
not be violating the laws.

Accordingly, the United States delegate, Captain Crozier, suggested a
change of wording in the article to omit the details: "The employment of bullets which inflict uselessly cruel wounds, such as explosive bullets and in general every kind of bullet which exceeds the limit necessary in order to put a
man *hors de combat* at once, is forbidden." This new wording clearly makes the
prohibition weaker and less clear by throwing out the technical details of the
bullets' construction (such as their shape, their structure, how they enter the
body, what they do there) and adding subjective assessments such as "inflict-
ing uselessly cruel wounds," blurring what is prohibited and what is not. The
judgment is left to each state to determine whether a particular bullet inflicts
"enough" pain to be included in the prohibition, which lessens the obligation
and precision of the article. The president of the meeting, Belgian delegate
Beernaert, asked, "What would remain of the article if they were to accept
[this] modification?" Agreeing with the president, the Russian delegate and
the Dutch delegate also remarked that this new wording was "far too vague."[33]

Similar to this debate in terms of states' desire to clarify or blur their obligations under certain articles, an intense discussion occurred when Article
55 in the Draft Convention (Article 59 in the final text) came up. This article
stated:

A neutral State may authorize the passage through its territory of wounded or sick belonging to the belligerent armies, on condition that the trains bringing them shall carry neither personnel nor material of war. In such a case, the neutral State is bound to take whatever measures of safety and control are necessary for the purpose.

The delegate from Austria-Hungary wanted to add "which exceed the amount necessary for the care of the sick and wounded of the convoy" after the phrase "personnel nor material of war." Mr. Beernaert (Belgium) said that that was really the sense of the article, so they decided to mention the interpretation of the article in the minutes of the meeting without adding it to the final text. This incident is another example that even when the exact meaning of an article was evident and there was no need for explanation in the actual article, states wanted at least to mention it during the conference and insert the explanation into the conference minutes when they wanted the obligations to be clear.[34] Given that the phrase "family honor and rights" in Article 46 has no such self-evident meaning and clearly needed explanation, and given that a delegate actually mentioned this situation and demanded some clarification, we can only conclude that states' resistance to clarification of this content was intentional.

Going back to the debate over Article 55, we find a rather long debate over General Mounier's (France) proposal to substitute "may authorize" with "shall authorize," in order to make sure that neutral states would treat belligerent parties equally so that there would be no special advantages to one of the parties. Mounier speculated that the passage of the wounded across the neutral territory might grant advantage to one side by opening up a line of communication to the army. This proposal to impose a clear obligation on neutral states met with strong protests from the small states at the conference. Delegates from Belgium in particular vehemently opposed any such obligation, since as a small neutral state "often trampled cruelly" between the longstanding rivals of the time, France and Germany, Belgians did not want to find themselves in an impossible situation (in which they would be forced to allow passage against their own interests). Rather than putting themselves under such obligations, they said they would prefer the status quo—that is, the absence of any regulations regarding neutral states conveying wounded soldiers. Their objection to this change came even though in previous debates they continuously emphasized their desire for clear laws regarding the rights and duties of the neutral states.[35]

As we can see from these examples, which are just a few among many, states do not want to sign on to obligations they believe they cannot adhere to (whether due to inability or lack of desire). When such a possibility arises, they try to make the obligation as vague as possible in order to avoid being portrayed as a violator in case such an incident happens. They want to be able to say that the prohibition does not include the specific act that they committed (such as using dumdum bullets that do not inflict "too much" suffering or committing rape, which may not be included in the provision regarding the protection of "family honor and rights"), and therefore there is no violation.

In order to understand why states believed that they could not comply with a law prohibiting rape and so preferred that Article 46 omit it, we need to turn to the normative context in which the Hague Regulations were written.

The Normative Context

Since we are trying to understand the social conditions under which the international laws not protecting women (as opposed to private property) emerged, it is necessary to look at the normative context, or the environment of the web of intersubjective meanings shared by the European states in the nineteenth century with respect to women. Therefore, my next focus will be on the treatment of women by the law, especially in relation to property.

Ursula Vogel argues that in nineteenth-century Europe, man's property rights over woman's body merged into the demands of public good and were under the protection of the state.[36] This merge happened because of the emancipatory potential of political modernization for women. Ensuring that women's chastity was the sexual property of their husbands was a way of controlling the process of political modernization.[37] According to John Stuart Mill, in the nineteenth century "the wife is the actual bond-servant of her husband: no less so, as far as legal obligation goes, than slaves commonly so-called."[38] The fact that a wife was the property of her husband in common law was one of the most important signs of this marital slavery.[39] Friedrich Engels also wrote, in 1884, that modern families, which had their roots in the victory of private property, are established on the domestic slavery of the wife. According to Engels, the preservation and inheritance of property required the establishment of monogamy, which in fact expected monogamy for the wife but allowed hetaerism for the husband, and male supremacy, especially for the ruling classes. As a result, sexual acts outside of marriage were considered crimes for women—with serious legal and social consequences—but they could be honorable or just a slight moral blemish for men that they wear with pleasure.[40]

In order to understand the normative context surrounding the writing of the Hague Conventions, I will look at the elements of this process of women's subjugation in Europe, mainly in Victorian England and post-Revolutionary France as its centers. First, I will examine the law, in particular marriage laws and the laws regulating adultery, as well as property laws. Second, I will investigate the social class element in this context, which can help explain the vague treatment of rape in international law, which was written by people from a certain class. Third, I will turn to the issue of sexual violence.

The Law

Nineteenth-century Europeans constructed women as both powerful and powerless, as sexual agents but also victims, as dangerous but also in need of protection. Regulating the female body became a priority, which was done through the introduction of more sophisticated legislation.[41] Marriage and property laws are the most important areas of legislation that reinforce men's and states' rights over women's bodies.

Marriage and Adultery Laws

According to Carol Smart, "marriage was a major signifier in the process of constructing the meaning of Woman in legal discourse in the latter part of the nineteenth century, a systematic mode of regulating the dangers . . . posed by the potential unruliness of women's bodies."[42] Two major parts of marriage laws are significant for our purposes: (1) divorce and adultery and (2) sexual violence within marriage.

Nineteenth-century English divorce laws treated male and female adultery in completely different ways. The only ground for "*divorce a vinculo*" (divorce granted by the Parliament) was a wife's adultery. The distinction between the adultery of a husband and a wife was based on, Keith Thomas argues, "the desire of men for absolute property in women."[43] In 1854 in the British Parliament, Lord Cranworth said that it would be too harsh to bring the law to bear against a husband who was "a little profligate."[44] Through law, then, the state tried to manage the "unruliness" of the female body by denying women the right to divorce an adulterous or violent husband while stripping her of all rights (such as continuing her marriage or gaining custody of her children) if she committed adultery. According to Ursula Vogel, these adultery laws were established "on the assumption that any leniency on the part of the law would be exploited, to the disadvantage of men, by the depraved members of the female sex."[45]

Since what people considered a danger to the well-being of the society, and therefore what the state wanted to regulate, was the female body rather than the male body, sexual violence within marriage was a nonissue.[46] In 1888 a judge declared:

> The sexual communion between . . . [married couples] is by virtue of the irrevocable privilege conferred once [and] for all on the husband at the time of the marriage, and not at all by virtue of a consent given upon each act of communion, as is the case between unmarried persons.[47]

One nineteenth-century feminist, Elizabeth Wolstenholme Elmy, wrote in relation to marital rape laws: "The only absolute right I should claim for a woman as against a man is that she should never be made a mother against her will."[48] The Parliament, however, did not agree with her. The list of possible aggravations that could justify a woman seeking divorce (in combination with adultery) that was debated in the House of Lords included rape, sodomy, desertion, transportation, penal servitude, incest, bigamy, and cruelty. Out of these possibilities, the Parliament agreed only on incest, bigamy, and cruelty in the Divorce Act of 1857. As Mary Shanley puts it,

> they did not regard crimes of sexual violence or prolonged absence by the husband as fatal to the marriage bond. The Lords did not even consider sexual violence within marriage. A husband had the [exclusive] right of access to his wife's body, and by definition could not be charged with marital rape.[49]

In post-Revolutionary France, the initial revolutionary enthusiasm and egalitarian spirit that had begun to give women more rights, including property and divorce rights, subsided soon after, and the bourgeois fear of inheritance going to the children of adultery shaped marriage and adultery laws.[50] The risk of bringing bastards into the family was too much to for the nineteenth-century state, and it firmly established inequality between men and women by bringing back into the new penal code (1810) the crime of adultery, which the revolutionary codes had abolished.[51]

According to Alexandre Dumas, French obsession with adultery began with the Napoleonic Civil Code (1804). The abolition of primogeniture (right of the firstborn child or eldest son to receive the family inheritance) was one of the first policies of the new regime, due to its inherent inequality and because the new regime's objective was to divide large estates for a more equitable wealth distribution.[52] This legal change made adultery, considered more of an embarrassment or a joke called cuckoldry in the seventeenth century, a crime. The husbands who were sure that their first male child was their own and would inherit their title and fortune felt comfortable under primogeniture, but when the Napoleonic Code required equal division of wealth among children, they became obsessed with preventing children who were not theirs from inheriting any of their estate.[53] Besides, the association between the lifestyle of the aristocracy and adultery in the minds of the people contributed to the post-Revolutionary hatred toward adultery.

The Napoleonic Code suppressed women's rights by retreating from the Revolution's ideas about equality. It restricted divorce to cases of adultery by the wife, adultery by the husband if he kept his concubine in the family home, cases of brutality, and conviction of a serious crime. It made divorce by mutual consent of the spouses tied to so many conditions that it became awfully difficult to obtain one.[54] In addition to the laws establishing women's inequality, many "scientific publications" sought to rationalize women's subordination—one of their rationales being women's reproductive functions.[55]

Similarly, in England, adultery by the wife could be a basis for divorce, but adultery by the husband could not, unless there were other aggravating offences. In 1853 the Royal Commission on the Law of Divorce stated that "the difference between the adultery of the husband and the adultery of the wife (socially speaking) is boundless."[56] It was evident that this "boundless" difference had its roots in the vital importance of protecting property rights through rightful inheritance. In 1857, during a speech in the House of Lords, Lord Cranworth said:

> A wife might, without any loss of caste, and possibly with reference to the interests of her children, or even of her husband, condone an act of adultery on the part of the husband: but a husband could not condone a similar act on the part of a wife. No-one would venture to suggest that a husband could possibly do so, and for this, among other reasons, . . . the adultery of the wife might be the means of palming

spurious offspring upon the husband, while the adultery of the husband could have no such effect with regard to the wife.[57]

With the advent of modern civil law, ownership rights over another person (like slavery and feudal servitude) lost their legitimacy; however, the husband's right to the wife's body did not, Vogel argues, because "it is sheltered by claims made on behalf of the public good."[58] In 1840, for instance, in the case of a husband who imprisoned his wife in her room because she wanted to leave him, a judge in England ruled that the husband can do so because the law, "reflecting public opinion," allowed a husband to enforce his right to his wife's body by a writ of *habeas corpus*.[59]

Another good signifier of the situation reflecting women's place in nineteenth-century England is the action for criminal conversation, which was the action of a husband suing a man to charge him with adultery with his wife. If the defendant is found guilty, the husband recovers "damages." The wife was not a party to these transactions and she was not allowed to testify, since it was an action between men for damage to the husband's property.[60] Historically and conceptually, Vogel argues,

> the rights that the adulterous woman violates refer to different claims as well as different claimants. They refer to a man's ownership of children, to his control over property (estates) and lineage, and to his right of exclusive access to the wife's body and sexuality. But it is not only the property right of a private person that is at stake here, but the collective interest of society represented by the state.[61]

Society's interest required women to be chaste and lineages to be pure, so that inheritances would go to the rightful children[62] and the families would be "in order," making social order possible.

This situation was particularly evident in post–Revolutionary France. Although the government built the whole system of private law on the principles of individual liberty and equality, the civil code became a double standard because of the reactions that came after the Reign of Terror. Divorces that women initiated were seen as the symbols of a society in disarray, so the government designed the laws in a way to ensure "social disorder" did not happen. The argument was "that the wife's adultery might result in a 'foreign child' usurping the husband's property and that as a consequence the order of the society itself would descend into anarchy."[63]

Adultery committed by a woman required her to be punished (for example, through divorce), but in fact her adultery was not regarded as the act of a real, legal person; rather, she was just the tool and her role in the act required the communication of two men, especially when it came to law. This situation resonates very much with the case of rape. Rape, especially during war, is a form of male communication, women being just the instruments of that communication.

Since society considered women not only tools of communication between men but also men's property, both socially and legally, their property also belonged to their husbands. In nineteenth-century England, common law doctrine of spousal unity eliminated a woman's legal personality upon marriage, rendering her ineligible to hold property in her own name. That was because "a wife was herself the 'property' of her husband, since he could claim her earnings and her body when she cannot make similar claims upon him."[64] Later in the century, several social and economic trends encouraged legislators to reform the marriage law (with respect to property), and they reformed women's property rights under certain conditions, all of which benefited the interests of certain men. For example, the shift of wealth from land to movable property and the uncertainties of nineteenth-century economic life made men want their wives' property to remain free from their creditors in case they went bankrupt.[65] Businessmen were engaging in trade and transactions that could easily result in bankruptcy (unlike the stability that being part of the landed aristocracy ensured), and they did not want to lose all of their property in such a case. Instead, they wanted their wives to hold some of their property separately, immune from sequestration, which proved a safer economic path. In addition, creditors who gave credit to a woman before she got married wanted legal protection so that they could get their money back from the husband who owned the woman's property after marriage. These fiscal reasons for married women to hold on to their own properties encouraged the Parliament to pass the Creditor's Bill (Amendment to the Married Women's Property Act of 1870) in 1874. The Parliament found the idea of tradesmen being cheated insupportable, while it did not care that "married women should be deprived of all their property except their earnings."[66]

We can conclude that in the nineteenth century, the lawmaking process excluded women and their interests, although women resisted the process in many ways.[67] It is not surprising that the treatment of women by international law at the time was so inequitable, especially given the lack of space for women's resistance. While international law worked vehemently to protect men's property, the most profound attacks on women's bodies did not find a place in the laws of war. Even if we assume that "family honor and rights" in Article 46 of the Hague Conventions implicitly referred to women's bodies, it was to the extent that they were some men's property.

What about men who were not major property owners? What about "their" women? Who is supposed to be protected against whom by the law? Who has "family honor and [hence property] rights" and who does not? These questions bring us to an important social factor in Europe: class.

Class

In nineteenth-century England, political leaders designed public policy under the assumption that violence against women was mostly a phenomenon of the lower classes.[68] The bourgeois moralist culture portrayed lower-class men as "an animalistic mass."[69] Even one of the feminists of the time, Harriet Taylor Mill, wrote:

> The truly horrible effects of the law among the lowest of the working population, is exhibited in those cases of hideous maltreatment of their wives by working men, with which every newspaper, every police report, teems. Wretches unfit to have the smallest authority over any living thing, have a helpless woman for their household slave. These excesses could not exist if women both earned, and had the right to possess, a part of the income of the family.[70]

Although most feminists believed that violence against women existed in all classes, they used the stereotypical "picture of the brutal male drunkard abusing his wife" to push for legislation dealing with violence against women because the Parliament could only accept making laws "to discipline working-class males and save decent working-class women from brutal husbands" rather than acknowledging systematic violence against women.[71] Irish social reformer and suffragist Frances Power Cobbe wrote:

> The dangerous wife-beater belongs almost exclusively to the artisan and laboring classes, . . . drunken, idle, ruffianly fellows who lounge about the public-houses, instead of working for their families. Some of their victims are "hopelessly depraved" [but] there are among them at least as many good women as bad. . . [S]ober, honest, chaste, and industrious.[72]

Class considerations also played into the adultery and divorce laws with respect to property and inheritance. As Shanley argues:

> The notion that only a wife's adultery justified severing the marriage bond assumed that a man's sexual authority and the legitimacy of his offspring were the basic consideration of the marriage contract. Parliament's disregard of the threat to a family line posed by a husband's adultery reflected the assumption that men committed adultery with women who did not belong to the "respectable classes" and whose family life was consequently considered unimportant. If a man did seduce the wife of a gentleman, her husband could divorce her to protect himself against illegitimate heirs.[73]

Similarly, in France the concerns about the property of the upper classes and its passage to the rightful heirs shaped the fate of women with respect to marriage, divorce, and adultery laws. An influential eighteenth-century treatise eventually canonized in the Napoleonic Code said:

> Adultery committed by the wife is infinitely more injurious to the proper organization of civil society since it tends to plunder the family and result in the transference of property to adulterine children who are alien to it. Adultery committed by the husband, however, although extremely criminal in itself, is, in this regard, without consequence. Furthermore the wife, who is an inferior, does not have the right to police the conduct of her husband, who is her superior. She must assume that he is faithful, and jealousy must not lead her to investigate his conduct.[74]

Given this kind of mentality, how could we expect to see rape laws that would protect women? Given that what mattered was the protection of the property of the "respectable gentleman," his inheritance, and his family line against lower-class men's excesses, it was to be expected that the law would protect "family honors and rights" of the "respectable gentleman" rather than women who belonged to either upper or lower classes. When it comes to rape in war, therefore, Article 46 of the Hague Conventions would protect women who belonged to the men in upper classes, who had "family honors and rights," while lower-class women were of no concern.[75]

Sexual Violence

In the nineteenth century, Europeans viewed rape as a sexual activity rather than as a form of violence. The abduction of heiresses that happened at the time, for example, became a concern about sexual activity rather than one of property or the well-being of the women, even though women themselves were considered property.[76] Looking at Victorian England as an example of a common law legal system, and post-Revolutionary France as an example of the civil law legal system in Europe, will help us understand the way rape was excluded from the Hague Conventions.

England

In the nineteenth century, the British considered the protection of and attention to female chastity and honor to be a sign of "England's high civiliza-tion."[77] Rape, as an attack on this honor, was considered one of the most im-portant reasons for excluding women from the public sphere. "Magistrates, judges, and journalists dealing with rape cases began to introduce the idea that rape emperilled women's safety in evening streets; while men could travel freely, 'respectable' women would be safe only at home."[78] It is particularly significant that the women who were considered to be under grave danger and who needed to stay in the safety of the private sphere were middle- and upper-class women. Poor working women were open to both sexual and non-sexual male violence, and there is no evidence that the judges, magistrates, journalists, and other men handling rape cases cared about them. In fact, they even indicated that lower-class women were inherently seductresses, tainted, and inviting, and therefore not able to be true rape victims.[79] By the nineteenth century, chastity, which included not only physical chastity but also obedience to father (for unmarried women) and husband, increasingly came to be considered a middle and upper-class phenomenon because of its relation to property passing on to the rightful heirs. The chastity of lower-class women had no repercussions for property rights and was therefore of no concern to the state. Lower-class women could not be raped because they were not valuable property, owned by a gentleman and hence not the sub-jects of a crime against property.[80] When lower-class women were sexually assaulted, the incident was usually disregarded because lower-class women, with their "loose" or "unchaste" behavior, would either "consent to violence" or "deserve their fate."[81] These ideas about consent and the victim being the "dirty" part of a rape also existed in popular music of the time springing from traditional folk music. These songs portrayed violence as a form of seduction, which was not a crime when committed against lower-class women whose "no" meant "yes." For example, in a song called "By the Light of the Moon," the man sings:

> How this fair maid blushed and grumbled
> Let me alone, I pray forbear;
> Pray be easy, do not tease me,
> Touch me again and I'll pull your hair;
> How this fair maid blushed and grumbled;
> You have spoiled my gown and new galloon.
> But well pleased my Sally by the light of the moon.[82]

According to Anna Clark, this situation was another example of the fact that the ruling elites create and manipulate particular ideas about rape at particular historical moments.[83] In the nineteenth century, although chivalry was glorified for men, and chivalry included control of sexual desires, this control was exhibited only toward chaste (probably upper-class) women. When rape occurred, it was considered as a "regrettable loss of self-control" by the man, not a criminal deed, because people believed that it is very difficult to control passion.[84] Even when the perpetrators of rapes admitted to rape, they would often claim that they had been "intoxicated," and did not remember using force.[85] The fact that an innocent man could be accused of rape by a deceitful (particularly lower-class) woman was so haunting to the lawmakers that they were clearly resistant to even believing a possible incident of "regrettable loss of self-control."[86]

Despite this loose understanding, legally rape was a serious crime (a capital crime until 1841). But rapists were punished only when they violated the property rights of some men—specifically, the father or the husband of the rape victim. One of the reasons that nineteenth-century British rape laws required ejaculation as a proof of rape was this matter of women's chastity being men's property. Ejaculation meant both "physical pollution" on her body and the possibility of an illegitimate child.[87] Still, courts tended to ignore physical evidence in rape cases because "lawyers, doctors and moralists wished to invest the power of proving rape in their own moral judgments, not in women's words or bodies."[88]

In fact, nobody wanted women to talk about rape. They considered lower-class women, who were supposedly immodest already, to be incapable of being raped. Upper-class women, on the other hand, were considered too modest to comprehend and talk about what happens during rape because discussion of any sexual matter was indecent in upper-class society. The press also refrained from reporting sexual crimes, and even when it did report on some cases, the details were obscured as "unfit for publication."[89] Whenever women raised their voices about rape, newspapers and judges silenced them because "respectable women were not supposed to know of or speak about any sexual matter," which meant the loss of the word *rape* for women to define their experiences.[90] If a woman did talk about what happened to her, she would be considered immodest and incapable of being a rape victim. If she did not talk about it, then it meant there would be no complaint and no case against the rapist. A Lambeth magistrate's point about rape illustrates this mentality clearly when he said, "the more decent or respectable females were, the more reluctant they were in coming forward to give public details of such gross outrages."[91] As a result, women usually could not use the word *rape* to define what happened to them because it would be perceived as immoral (their immorality) rather than criminal.[92] The fact that reporting and testifying on rape was blocked and women were silenced is well illustrated by a British newspaper in 1826:

> no female not uninitiated into vice, or neglected in education, can possibly go through the ordeal of a public trial; and the father is not to be envied who would not rather allow the injury to his daughter to escape punishment, than hear the daughter answer those questions, which . . . must be put to her, before a conviction can be obtained.[93]

Public morals, which were damaged by the "shame" created by all the indecent talk about the details of a rape case, were more important to judges and jurists than punishing rapists. Judges sometimes directed juries to acquit (or even imprison rape victims) in order to prevent the case from going further and damaging public morals.[94]

The indirect silencing of rape victims included untruths about rape and the sexual act, fallacies that became common beliefs perpetuated by the medical jurisprudence—for example, that it was not physically possible for a man to rape a healthy adult woman, or that conception indicates desire during sexual intercourse and thus could prove the rape victim consented— which made rape cases even more complicated.[95] Especially for lower-class women, not being the property of a husband or a father meant they could be considered the property of all men, particularly if they acted as such according to the nineteenth-century (middle-class) standards by acting outside the range of accepted female behavior.[96] For example, in 1817, after Mary Ashford, a servant, was raped and killed, her rapist and murderer was not convicted because they met at a public house dance. A priest distributed copies of the inscription on her grave, which offered a warning of the times. The inscription said:

> As a warning to female virtue, and a humble monument to female chastity, this Stone marks the grave of Mary Ashford, who, in the 20th year of her age, having incautiously repaired to a scene of amusement, without proper protection, was brutally violated and murdered on 27th May, 1817.[97]

Similarly, in 1868, a weaver, Anne Keystone, was gang-raped in front of 100 people, but the rapists were not convicted because the victim had been drinking in a pub before the event.[98]

British laws aimed to preserve public morality and women's chastity as a form of men's property. They did not aim to protect women from violence. That is why they did not let women speak about rape, and they particularly thwarted lower-class women from accusing their rapists in courts. Even when the women found the strength to go to court, it very rarely resulted in convictions. Courts even prosecuted some rape victims for perjury when a prosecution for rape failed.[99] What people expected from women was to stay in their homes and not to go out without a man to protect them. According to society's rules and expectations, if women did go out without male protection and other men lost control of their passions and attacked them, women should resist their attackers, even if it meant death. If they could not resist, they should continue living their "dirty" lives without accusing anyone for the rape, or kill themselves in order to sponge away the dishonor they brought on their family with their "impure" bodies.[100]

France

Before the nineteenth century, rape was very common in France as part of a system of violence. It was also harshly condemned by the laws of the ancien régime. Rape was defined as an "execrable crime" that "destroys families and defies the king," "a capital crime that is punished by death; the act of a famished tiger, the deed of a stinking billy-goat, requiring a solemn and public vengeance."[101] Rapes committed against virgins were considered the worst because of the harm caused to society by making these girls unmarriageable.[102] These denunciations do not mean rapists were adequately punished (by feminist standards). In fact, French law tolerated rape, especially when it was committed against women who were behaving "improperly," as if they belong to no one, and so belong to everyone. Complaints were rare, and judges resisted convicting in the few cases brought to court.[103] During the fifty-nine-year reign of Louis XV, only five rapists were punished, all in cases involving victims under ten years old. However, in terms of the general tolerance by society and the courts, rape was lumped with other types of violent crimes as the cruel deeds of "infamous and execrable monsters of nature."[104]

The class of the victims and perpetrators was significant in terms of the willingness of the judges to convict; they would determine the gravity of the crime and the degree of punishment, if any, based on the rank of both the victim and the perpetrator. Treatises even mentioned formulas on the matter: "The quality of the person to whom the violence is done increases or diminishes the crime. Thus an act of violence against a slave or a serving maid is less serious than that against a girl of respectable condition."[105]

This rank-differentiation in the treatment of rape cases was common in other violence cases as well. The practice of settling outside the court, for example, was common to all violent crimes and clearly favored wealthy perpetrators against lower-class victims.[106] A legal hierarchy of violent crimes placed rape below highway robbery and above murder. This hierarchy on paper did not translate into practice, however, because of courts' unwillingness to prosecute rape, which remained different from other violent crimes in terms of the shame and blame it brought on the victim. "Lust by force," "crime of lewdness which is committed by force," and "forced debauchery" are some of the expressions French laws used to describe rape in the seventeenth and eighteenth centuries.[107] In this sense, rape was a moral crime rather than a violent crime. French law and the society saw the rapist as an evil man committing a crime against morality and religion rather than against a person.[108]

In nineteenth-century France, we see major breaks from the ancien régime in the way the French understood and handled rape. Authorities still rarely brought rape cases to trial, and rape still came below property crimes in the hierarchy of crimes, but it lost its place as the second on the list. The ancien régime's "highway robbery, rape, murder" listing became "murder, theft, forgery" in the nineteenth century, and rape was no longer on the top of the list.[109] There were, however, some drastic changes. First of all, the idea that uncivilized practices such as rape did not belong to the urban world of modernity—that they can only happen in villages and hamlets left behind by progress—became prevalent. They thought rape happened where there is ignorance and stupidity and did not happen where there is progress and civilization.[110] Second, new expressions for rape (such as "indecent assault") came into use, which resulted in the downplaying of serious sexual crimes by virtually eliminating the word *rape* from usage.[111]

France's Code of 1810 was an important novelty in terms of establishing, for the first time, a hierarchy of different types of sexual violence according to their gravity. It also recognized some of these "indecent assaults" as acts of physical violence rather than of immorality.[112] Under the heading of "offences against decency" where indecent assault was placed, however, the code added adultery (almost exclusively by the wife), incitement to immorality, and bigamy. By confirming the inequality between men and women in this way, these additions not only strengthened the logic of female inferiority but also "legitimized the persistent suspicion of women in rape trials."[113] As far as the way the press portrayed rapes, the class factor continued to be important. On the subject of a gang-rape case in 1844 in Paris, for example, the *Gazette* said that the fact that the perpetrators were twenty-year-old factory workers confirmed the "almost congenital immorality of the working classes."[114] In the mid- and late nineteenth century, the newly emerging public sensibilities against violence and bloodshed led to increasing condemnation of sexual violence, especially the acts against children. In the cases of rape of adult women, however, the number of complaints and the conviction rate remained low.[115] Nineteenth-century France, then, witnessed a major change in the way law defined, categorized, and understood rape, but little change in the way courts judged it.

By the end of the nineteenth century, with the influence of evolutionary theory and the obsession with progress, the way science and society portrayed rapists changed as well. It was no longer the "evil men" of the ancien régime that were committing these crimes, but the "primitive organisms" who were left behind during the course of evolution because of the regressive tendencies in their genes. They were closer to animals on the evolutionary scale, with their lust for blood and instinct for rape. This new interest in the criminal himself even led to the first use of the word *rapist* to mean a pervert rather than perpetrator of rape.[116] However, in any case, in the public imagination, the rapist almost always came from the poor; rape remained "an act of slums."[117]

As we can see in both the British and the French cases, throughout the nineteenth century society continued to see rape as an act perpetrated by an individual (who is evil or unevolved or, in the case of war, a soldier deprived of sex for too long) against another (usually the men who "owned" the victims), rather than a social practice and institution degrading women. Since law is an expression of the normative context, the way people think about a practice, it is not surprising that neither domestic nor international law handled rape as an oppressive institution that needed to be addressed.[118]

The Actors

Nineteenth-Century Feminism

In the nineteenth century, women started to assert themselves more forcefully, in large part due to the increasing constrictions put on them by the Victorian (class-based) ideals about "true femininity."[119] Victorian feminists concentrated on liberal political theory, with its emphasis on individual liberty and bodily autonomy, in order to struggle against the ideological and legal subordination of women.[120] They intervened in the Parliamentary debates on many issues, such as the Divorce Act, married women's property, child custody rights, and suffrage. In her book, *A Plea for Women*, Marion Reid, an important feminist of the time, argued that the private sphere limits women, especially in terms of intellectual development. Even though Reid did not renounce the domestic responsibilities of women, she instead argued for more rights for women in the public sphere (such as the right to vote and property rights) along with their traditional roles in the private sphere. The fact that nineteenth-century liberalism was blind to the inequalities in the family realm was due to its public-private distinction. Liberalism's individualist ideas were severely limited by its assumption about "the inevitable existence and legitimacy of the patriarchal family," and these ideas made it impossible for principles of equality and consent to be applied to the relationship between men and women as well as women and the state.[121]

These limitations have their roots in the fact that, throughout the centuries, a functionalist mode of thinking about women dominated society, political theory, and the law. What were women good for? Reproduction? The answer to that question had been yes, since women's place in society, as well as in war and in the law, were determined by the necessities of the patriarchal family, society, and the state. The public sphere—political and economic life—depended on women performing their functions as wives and mothers secluded in the private sphere. Even the liberal society and the liberal state required this arrangement.[122] For male citizens to participate in politics and economic life, women needed to take care of the house and the children. To ensure that the heirs to the property of the male citizens were legitimate, women had to be constricted as much as possible.

The liberal state did not fulfill its promise of protecting individual interests for women because it treated the family, rather than the individual, as the basic political unit. The family's interests were protected, which meant the interests of the male heads of the families. Women's interests were automatically assumed to be the same as those of their families.[123] Therefore, the state never took women and their political and legal rights into consideration when making decisions. These decisions included the making of international law.

Some important elements of liberalism, however, would ultimately help feminists, particularly the idea of progress. John Stuart Mill, one of the important theorists of the time, wrote extensively on the subordination of women in British society from a liberal perspective. According to Mill, if a society, as well as an individual, is not constantly progressing, it means it is deteriorating. The subordination of women hinders the progress of society not only by clinging to the morals of an underdeveloped time, the time that enslaved women, but also by preventing the potential individual contributions of half of the society to further improvement.[124] A family based on a relationship of power and obedience between man and woman cannot produce future citizens who understand and appreciate freedom and who will have the proper moral training to contribute to human progress.[125] These arguments about the loss of potential contribution from women to the improvement of mankind became very important for nineteenth-century feminists in their struggles for political and legal rights.

Although these feminists concentrated primarily on suffrage, access to education and jobs, and property, divorce, and custody rights, they occasionally become involved in anti-rape activism. In the United States, for instance, in 1868, prominent suffragists Elizabeth Cady Stanton and Susan B. Anthony took up the cause of Hester Vaughan, a domestic servant in Philadelphia who was seduced, impregnated, and fired by her employer and then convicted for the death of her infant. Cady Stanton and Anthony persuaded the governor to pardon Vaughan and used this case as an opportunity to draw attention to the sexual vulnerability of women. Their newspaper, *Revolution*, supported the death penalty for rapists as well.[126] Late in the century, women raised their voices against the systematic sexual abuse of black women in the intersection of sexism, racism, and economic oppression.[127]

In England, feminists successfully pushed for the repeal of the Contagious Diseases Acts of 1864, which allowed the government to examine women suspected of prostitution around army bases for venereal diseases. Out of this campaign came the social purity movement of the 1880s, which fought against prostitution, rape, incest, sexual abuse of children, and other types of sexual harassment. The feminists in this movement argued that the "male sexual urge was a social and not a biological phenomenon," and male sexual behavior that is damaging to women should be changed by enjoining chastity upon men.[128] British suffragists such as Elizabeth Wollstenholme Elmy and Frances Swiney wrote extensively on the sexual oppression of women, both within and outside of marriage, and they promoted sexual self-control for men in order to ensure full control for women over their own bodies. These feminists unsuccessfully campaigned against the Criminal Code Bill (1880), which denied the possibility of marital rape.[129]

In France, feminists not only fought against the Civil Code (1804), which eliminated the right to divorce and established subordination of women in marriage and absolute paternal authority, but also fought against the vulnerability of women to rape, which was reinforced by the absence of legal protection. French feminists like Suzanne Voilquin published stories about rape in order to draw attention to this social fact and to the sexual oppression of women in general.[130]

European feminists also began to organize beyond their own borders starting in the mid-nineteenth century. In 1848, European and American suffragists came together for the first time at the Seneca Falls (New York) Convention.[131] Their agenda for women's rights called for suffrage, egalitarian marriage, divorce and property law reform, and equal access to employment, education, and the church, among other things. There was no mention of rape, sexual violence, or the laws regarding it. These seeds of international feminism that flourished in the aftermath of the European Revolutions of 1848 helped feminists view their local struggles as part of an international movement and activated the connections between feminists with radical views across borders. This first feminist movement was weakened by the 1860s as a result of the U.S. Civil War and the increasing political repression in Europe.[132] The late nineteenth century would witness the rise of an international (Western) women's movement, which would ultimately tackle the issue of rape, but not before the early twentieth century.[133]

Feminists' concerns about sexual violence against women could not reach The Hague in 1899, not when there were no women state delegates and no women's organizations with an agenda set on sexual violence. In 1907, the International Council of Women (ICW), an organization made up of women's groups from 23 countries, participated in the peace movement's enthusiastic appeal to the Second Conference to ensure peace and disarmament. The ICW submitted a petition signed by two million people demanding peace.[134] Yet sexual violence was not on their agenda.

Feminists would eventually start raising their voices against the effects of war on women in the international arena, but not until after 1907 and not as forcefully as they would almost a century later. In 1913, the Peace Committee of the ICW decided to focus on the issue of rape in war. Carrie Chapman Catt, founder and president of the International Woman Suffrage Alliance,[135] argued that the "conditions of war subvert the natural instincts of many men of all races, who temporarily return to the brutal practices of the most savage primitive races." Similarly, Rosika Schwimmer, a Hungarian suffragist and peace activist who was also active in the International Woman Suffrage Alliance, said the "victimizing of children, young girls, and women of all ages so common in peaceful times, because under the double standard of morals men are not outlawed for sexual crimes, is multiplied in war time." The alliance called women to come together internationally so that they could influence the upcoming Hague Conference:

> the moral and physical sufferings of many women are beyond description and are often of such a nature that by the tacit consent of men the least possible is reported. Women raise their voices in commiseration with those women wounded in their deepest sense of womanhood and powerless to defend themselves.[136]

In its May 1914 meeting, the ICW adopted a resolution called "Woman and War." Although it largely concentrated on peace and suffrage, the resolution also called for women's concerns to be included in the next Peace Conference at The Hague, which was scheduled to be held in 1915. The resolution specifically mentioned the need for the protection of women from rape in war by international law.[137] This resolution is particularly interesting because, besides mentioning the word *rape* and breaking the silence in this respect, it demanded a practical solution to the problem of rape in war (among other things) and it attempted, briefly, to explain the phenomenon as the expression

of violent inclinations in some men that surfaced due to the violent environment of war:

> the International Council of Women, protesting vehemently against
> the odious wrongs of which women are the victims in time of war,
> contrary to international law, appeals to the next Hague Conference to
> consider how a more effective international protection of women may
> be secured, which will prevent the continuance of the horrible viola-
> tion of womanhood that attends all wars ... In the late Balkan war non-
> combatants (generally women) were not only starved but massacred,
> while rapes and mutilations were reported. Outrages upon women are
> common in all wars; bestial horrors, which are crimes indeed, await
> the women of a country. The brutality lying dormant in some men is
> kindled by bloodshed; the ape and tiger, the "tooth and claw," come to
> the surface. War seems to be a concentration of crimes. Under its stan-
> dard gather violence, malignity, fraud, rage, perfidy, and lust.[138]

Similarly, during the First World War, women's groups brought up (though
infrequently) the issue of rape in war in their publications. In the April 1915
issue of *Jus Suffragii*, the monthly organ of the International Woman Suffrage
Alliance, one prominent British suffragist, Millicent Garrett Fawcett, wrote:

> It is idle to attempt a sum in arithmetic, and exactly compare the suf-
> ferings of men and women in war time. The agony of both is incred-
> ible, and not to be measured. Let any man imagine, if he can, what
> must be the mental and moral anguish of a woman condemned to
> bear a child begotten in rape and hatred by a victorious enemy. Such
> women, in no small numbers, are facing their shattered lives to-day,
> and in one case, at any rate, a Government has considered in what way
> such women can best be helped to bear their almost unfathomable
> misery. However hideous the sufferings of men in war, have they had
> to face any position which makes them loathe their own flesh and the
> light of day?[139]

It is particularly interesting to see the subject of forced pregnancy as a result
of wartime rape put on the agenda in 1915, since it will ultimately be one of
the basic tenets of feminists' framing of "rape as genocide" in their campaign
leading to the prohibition of rape in war in the 1990s.

These voices, however, were unheard—not only because there was a World War going on but also because, even after that war, no one was willing to listen to them. Just like the voices of the victims of domestic rapes, the voices of the victims of wartime rapes and the voices of the feminists were not heard. Advocacy by women's organizations, like the First International Women's Congress in The Hague in 1915, were ridiculed as "amiable chatter of a bevy of well-meaning ladies" among other things.[140] As for the records of rape in war, the silence and invisibility that we see in the domestic rape cases in nineteenth-century Europe are also evident in the works of historians. Between 1746 and World War I, it is particularly difficult to find documentation of rape in war, whereas the periods before and after provide more sources and documentation.[141]

In the end, the normative context can explain the silence of the Hague Conventions on rape as an attack on women. According to nineteenth-century Europeans, women (especially lower-class ones) were simply not human enough to be protected. Yet it does not explain why they were not even property enough to be protected. It is necessary to turn to the way rape, rape in war in particular, was conceptualized by the European society (and states), which can explain why states did not want to place themselves under the obligation of preventing rape in war.

Understanding Rape in War

Because nineteenth-century Victorians assigned the sexual characteristics of purity and morality to women and inherent lust to men, they interpreted rape as a deprivation of the victim resulting from her inability to control the natural behavior of the attacker (hence the blame was on her).[142] Prominent behaviorists of the time compared male sexuality to its counterparts in the animal world as "the active motile element," as opposed to the "passive quiescent" females.[143] Sexually aggressive or "unchaste" women who did not conform to the standard of the passive female (that is, having the demeanor of modesty) were considered to be either socially depraved (as in the case of lower-class women) or biologically dysfunctional, due to various gynecological causes (one of which was overproduction of male hormones).[144] These underlying assumptions about male aggressiveness and female passivity with respect to sexuality normalized the "male urge to rape," tying it to the biological characteristics of men, such as their hormones, whose abundance in a woman would lead to sexual aggressiveness as well.[145]

As we saw in the way domestic rape cases were handled, this understanding of rape as a "natural" phenomenon was prevalent. "Loose" women were already fair game, and their rapists usually escaped punishment. Rapes of "chaste" women who conformed to middle-class standards of feminine behavior, however, did not bring about many convictions either. If a chaste woman was raped, society found her at fault for three reasons: First, she should not have put herself in a situation where she could be raped. The fact that she left the private sphere without proper male protection made her a target, so it was her fault that she was raped. Second, if she put herself into that situation, she would be expected to defend her chastity at all costs, resisting until death. If she did not, it was her fault. Last, and most important for our purposes, if she did anything considered remotely provocative (such as being in the wrong place), the rapist's actions were justified, since men could not be expected to control their urges.[146]

The prevailing nineteenth-century sentiment about rape was that it was "an extension of the social construction of male sexuality as active, dominant, and aggressive."[147] Particularly in the context of war, where being "active, dominant, and aggressive" is the norm and "sex-starvation" of the soldiers in the barracks happens a lot, the merger of sexuality and aggression made even more sense to people. When Friedrich Nietzsche declared in 1883 that "man should be trained for war and women for the recreation of the warrior: all else is folly,"[148] he was expressing an idea that was not too far from commonly held beliefs.

In the 1880s and 1890s, the first sexologists, Richard von Krafft-Ebing and Havelock Ellis, who were influenced by the Darwinian doctrine of sexual selection, proposed theories that contrasted with the Victorian picture of pure and chaste women, yet reaffirmed the notion of ultimate female passivity and need for domination. Krafft-Ebing declared that "gratification of the sexual instincts [is] the primary motive in man as well as in beast."[149] Ellis also argued that women hide their sexual desires by "playing the role of hunted animal and adopting a demeanor of modesty" in order to make the men more eager and forceful. This makes the hunt more "sexually charged" and contributes to natural selection because a woman who says "no" to "the assaults of the male" will be "putting to the test man's most important quality, force," so in fact she is saying "yes."[150] These theories became part of the popular culture throughout the twentieth century and influenced how men (and states and militaries controlled by men) thought about sex, violence, and rape.[151]

In Victorian England, soldiers were considered to be slaves to their "animal passions," not only because of the assumptions about men's uncontrolled sexual drive, but also because of the military lifestyle. Society saw as inevitable the brothels that emerge around army garrisons and camps; in fact, the British Army even maintained brothels in India for its soldiers.[152] Although soldiers' sexual behavior led to widespread venereal diseases and loss of efficiency, the army did not try to regulate soldier behavior. Instead, British military authorities sought to regulate prostitution by checking women regularly for venereal diseases and detaining the infected ones. The state did make various efforts to "civilize" the soldiers in many areas and according to Victorian morality, but these efforts never included civilizing their behavior as "sexual brutes."[153]

In 1854, just after the arrival of Admiral Matthew Perry in Okinawa, the first incidence of rape of Okinawan women by U.S. military personnel occurred. It was also the first incidence on record of not viewing rape by a soldier as a crime. Perry responded to his crew member's action by demanding the prosecution of the local men who had chased the rapist, a chase that resulted in the man's fall and death. While the local men were prosecuted and sentenced to banishments, "Perry demonstrated his 'keen sensitivity' by presenting to the rape victim a 'handsome present' consisting of a few yards of cotton cloth."[154]

Even when rape in the domestic context saved itself from the image of the "normal" extension of uncontrollable male sexuality, it could never escape it in the context of war. In France, for instance, one exception to the picture of the evil rapist attacking morality drawn by the laws of the ancien régime was rape in war. It was considered to be a symbol of the conquest of a territory rather than a deed by an evil man. Stories described "Rapes of young girls and young boys, children torn from their parents' arms, mothers of families abandoned to the enjoyment of the victors," and "women who always love soldiers more than the rest, their violence only increasing their appetite."[155]

Given this normative context with the core norms of women's inferiority and property status reflected on the domestic marriage, divorce, adultery, and property as well as rape laws and cases, it is not surprising to see the exclusion of rape from The Hague Conventions as a prohibited act against the citizens of the rival state. Clearly, the absence of women during the conferences, both as delegates and members of a strong international women's movement, affected the lawmaking process as well. The international women's movement was very young, and, lacking political rights in most countries, women were missing in the state apparatus of the parties at The Hague.

However, the nonexistence of rape, even as a property crime, is a question that requires us to turn to another part of the normative context: the gendered ideology of rape, that is, the beliefs of the nineteenth-century states and societies about what rape was. The fact that rape was thought to be inevitable because of the biological nature of men and women made it virtually impossible, in the eyes of the states, to prevent it, especially in war. Therefore, not wanting to commit to a prohibition that was bound to be violated by their armed forces, states made sure that they would not be accused of the violation of international laws.

Changes and continuities in the legal and ideological situation in the twentieth century, as women's participation in both domestic and international politics increased, are the focus of the next chapters.

Chapter 4

The Prohibition of Rape in War:
First Steps: The Geneva Conventions and
the Additional Protocols

Rape entered into international law immediately after World War II, with the next important text of international humanitarian law after the Hague Regulations (1899, 1907), namely the Geneva Conventions (1949). After the end of World War II, at the initiative of the International Committee of the Red Cross (ICRC), another conference to write a convention on the conduct of war convened, this time to concentrate on the protection of the victims of war. The fact that the atrocities of World War II were still fresh in people's minds contributed to the success of the conference. Fifty-nine states initially signed the conventions, and over the years 199 states (to date) have ratified it.

At the start of the postwar period, we begin to see slight changes in the way international regimes and laws approached rape, if not in its prevalence in armed conflicts. With both the Geneva Conventions of 1949 and the Additional Protocols of 1977, significant advances occurred, although they ultimately failed to provide a prohibition regime against rape in war.

The Geneva Conventions (1949)

The Law

It is important to note that the Geneva Conventions' treatment of rape is a huge improvement over that of the Hague Regulations, as the Geneva Conventions at least mentioned rape as an unacceptable practice. It still has significant problems, however, with respect to obligation and delegation. Article 27 says, "Women shall be especially protected against any attack on their honor, in particular against rape, enforced prostitution, or any form of indecent assault." The provisions are protective, not prohibitive.[1] In fact, if we look at the writing of the Geneva Conventions, we can see how states wrote and kept Article 27 as a moral declaration rather than a prohibition that would be sanctioned.

In order to trace the writing of this article, we need to return to the Preliminary Conference of National Societies of the Red Cross (Conférence Préliminaire des Sociétés Nationales de la Croix-Rouge) in 1946 and the Conference of Government Experts for the Study of Conventions for the Protection of War Victims (Conférence d'experts gouvernementaux pour l'étude des Conventions protégeant les victimes de la Guerre) in 1947, both held in Geneva. The Red Cross Conference (1946) began writing a draft with the idea that the terrible experiences of World War II and the urgency of international regulations relative to the protection of civilians, as well as the insufficiency of the Hague Regulations, required a new law.[2] The commission that dealt with the protection of civilians thought that violations of the conventional arrangements should be considered as war crimes and punished accordingly.[3] The Conference of Government Experts started its work with these ideas and prepared a draft that would be submitted to the Red Cross Conference in 1948. That Conference then completed the draft and submitted it to the Geneva Conference in 1949, which would give the Geneva Conventions its final form.

The preliminary documents submitted to the government experts by the Red Cross begin by saying that "the International Committee consider that the measures suggested in favor of civilians of all nations, and consequently the nationals of any belligerent State, should include treaty stipulations regarding . . . the principle of the protection of women against every form of outrage."[4] After these general remarks comes the most important and interesting part regarding the situation of women in time of war. Chapter III of the same document, titled "Protection of Women," says,

Article 46 of The Hague Regulations of 1907 prescribed the recognition of "family honor and rights, individual rights and the respect of private property, religious beliefs and their observance." The question of respecting the decency and dignity of women calls for more precise definition in the new treaty stipulations. Countless women of all ages, and even small girls were the victims of the most abominable outrages

during the war. In occupied territories, very many cases of rape occurred, and unheard of brutalities were perpetrated, sometimes accompanied by mutilations and indecent assault upon women and
young girls. Wherever troops have passed or been stationed, venereal
diseases have increased to an alarming degree. Thousands of women
were placed in disorderly houses against their will, or were obliged
to submit to the troops. When contaminated, they were cast out, or
sent to concentration camps or prison hospitals. A principle should
be embodied and proclaimed in the new Convention, to provide that
the women of all countries of the world, irrespective of nationality,
race, religious belief, age, description or social standing, have the right
to be treated with unconditional respect to their honor, decency and
dignity, in all circumstances whatsoever.[5]

We should stress a couple of points regarding these comments. First, the
commission makes the observation that Article 46 of the Hague Regulations
regarding protection of "family honor and rights" is not precise enough in
terms of calling for the protection of women. Second, the outrages women
had to face during World War II, especially in the occupied territories (under
German and Japanese occupation), proved that a new form of handling of the
issue was required. And last, this new form would be a principle proclaimed
in the convention to provide women with respect to their honor, decency,
and dignity.

The way these remarks were incorporated into the recommendations
to the conference gives us a better idea of what the commission meant
by "principle" and "respect" (instead of prohibition), as well as what they
meant by "precise." Article 4 of the recommendations says, "Women shall
be treated with all consideration due to their sex, and children with all consideration due to their age and their helplessness."[6] This language stands
in contrast to some of the subsequent articles—such as the ones regarding
reprisals and hostages, which openly *prohibit* these practices by saying they
are prohibited.[7]

The 17th International Red Cross Conference in Stockholm in August
1948 wrote the final Draft Convention and submitted it to the Diplomatic
Conference in Geneva in 1949. It is particularly important, therefore, for us
to understand what happened at Stockholm and thereafter with respect to
the status of women and other related topics, like the issue of grave breaches.

If we start by looking at the writing of the preamble of the Civilians

Convention (which is the Fourth Geneva Convention relative to the protection of civilians), we see a list of things that the Subcommissions of the Legal Commission (Sous-Commissions de la Commission Juridique) proposed for prohibition. Among these propositions are

- the persons will be protected against all attacks on their dignity,
- taking hostages is prohibited,
- there will not be any executions without prior judgment pronounced by an instituted regular tribunal and assorted indispensable judicial guarantees like those recognized by the civilized peoples, [and]
- all torture is prohibited.[8]

After a discussion about adding an article about prohibiting medical experiments (demanded by the Danish delegate), the phrase "and bodily integrity" was added to the first article of the preamble.[9] The resulting document submitted to the conference consists of these same prohibitions and, therefore, it does not mention rape. Part III of the final draft of the Red Cross Conference on the Status and Treatment of Protected Persons forbids several practices—such as torture and corporal punishment (Article 29), measures of reprisals, the destruction of movable property or real estate (Article 30). Article 27, on the other hand, says, "Women shall be specially protected against all attacks on their honor or dignity,"[10] with no specific reference to rape. Interestingly enough, it refers to "dignity," which we will find omitted from the related article in the Geneva Conventions (1949).

This draft's treatment of grave breaches[11] is very important in terms of the creation of prohibition regimes by the Geneva Conventions, since in this case grave breaches fulfill the obligation and delegation aspects of lawmaking. An ICRC report to the conference states that "The humanitarian Conventions resemble other national and international laws in this respect: if they are to be observed, there must be provision for sanctions. Without any such sanctions, even intensified supervision over the implementing of these Conventions would be of no avail."[12]

Therefore, the Draft Convention's Article 130 was

Each contracting party shall be under obligation to search for the persons alleged to be guilty of breaches of the present Convention, whatever their nationality, and in accordance with its own laws or with the conventions prohibiting acts that may be defined as war crimes, to indict each person before its own tribunals, or to hand them over for judgment to another Contracting Party.[13]

We see that after the Stockholm Conference, the ICRC revised the first draft and Article 130 became

> Within a maximum period of two years, the governments of the High Contracting Parties shall, if their penal laws are inadequate, enact or propose to their legislative assemblies the measures necessary for the repression, in time of war, of all acts contrary to the provisions of the present Convention.
>
> Each contracting party shall be under obligation to apprehend, regardless of their nationality, the persons accused of acts contrary to the present Convention, and in conformity with its own laws or with the Conventions prohibiting acts that may be defined as war crimes, to indict such persons before its own tribunals, or if it prefers, to hand them over for trial to another Contracting Party.[14]

Finally, in the final text sent to the governments along with the invitation to the Diplomatic Conference of Geneva, those breaches that needed to be sanctioned, which the first documents generalized as "prohibited acts" or "war crimes," were further specified and the exclusion of rape became even more evident. The text had an additional article, Article 130bis, defining and itemizing grave breaches. Acts considered to be grave violations are "murder, inhumane suffering, grave attack on physical integrity or health, on liberty or dignity of persons, important destruction of goods/possessions, acts by their nature or repetition manifesting a systematic contempt of this convention."[15]

As a result, the draft that the ICRC prepared in cooperation with government experts did not mention rape either as a word (at first) or as a prohibition to be sanctioned—despite the initial calls for making protection of women more precise, in light of what happened during World War II. Looking at how this draft was written, we see that rape was not even considered an issue for debate. Likewise, as we go into the Diplomatic Conference of Geneva, we will see many discussions in many committees about the inadequacy of many prohibitions that lasted for months, but we will not see any major discussion about the inadequacy of the single article that is supposed to protect women, nor the idea of sanctioning this single article through its inclusion among grave breaches.

Before we look at the Geneva Conference, however, we need to address one major historical intervention that came just before it: the changing of the wording of Article 27 of the ICRC Draft, thanks to two nongovernmental organizations—the International Alliance of Women (IAW) (Alliance Internationale des Femmes) and the International Abolitionist Federation (Fédération Abolitionniste Internationale). In the report of its 15th Congress, the IAW wrote:

> When the Alliance Board met in London in March 1949, the President reported that she had been asked to support in the name of the Alliance a clause defining rape, enforced prostitution, and offences against women's honor and dignity as crimes against which women should be specifically protected. This she had done, and the clause had been incorporated in the Draft Convention to be submitted to a Diplomatic Conference in April. The Alliance societies had been asked to support the Draft Convention with their Governments and to get women included in the delegations to the Conference.[16]

Who among the board members asked the president to make this intervention and why the IAW did not incorporate certain parts of the suggestion, such as a definition of rape, are unclear. It is understandable that they wrote the article by referencing rape as an attack on honor, since it was likely that states would not accept it any other way, given the normative context of the day.[17] In fact, it is praiseworthy that they dared to mention the word *rape* in their proposal for the article, given the tendency to avoid the word as "distasteful." Even the French prosecutor at the Nuremberg trials, "when asked about the rape of French women said 'the tribunal will forgive me if I avoid citing the atrocious details.'"[18] Given this assertiveness, the reason that the IAW became inactive during the writing process at the conference and did not work for the inclusion of rape among the grave breaches is not known.

It seems as if the IAW did not think of this intervention and the resulting achievement as significant. The alliance refers to the Geneva Conventions as the "Red Cross Convention for the Protection of Civilians in War," which implies that the group viewed it as a convention limited in scope. The IAW also apologized in the report because in the previous years between 1946 and 1949, it had not made important achievements due to lack of funds, sufficient staff, and time.[19] The report also did not mention this addition to the Geneva Conventions among the list of developments that it considered noteworthy.

The list included the recognition of the equality between men and women by the United Nations Charter and the Universal Declaration of Human Rights (UDHR), but nothing on the Geneva Conventions.[20] In fact, the only place the IAW mentioned the Geneva Conventions in the 1949 report was in the quote above.

The IAW program for 1949–1952 called for concentration on the enfranchisement of women, political equality, economic and social equality, educational opportunities, equal pay, appointment of qualified women to policy-making posts, and increased opportunities to receive training for such posts.[21] It also advocated working toward the widest possible circulation and discussion of the UDHR and toward strengthening the UN, as well as studying and supporting the Draft Covenant of Human Rights, the Draft Convention for the Suppression of Traffic in Persons and the Exploitation of the Prostitution of Others, and the Convention on Genocide (to secure ratification).[22] No such plan was made for working on strengthening or securing the ratification of the Geneva Conventions. In fact, the IAW did not stipulate any intervention into the writing of the Geneva Conventions in its 1946 congress.[23]

In any case, as a result of this small-scale intervention by this women's organization, the Geneva Conference started with a text that included an Article 27 stating: "Women shall be specially protected against any attacks on their honor, in particular against rape, enforced prostitution and any form of indecent assault."[24]

Despite this change in wording, which I will explain further when I discuss precision, the fact that the text treated rape differently from other practices gives the impression that states would not be legally obligated to prevent it from happening, but that they were encouraged to try to protect women from this unpleasant practice. Therefore, in terms of obligation on preventing rape in war, the Geneva Conventions are at the lower end of the legalization spectrum.

Although the Geneva Conventions is the first international legal document to mention rape, Article 27 has only moderate/low precision when it comes to rape because there are "broad areas of discretion."[25] What constitutes rape and whether it is prohibited are ambiguous, since the article uses the language of protection, which does not have a clear meaning. If we go back to the debates during the conference, however, we will see that virtually every word written down was discussed and chosen with utmost care, and the delegates knew exactly what they meant when they used different terms in different articles. Thus, it is reasonable to assume that in the case of rape, when delegates retained the "protection" language that existed in the draft before them, they did so consciously.

Take, for instance, the long discussions on Article 29A (Article 32 in the final text). During the 26th plenary meeting, French delegate Mr. Cahen-Salvador pointed out a disparity in terms between Article 2A (Article 3 in the final text) of the preamble and Article 29A, which dealt with the same issues of prohibiting violence to life and person, taking of hostages, outrages upon personal dignity, and sentences and executions carried out without previous judgment. He said this "slight" disparity caused him a certain anxiety, and that the two articles' terms should be harmonized because:

> Our Convention is intended to become an integral part of international law, and in my capacity as a lawyer I have to point out to you that it would be extremely dangerous to allow any discrepancy to exist between the terms used, because as soon as there is disparity lawyers and legal authorities—which might here be the High Contracting Parties—might discuss indefinitely the reasons for this difference. Any Powers, the good faith of which was in doubt, might use such a discrepancy as a pretext to renounce the obligations which we have just established.[26]

Cahen-Salvador's legal opinion about the importance of terms used in writing international law is further supported by the debates over several other articles and words, including the importance of the term "prohibition." For example, during the tenth meeting of Committee III writing the Civilians Convention, a very interesting discussion came up with regard to the prohibition of corporal punishments and torture in Article 29 (Article 32 in the final text). The Soviet delegate, Mr. Morosov, said that the acts committed during the last war would remain one of the darkest chapters in human history. The provisions of the convention must take account of the lessons of the last war in order to render any repetition of such crimes impossible and the text as drafted seemed inadequate. He wanted to replace "torture and corporal punishments are prohibited" in Article 29 with "the contracting States undertake to qualify as a serious crime, murder, torture and maltreatment causing death including medical experiments as also all other means of exterminating the civilian population." Mr. Clattenburg, the U.S. delegate, could not agree because the Soviet amendment dealt with war crimes, which was the purview of the Joint Committee, so any discussion or proposal regarding war crimes should be referred to that committee. The subject of the amendment was similar to the Genocide Convention under consideration by the UN as well, and the English text of the Soviet proposal—"torture and maltreatment causing death"—could be read as meaning that torture that did not cause death was permitted, a defect all the more regrettable because the Soviet amendment suggested the deletion of the words "torture and corporal punishments are *prohibited*." For these reasons, the American delegate argued, Article 29 should be retained as it stood. The Australian delegate, Colonel Hodgson, said he was certain that no delegation wished to avoid discussion on the substance of the Soviet amendment. He said it should be noted, however, that the amendment seemed to be a *moral declaration* rather than a prohibition, and might therefore overlap with the preamble. Acceptance of the amendment as submitted would mean that the words "torture and corporal punishments are prohibited" would be omitted and would not be replaced by *any prohibition properly so called.* The expression "undertake to qualify as a serious crime" could hardly be interpreted as a formal prohibition. Nevertheless, the Australian delegation was prepared to consider the proposed amendment, regarding it as a list of prohibited atrocities.[27] But this discussion did not end there.

During the next committee meeting, the issue came up again. The U.S. delegate remarked that it would be dangerous to give way to emotional impulses, that crimes could not be outlawed merely by drawing up a convention, that the aim of the conference was to define, as simply as possible, the duties of governments toward war victims, and that the duty of those governments was to apply in good faith the Convention they had ratified. He continued to state that the use of vague phraseology might lead to unforeseen interpretations of the convention. The National Socialists had resorted to torture, he reminded the committee. It would be regrettable, he argued, if torture were not *specifically prohibited* under Article 29. The American delegation proposed a new amendment, which eventually ended up as the final text's Article 32.[28]

Committee III's report to the plenary assembly further illuminates the fact that the writers of the convention made a specific differentiation between acts that the convention prohibited and acts it did not prohibit but were subjects of moral declarations. When talking about the article about the protection of women (Article 25 at this stage, as it was combined with the original Article 25), the report said: "The new second paragraph was transferred here from Article 27 because it lays down an equally general principle i.e. respect due to women."[29] When discussing the other articles, the report's wording completely changed: "Articles 29 to 31 (including 29A) lay down certain prohibitions which, in the light of the principles underlying our Convention, take first place and which unreservedly condemn the atrocities committed during the last war. A certain number of these prohibitions already appear, as regards occupied territory, in the Laws and Customs of War on Land (pillage, Article 47, collective penalties, Article 50)."[30] Moreover, the report suggests that even a slight change in the wording could weaken a prohibition. So, for example, with respect to Article 30 (Article 33 in the final text), the commission dropped the word "formally," which appears in Article 47 of the Laws and Customs because the members believed that since the word was not used in the other prohibitions, its use in Article 30 would weaken them. The report declared that "All the prohibitions under consideration are absolute, and adverbs, be they ever so incisive, add nothing." They were referring to the prohibition of pillage, which was added to this article as a new second paragraph.[31]

As opposed to these delicate arguments about these various practices (including pillage) that needed to be prohibited, the Conference meetings did not offer a comprehensive and careful handling of Article 27 on the issue of rape. Article 27 came up as a subject of discussion only in the ninth and tenth meetings of Committee III. (It was not mentioned at all during the plenary meetings.) Only two delegates commented on the article's section related to women. The first was the Indian delegate, who suggested that the standard of treatment to be given to the category of persons to whom Article 27 related should not be better in the national territory than the treatment given to the nationals of the country, while in occupied territory it should be no worse than the standard prevailing in the occupied country prior to the occupation. The Italian delegate suggested that, "in view of the extreme gravity of offences against the honor and dignity of women, a specific reference should be made to the responsibility of the commander of the armed forces as in the similar provisions of Article 51 of the Hague Convention."[32] Looking at the final text, we can see that the conference did not take these suggestions, and looking at the meeting minutes, we can see that they did not even discuss them.

What should we conclude from all this explicit discrimination against rape in terms of being excluded from the prohibitions, as well as from the conference's discussions? Obviously, the call for more precise measures to ensure respect for women during wars—made at the Government Experts Conference in 1947—played out in Geneva in two ways: some more precision (at least compared to the Hague Regulations) emerged thanks to the efforts of two NGOs, but the measures remained in the gray area of "respect," "protection," or "moral declaration," rather than prohibition. Apparently, no one took Article 27 seriously enough to discuss its wording (as opposed to other articles included in the Conventions' prohibitions, as I discuss in the case of pillage) or applications, and it remained outside the scope of the main prohibitions of the convention as a low-precision regulation.

The Geneva Conventions have a high degree of delegation with regard to the provisions on the enforcement when it comes to grave breaches, since it obligates states to either bring the perpetrators before domestic courts or hand them over for trial by other parties.[33] What about rape and its status with respect to delegation? Article 130 of the Draft Convention (Article 147 in the final text) says:

> Grave breaches to which the preceding Article relates shall be those involving any of the following acts, if committed against persons or property protected by the present Convention: wilful killing, torture or inhuman treatment, including biological experiments, wilfully causing great suffering or serious injury to body or health, unlawful deportation or transfer or unlawful confinement of a protected person, compelling a protected person to serve in the forces of a hostile Power, or wilfully depriving a protected person of the rights of fair and regular trial prescribed in the present Convention, taking of hostages and extensive destruction and appropriation of property, not justified by military necessity and carried out unlawfully and wantonly.

The article does not mention rape, and judging from the effort that was put into writing this article and ensuring its clarity, including the use of the words "grave breaches," before and during the conference, we can conclude that it is not something delegates forgot to include. In addition, none of the other acts mentioned in this article could be interpreted as implying or meaning rape.

Going back to the Stockholm Conference (1948), we know that the ICRC strongly recommended a provision for sanctions to make the convention effective[34] and added Article 130 and 130bis to its draft, defining breaches of the convention and how they would be sanctioned.[35] These issues came up several times during the committee meetings in Geneva as well as at the plenary meetings. The Soviet delegate's insistence on using the word "crime" for violations of the convention especially stirred up debate. The Soviet delegation submitted several proposals both to Commission III (Civilians Convention) and to the Joint Committee (articles common to all four conventions)

Preliminary Provisions (1)

The following acts shall be prohibited and shall remain prohibited at any time or in any place whatsoever:

a) human beings shall not be subjected to attempts against their life or injury to their physical integrity. The following shall be considered grave crimes: murder, torture, mutilation, including scientific experiments, as well as any other means for the extermination of the civilian population;

b) the taking of hostages;

c) deportations, either individual or collective;

d) attacks against the dignity of persons, in particular humiliating or degrading treatment or discriminatory treatment based upon differences of race, colour, religion, beliefs, sex, birth or social status;

e) the pronouncement of sentences and penal sanctions carried out without preliminary trial by a regularly constituted tribunal giving all the necessary legal guarantees recognised by civilised nations as indispensible.

f) Collective penalties as well as any measured of intimidation or terrorism; the destruction of any real and personal property belonging to private individuals or to the State, as well as to social or cooperative organisations when this is not rendered absolutely necessary by military operations;

(1) It will be necessary to delete the following items from this text:

Article 29:   the words "torture and" in the second paragraph;

Article 29 A:

Article 30:   the second sentence of the first paragraph;

Article 31:

Article 45:   first paragraph;

Article 61:   first paragraph.

Figure 1. Civilians Convention, Text Adopted by the Working Party—Corrigendum, 8 July 1949. (SFA)

by arguing that the text using the term "grave breaches" was too vague and seemed nothing more than a recommendation.[36]

Although the majority rejected the proposal because of the idea that "crime" was a technical term used in Penal Law and thus had a specific meaning that did not suit this Convention,[37] some delegations supported the Soviet proposal, considering what had happened in the last war.[38] As a matter of fact, the issue of what to include in grave breaches became the topic of long discussions during the Joint Committee meetings. A Finnish amendment to replace the expression "maltreatment"—which was used in an earlier draft and considered unduly vague—with "inhuman treatment" was accepted.[39] Nevertheless, the Soviet delegate's proposal that express mention should be made of certain acts Article B (of Article 130) did not cover and which are also grave breaches was rejected.[40] As a result, the Special Committee wrote the grave breaches language we see in the final text and reported that:

> In order to allow for reluctance to include all breaches even trifling ones in penal legislation, we limited the obligation to enact legislation to grave breaches which no legislator would object to having included in the penal code, and left the Contracting Parties free to take their own measures for the repression of breaches which do not come within the category defined as grave breaches. This category has been carefully defined, so as to avoid including acts which allow for various degrees of gravity and could not therefore be considered to be grave breaches if only committed in their less serious forms.[41]

In the end, whether the writers of the convention thought of rape as an insignificant thing that naturally occurs in wars or whether they thought it had various degrees of seriousness (perhaps depending on the degree of "honor" of the victims), they did not list it among the grave breaches; in fact, they did not even discuss it.

Therefore, on the hard-soft legalization scale, the Geneva Conventions are soft for rape, since rape is not included among the grave breaches. This flaw in delegation, combined with the problems with obligation and precision, makes rape in war open to manipulation, which not surprisingly occurred many times after World War II in various conflicts with legal and political impunity.[42]

We can only conclude that the Geneva Conventions (1949) do not fulfill the obligation and delegation requirements of a prohibition regime, although they mark an important step in terms of increasing precision by mentioning the word *rape*.

The Normative Context and the Main Actors

What Changed?

The two world wars had been stages for previously unseen range and forms of violence against civilians. The horrors of the Second World War especially triggered the creation of a legal framework for preventing similar events.[43]

The post-World War II tribunals, however, did not deal with rape properly given its widespread occurrence during the war. The Nuremberg Tribunal did not mention rape in its charter or in its decisions, and did not prosecute anyone for rape; the Tokyo Tribunal prosecuted some individuals for the rapes in Nanking, but did not prosecute anyone in cases involving "comfort women."[44]

Although the Universal Declaration of Human Rights, adopted by the UN in 1948, does not mention women's right to be free from violence and rape, it has provisions stipulating equal rights for men and women. Women's organizations managed to get similar provisions on gender equality into the UN Charter (1945), and led the way for the establishment of the United Nations Commission on the Status of Women (CSW) to further women's causes and increase women's presence in the international arena.[45]

After the achievement of suffrage in most Western countries by the 1930s, women increasingly participated in their countries' governments. At the 1949 Geneva Conference, women made up 5.8 of all state delegates. At last, women's voices were present. When the issue of whether to call grave breaches "breaches" or "crimes" was being debated, the Romanian delegate, Mme Manole, as the only woman delegate who spoke on the issue of grave breaches, said that she did not understand why new repressions aimed at the perpetrators of such grave crimes should not be created. She asked, "Why should we pity the perpetrators of such brutalities towards men, women, and children, of torture, arson?"[46] She was the only delegate to mention women in regards to the subject of grave breaches.

The first attempts to specifically outlaw rape in war were not made until 1949.[47] By participating in the drafting of the UDHR in 1947 and 1948, however, women at least ensured that the language of the declaration encompassed women within the framework of human rights. These women included not only the female delegates (and the chair, Eleanor Roosevelt) of the Commission on Human Rights and the Commission on the Status of Women, but also representatives of NGOs such as the International Council of Women, the International Union of Catholic Women's Leagues, and Women's International League for Peace and Freedom.[48] Women were also becoming more and more aware of the shortcomings of the existing gender ideology and the law in terms of protecting women from sexual violence. Ruth Herschberger, an American poet and writer, described the intricate relationship between force, rape, and war in her 1948 essay "Is Rape a Myth?"[49] The women working for women's rights in the international arena were certainly aware of this situation, too.

As I previously mentioned, the IAW was one of the leading women's organizations of the time. It was granted consultative status in the UN in early 1948 and became very active in the drafting of the UDHR.[50] As a reformist organization, it learned not to scare states by being too radical. In 1930, for instance, the League of Nations organized a conference at The Hague, the International Conference for the Codification of International Law, in order to clarify and coordinate the existing body of international law. The IAW saw this as a great opportunity to further its cause at the time, equal nationality rights for women. It sent a proposal to the conference, demanding that women be given the right to control (retain or change) their own nationality after marriage, as men were able to do. The League of Nations found this proposal too radical, and excluded the IAW (and all other women) from the drafting process. Women were even banned from the grounds of the Conference to prevent them from "harassing" the (all-male) representatives.[51] In light of this event (and probably other similar ones), the reason that the IAW would later write Article 27 of the Geneva Conventions (1949) with a relatively imprecise definition of rape referring to "honor" and "protection" becomes clearer.

Although women's organizations were not among the official participants of the Diplomatic Conference in Geneva (1949),[52] they participated in the writing of the Draft Convention by the ICRC Conference in 1948. For example, the World's Young Women's Christian Association (WYWCA) asked the ICRC to consider its input on certain articles regarding women during the ICRC Conference held in Stockholm in 1948, which (as we learned previously) produced the Draft Geneva Conventions. In her letter to the vice president of the ICRC, WYWCA Secretary General Helen Roberts proposed several amendments to the articles concerning women in the Convention on the Amelioration of the Condition of the Wounded and Sick in Armed Forces in the Field (Convention I) and the Prisoners of War (Convention III). For instance, for Article 13 of the Draft Prisoners of War Convention, she stated:

> Our various and numerous experience in the service of the women and the girls in about 70 countries, allows us to estimate this article at its fair value. There are in effect numerous countries, particularly in the East and in Africa, where women, even if they acquired constitutional rights equal to those of the men, are indeed often considered and treated by tradition as inferior to men, and it appears to us fair and essential to have . . . a provision such as: "and in all cases benefit by treatment favorable as that granted to men."[53]

For Article 20 of the draft, on the places and methods of internment, again, Roberts had several demands for special treatment of women, specifically for separate accommodations.[54] With regard to the Civilians Convention, she simply said it had already taken into account their previous comments.

In a response to Roberts's letter, the ICRC stated that it accepted the WYWCA's proposition on draft Article 13 and said that it was still studying the question with regard to the draft Article 20 concerning how to specify more precisely the separation of sexes in internment camps.[55]

The International Council of Women (ICW) also requested participation in the ICRC Conference. In a letter of acceptance to the ICW, the ICRC said, "the delegates of the international organizations invited to participate in this conference will have not only advisory voice in the plenary sessions, but will also be able to take part in the workings of the envisaged commissions and to introduce proposals," and that the ICW could participate and introduce its opinions.[56] Similarly, the International Federation of University Women was invited to send a representative to the conference in the capacity of a visitor.[57]

What Had Not Changed?

Despite the fact that women started to participate in politics both domestically and internationally in greater numbers, despite the fact that human rights emerged as a powerful framework in which women were included at least on paper, despite the fact that sexual violence was "shockingly" widespread during World War II, and despite the intervention of the IAW in the wording of Article 27 of the Geneva Conventions, rape was still excluded from the list of grave breaches. The idea that rape in war is inevitable was still prevalent, and it seems to be largely responsible for the lack of legal change.

Even when historians or writers talked about rape in war as an atrocity, the mentality that it was inevitable surfaced. For example, in his propaganda book on the German atrocities during World War I, Newell Dwight Hillis describes how German soldiers were tested for syphilis in order to qualify to "use" the women kept in the military camps; the punishment for disobedience by a disqualified soldier was death, so that the disease would not spread in the army. "Under this restriction," Hillis writes, "the syphilitic soldier has but one chance, namely to capture a Belgian or French girl."[58]

General George S. Patton, a U.S. army general in World War II, wrote that "in spite of my most diligent efforts, there would unquestionably be some raping" by the soldiers under his command.[59] Another interesting recollection by General Patton on the perception of rape, in this case by the men of the occupied territory, reveals the widespread mentality on the inevitability of rape in war. In the part of his memoirs about the invasion of Italy during World War II, Patton wrote:

> One very funny thing happened in connection with the Moroccan troops. A Sicilian came to me and said he had a complaint about the conduct of Moroccans, or Goums, as they are called. He said that he well knew that all Goums were thieves, also that they were murderers, and sometimes indulged in rape—these things he could understand and make allowances for, but when they came to his house, killed his rabbits, and then skinned them in the parlor, it was going too far.[60]

Even many women thought rape was inevitable. In 1945, German women in Berlin waited in fear and anguish for the Soviet soldiers to arrive and the "inevitable" to happen. Days before the arrival, some women began dressing like men, and some tried to appear old and dirty so they could escape from the soldiers' "lust."[61] After the Soviet soldiers arrived, the expected happened to approximately 110,000 women.[62] Apparently, Stalin's declaration prohibited "this kind of thing," but as a Soviet officer said, "it happens anyway."[63] One of these victims describes rape as "something foreseen and feared," "all somehow part of the bargain," "a case of urges and instincts having been unleashed."[64] The Soviet officials in Berlin even invented an expression to avoid using the rather distasteful word *rape*. "This kind of thing" that "happens anyway" was called "forced intercourse," which gives an idea about the way rape in war was perceived as unpleasant yet unavoidable, and ultimately trivial.[65]

In his interview with Milovan Djilas, Stalin's comments on these rapes are even more revealing in terms of how "normal," "inevitable," and "excusable" rape was considered to be: "Does Djilas, who is himself a writer, not know what human suffering and the human heart are? Can't he understand it if a soldier who has crossed thousands of kilometers through blood and fire and death has fun with a woman or takes some trifle?"[66]

The fact that Stalin considered rape as "having fun" or found it understandable in a soldier who has passed through the difficulties of war—despite the fact that he formally prohibited it for Soviet soldiers—expresses the double standard about rape in war quite well. In what other instance does a state excuse the violation of orders by soldiers? Given that the whole military apparatus and the conduct of war depends on the maintenance of military discipline, chain of command, and the enforcement of rules and orders, it would be senseless for a leader to accept the violation of his orders by his soldiers and treat the situation with such understanding—except in the case of rape. Knowing that the violation of orders against rape were usually tolerated, soldiers did not hesitate to practice the "inevitable." Aleksandr Solzhenitsyn, who was a Russian soldier in World War II, wrote:

> For three weeks the war had been going on inside Germany and all of us knew very well that if the girls were German they could be raped and then shot. This was almost a combat distinction. Had they been Polish girls or our own displaced Russian girls, they could have been chased naked around the garden and slapped on the behind—an amusement, no more.[67]

After the war and the rapes were over, a Russian newspaper editor interpreted the rapes in a similar manner: "We were naturally not one hundred percent gentlemen; we had seen too much."[68]

Germany documented the use of rape by German soldiers during World War II, and these documents were presented at the Nuremberg trials in 1946. The reason that Germans documented the rapes was because they wanted to be seen as having a concern for legality, so much so that they were even gathering reports of unofficial atrocities. "The official German position was that 'uncontrollable elements' were responsible for the ugly excesses."[69]

Another mass rape occurred when the Japanese Army invaded the

Chinese city of Nanking in 1937. The case was brought before the Tokyo Tribunal after the war. The comments in its decision on the rape of Nanking, however, indicate that the Tokyo Tribunal did not rid itself of the idea of the inevitable (and excusable) rapes happening during the first days after a city's capture, as a result of the exhilaration of conquest. In its judgment convicting the perpetrators of rape, the tribunal explained:

> Even girls of tender years and old women were raped in large numbers throughout the city, and many cases of abnormal or sadistic behavior in connection with the rapings occurred. Many women were killed after the act and their bodies mutilated. . . The barbarous behavior of the Japanese army cannot be excused as the acts of a soldiery which had temporarily gotten out of hand when at last a stubbornly defended position had capitulated—rape, arson and murder continued to be committed on a large scale for at least six weeks after the city had been taken.[70]

One wonders whether the tribunal would have prosecuted the rapes in Nanking if the Japanese army did not continue raping for six weeks after the conquest and if the rapes did not accompany "abnormal" behavior like murder and mutilation, especially against children and old women. Would the tribunal have excused the "normal" behavior—that is, rapes—as acts of boys who got out of control?

Cynthia Enloe argues that one solution state officials have historically used for the problem of "inevitable rapes" is providing organized prostitution to soldiers. According to Enloe, officials consider rape and prostitution solutions to the long-held belief regarding soldiers' "need" for sex. In other words, the connection in the minds of states between the use of brothels and rape is tied to their beliefs about the impossibility of preventing rape in war; this attitude led to the tolerance, encouragement, or in some cases even active facilitation of the use of prostitutes by the armed forces. States imagine that providing organized prostitution to male soldiers prevents the same soldiers from raping women.[71]

The "comfort women," represent such a case.[72] During the 1930s and 1940s, the Japanese Army recruited and forced women into prostitution to serve in military brothels, giving "comfort" to the sex-starved soldiers of the Japanese armed forces. The Japanese military started the process in the early 1930s and accelerated the practice after 1937. According to the military correspondence of the Japanese army in the 1930s, there were various reasons for the large-scale use of "comfort women." First, Japanese soldiers had raped Chinese women in occupied areas on numerous occasions, which increased anti-Japanese sentiment and complicated the management of occupied territories. Second, soldiers' contact with Chinese women could lead to the leaking of military secrets. Third, the government wanted to control the spread of venereal diseases in the army in order to prevent the reduction of military effectiveness.[73] General Yasuji Okamura, the vice chief of staff of the Shanghai Expeditionary Force of the Japanese Army at the time, wrote:

> There were not *ianfus* (comfort women) in former years of military campaigns. To speak frankly, I am an initiator of the comfort women project. As in 1932 during the Shanghai Incident some acts of rape were committed by Japanese military personnel, I, Vice Chief of Staff of the Shanghai Expeditionary Force, following the example of the Japanese naval brigade, asked the governor of Nagasaki prefecture to send comfort women groups. As a result, rape crimes totally disappeared, which made me very happy. At present each army corps was accompanied by a comfort women group, as if the latter constitutes a detachment of its quarter-master corps. But rape acts did not disappear in the Sixth Division, even though it was accompanied by a comfort women group.[74]

Similarly, the German army kept prostitutes, in particular for preventing venereal diseases and increasing "morale," despite the Nazi regime's ideological opposition to prostitution as an institution not in line with the Nazi objective of "a nation of chaste families."[75]

During France's colonial rule in Indochina, the French Colonial Forces included a mobile field brothel. Advocates argued that this institution was "providing the soldiers with a controlled sexual release, thus cutting down on desertions, on rapes of hapless girls of the surrounding civilian population, and also on venereal disease."[76] General Patton, who believed in the necessity of such an arrangement to avoid "unpleasant" but "inevitable" incidents such as rape, wanted to institute this kind of arrangement for American soldiers during World War II. Patton had to give up the idea because of its potential consequences of outraging the wives and mothers of the soldiers and slowing down the war effort.[77]

These historical examples clearly show that the official use of prostitution had been a military response to deal with a practice they believed they could not prevent. By satisfying the "sexual hunger" of soldiers through the use of brothels, militaries tried to limit the number of rapes (among other things), but as the Japanese general in the Nanking case admitted, it had not proven to be an effective policy for the most part. Soldiers "revved up by war" seemed to resort to rape whether they were "hungry" or not. Therefore, writing a clear prohibition against rape into international law, when there was a high probability that some of your soldiers will inevitably rape anyway, did not seem attractive to states.

The Additional Protocols (1977)

The ICRC gathered four international conferences between 1974 and 1977 because of the increasing suffering of civilians during wars in the 1950s and 1960s and because of new weapons technologies and civil wars. The resulting protocols were ratified by 167 states, the United States being an important exception. As an extension of the Geneva Conventions (1949) in terms of their scope and tone, scholars consider the Additional Protocols to be somewhere in between the Law of the Hague (1899) (regulating both the methods of warfare and the conduct of hostilities) and the Law of Geneva (1949) (protecting civilian victims of war).

The Law

The two Additional Protocols to the Geneva Conventions revisited the issue of rape. In these additional texts, nothing changed in terms of delegation, because rape was still not included among the grave breaches. Some developments in obligation and precision, however, are worth reviewing. Although there is no change—in terms of the degree of obligation— in the First Protocol relating to the Protection of Victims of International Armed Conflicts, the Second Protocol relating to the Protection of Victims of Non-International Armed Conflicts, adopted a language of prohibition instead of protection. Also, in both protocols, rape is no longer mentioned as an attack on the honor of women.[78]

Looking at the handling of the issue of rape at the Diplomatic Conference in Geneva that met between 1974 and 1977, we get a deeper understanding of international lawmakers' perceptions and intentions. The Additional Protocols (1977) continued problems of obligation and delegation with regard to rape, even with the minimalist approach used here, which accepts high degrees of obligation and precision combined with at least a low degree of delegation to be the necessary requirements of a prohibition regime. Protocol I continued to use the language of protection instead of prohibition, creating the problem of obligation; and rape was excluded once again from the list of grave breaches, creating the problem of delegation.

Obligation Problem in the Additional Protocols

The problem of obligation in the Additional Protocols emerges out of Protocol I's use of the word *protection* rather than *prohibition* in relation to rape. Article 76 of Protocol I says, "Women shall be the object of special respect and shall be protected in particular against rape, forced prostitution and any other form of indecent assault." What does "women shall be protected against rape" mean? Who is supposed to protect them against attacks by whom? Will anybody be punished if they do not protect women from being raped, and will anybody be punished if they rape women? One might conclude that the difference between *protection* and *prohibition* is just a nuance and that the writers of the law did not even think of it as having different consequences. The evidence shows otherwise.

The importance of clarity and specificity in law is a known fact. The lawmakers who wrote the Additional Protocols were aware of this fact, too. Especially when their objective was to make these laws effective, we see a clear effort on their part to clarify even the smallest details on the subject. For example, during the debates on the protection of the civilian population, "certain delegates stressed the need for a still better definition of military objectives and civilian property, so that a clear distinction was preserved between these two concepts; such a distinction was essential in order to ensure effective protection for civilian property."[79]

Precisely because of the problem of clarity and specificity, the debates over Protocol II became troublesome and threatened its adoption or ratification until the delegation of Pakistan, after consultation with other delegations, prepared and presented a simplified version of Protocol II (CDDH/427 and Corr.1). Mr. Hussain, the Pakistani delegate, said they prepared it on the thesis that "its provisions must be acceptable to all and, therefore, of obvious practical benefit; the provisions must be within the perceived capacity of those involved to apply them and, therefore, precise and simple."[80]

Likewise, we can find indications of the significance of wording in many places. During the debates over Article 2 of draft Protocol II (CDDH/402), a proposal (CDDH/430) was made to add at the end of paragraph 1 the sentence: "It shall not be ordered that there shall be no survivors." On that note, the Canadian delegate, Mr. Miller said that the Canadian delegation had no objection to that amendment, but pointed out that the proposal's sponsor had based the wording on the text of Article 22 of draft Protocol II (CDDH/402). He suggested the use of the same wording: "It is prohibited to order that there shall be no survivors."[81]

Additionally, during the debates at Working Group B, "certain delegations stated that it was desirable that corporal punishment should be expressly prohibited."[82] Agreeing that such punishment should be described in the phrase "or any form of corporal punishment," the working group sent it to Committee I. At its 39th meeting, on April 11, 1975, Committee I considered Article 6 of the Draft Protocol II. It worked on the article fastidiously and voted on each phrase. The phrase "or any form of bodily harm" was rejected and "or any form of corporal punishment" was adopted by a 46 to 2 vote, with 11 abstentions.[83]

Another example of delegates' diligence about the wording of the law came in discussions of Article 65 of draft Protocol I (regarding fundamental guarantees). Mr. Herczegh from Hungary said that his delegation "supported the amendment by Ireland (CDDH/III/308), because the prohibition of torture could not be too strongly reinforced." He also said Hungary approved the amendment sponsored by Austria and the Holy See (CDDH/III/310) and viewed amendment CDDH/III/311 with sympathy, although it "feared that the obligation to accommodate as family units families held in the same place of internment could not always be fulfilled by countries in armed conflict" and "the insertion of the words 'as far as possible' would make it easier to accept the texts" on the subject (paragraph 4 of Article 65). Herczegh also supported the comment made by the Yugoslavian representative that "a better place for that paragraph would be Article 67, which dealt with the protection of women," which was the article dealing with rape. So, for Herczegh, the exclusion of Article 67, hence the issue of rape, from the fundamental guarantees did not constitute a problem, but the issue of family units that needed to be excluded from fundamental guarantees (due to the difficulty of its implementation) had to be moved to Article 67. He said that his delegation associated itself with the efforts made to enlarge the judicial guarantees that were the subject of paragraph 3, but it was a very complex question because of the differences between the criminal law systems of the various countries.[84]

The significance of this last discussion is that the Hungarian delegate not only supported a stronger prohibition of torture and was satisfied with rape not being among fundamental guarantees, but he also wanted to exclude something (accommodating family units in prison) from the fundamental guarantees by saying that they may not be enforced effectively. The delegate believed, therefore, that the language on this subject should be softened (by saying "as far as possible") and that this softened item should be put into the same article as the protection of women. In the end, accommodation of family units stayed in Article 65 (Article 75 of the final text), but the discussion provides insight into the way protection of women was viewed—at least by some of the delegations. This perspective regarding women could explain the lack of attention, hence lack of obligation, in the case of rape.

What is remarkable about the Additional Protocols is the situation with Protocol II that deals with civil wars. Rape was included in paragraph 2 of Protocol II's fundamental guarantees as a prohibition (Article 4, paragraph 2 (e) in the final text). This inclusion happened thanks to the suggestion of Madagascar's delegate, Mr. Rabary-Ndrano, who said that paragraph 2 (e) embodied the same concept ("outrages upon personal dignity, in particular humiliating and degrading treatment") as Article 6 bis (which was the article about "the protection of women" from rape in the Draft Protocol II). He proposed that rape should be mentioned in the sub-paragraph on fundamental guarantees.[85] Mr. Hussein, the delegate of Pakistan, supported that proposal and suggested that the word *rape* should be added after "enforced prostitution."[86] He also proposed the deletion of Article 6 bis, since the content of Article 6 bis was the same as that of paragraph 2 (e) of Article 6 (of the Draft Protocol, which would eventually become Article 4 in the final document).

Following Mr. Hussein's suggestion to delete Article 6 bis, the delegate of Canada, Mr. Miller, indicated that he would have opposed the change if it meant the deletion of the word *rape* from the protocol, but said that changing the location of the word was fine. He recalled that "his country had always been profoundly concerned with the question of the protection of women and children." Since the representative of Pakistan had agreed to add the word *rape* to paragraph 2 (e) of Article 6, however, he was satisfied and would not vote for the retention of Article 6 bis. Hence, Article 6 bis was deleted by consensus.[87] This was the only debate concerning the status of rape in the protocol.

It seems that the Madagascar delegate made this wording suggestion for the sake of parsimony, since there is no discussion on the matter of protection versus prohibition with respect to rape. It is interesting that these lawmakers, who parsed virtually every word regarding other issues, suggested and accepted such a change with no debate. Did they not think it was an important change? If so, why not make the same parsimonious change in Protocol I and put rape into Article 75 (fundamental guarantees), paragraph 2 (b), instead of leaving it as a separate article on the protection of women and children? What is the significance of the fact that Protocol II applies only to domestic wars and not to international wars? Is it possible that most delegations did not consider Protocol II to be as important as Protocol I, and therefore did not care to debate it? Does the American delegation's report evaluating the conference give a clue about this matter? According to the report, "the worst combination of results was achieved" because

> Committee III adopted relatively rigorous provisions for Protocol II, and Committee I adopted a relatively high threshold of application. . . . [A]s a result, the goal of strengthening the law applicable to internal armed conflicts has been dealt a serious blow; even if ultimately adopted by the Conference, . . . there is substantial doubt that the provisions of Protocol II would ever be applied.[88]

The American delegate to the conference, Mr. Aldrich, later wrote that:

> As for Protocol II, I regret that the Diplomatic Conference largely failed. Though of some value, that Protocol has much too high a threshold of application and too little in the way of substantive rules. The Conference allowed this to happen in order not to endanger Protocol I and because of the adverse reaction of many developing countries to the draft Protocol II developed by the three main committees at the Conference. So long as governments worry that they might enhance the status of rebels merely by agreeing to treaties restricting how rebels may be treated, the treaty route may not be the most promising way of developing the law.[89]

Alternatively, we can recall the difference between the Lieber Code (1863), which was written for a civil war, and the Hague Conventions, which applied to international laws, in terms of their inclusion and exclusion of rape. How much does the idea of inevitability of rape change according to the type of conflict under consideration? Commenting on the Vietnam War, which preceded the writing of the Additional Protocols and affected important aspects of them, Susan Brownmiller points to the fact that incidents of rape are fewer in civil wars[90] because they are seen as struggles of brother against brother. Given that rape was uncommon during the American Civil War as well, she attributes this rarity to the "code of honor" among men, which bans attacking "one's sister or one's buddy's sister."[91]

In light of these facts, the prohibition of rape in the Lieber Code makes more sense. The fact that Lieber, who included the prohibition of rape into the first codified law of war, wrote it for a civil war may help us understand why he included rape, whereas the drafters of the Hague Regulations did not. After all, Lieber was deeply involved in the war himself, being the father of three sons fighting on both sides, a literal fight of brother against brother. The stress of this situation gave Lieber not only a realistic approach to laws of war, but also a "strongly humanitarian feeling."[92] Perhaps he thought that rape should and could be avoided when it comes to women who may be the wives or daughters of your brother, instead of some unknown women belonging to the evil enemy. It is also necessary to reemphasize the fact that the Lieber Code was written as an army code, not international law. This means it would not bring any obligations on the United States the way a multilateral treaty like the Hague Conventions would. Hence it is possible to expect less attention to the possibility of compliance and less maneuvering on the part of a state to clarify or not clarify the exact obligation.

Although Protocol II brings about the most important change with respect to rape, there is one important development in Protocol I: the elimination of "honor" as the object of protecting women from rape. This development happened with the initial draft prepared by the ICRC. Mr. Surbeck, the ICRC representative at the conference, introduced the change by saying that

at the present state of international humanitarian law women were protected only by a few scattered provisions. That was evident in the Geneva Conventions of 1949, especially in the fourth Convention. Women who were not in a special situation such as pregnant women or those responsible for young children were protected as such only by Article 27, second paragraph which stated that "Women shall be especially protected against any attack on their honor, in particular against rape, enforced prostitution or any form of indecent assault." That wording had been repeated almost completely in Article 67 which was before the Committee. In the wider application of Section

III of Part IV of draft Protocol I, of which Article 67 was a part, paragraph 1 envisaged extending to all women without exception the protection which was granted to them by the second paragraph of Article 27 of the fourth Geneva Convention.[93]

The removal of "honor" from Article 67 is interpreted as a "minor drafting change,"[94] and there is no comment on its importance during any of the meetings. The wider application referred to here is about the extension of the scope of the article to all women in the territory of the parties to the conflict with no distinction, rather than only to those who fulfill the conditions of Article 4 of the Fourth Convention (those who are not the nationals of the power in the territory.)[95]

The Additional Protocols brought about important changes, both by getting rid of the word *honor* and by using the word *prohibition* in Protocol II. But Protocol I, as the one establishing the rules in international wars, continued to pose an obligation problem by failing to prohibit rape.

Delegation Problem in the Additional Protocols

The delegation problem in the Additional Protocols with respect to rape arises from their failure to include rape among grave breaches (as the Geneva Conventions of 1949 also failed to do). This failure is particularly surprising in light of new items the conference added to the list of grave breaches (with Article 85) and its attempt to establish an International Criminal Tribunal to handle cases related to grave breaches. I analyze this failure in three areas: first, the new grave breaches added to the conventions; second, the process of adding these during the conferences; and third, the failed attempt to establish an International Criminal Court.

New Grave Breaches. On a suggestion made at the 1971 Conference, a "questionnaire concerning measures intended to reinforce the implementation of the Geneva Conventions" was sent to the state parties. Using the responses, the ICRC prepared a new draft that extended the repression of breaches to include the breaches of the protocol.[96] This draft added a new article, Article 85 (Draft Protocol Article 74), to manage grave breaches.[97] Paragraphs 3 and 4 listed the new set of unacceptable behaviors that would be classified as grave breaches, in addition to those mentioned in Article 11, which describes the prohibition of medical and scientific experiments, mutilations, the removal of tissues and organs for transplantation, blood transfusions, and other acts that may endanger the physical or mental health and integrity of the person. These new grave breaches are

- making the civilian population or individual civilians the object of attack;
- launching an indiscriminate attack affecting the civilian population or civilian objects in the knowledge that such attack will cause excessive loss of life, injury to civilians or damage to civilian objects,
- launching an attack against works or installations containing dangerous forces in the knowledge that such attack will cause excessive loss of life, injury to civilians or damage to civilian objects;
- making non-defended localities and demilitarized zones the object of attack;
- making a person the object of attack in the knowledge that he is *hors de combat*;
- the perfidious use of the distinctive emblem of the red cross, red crescent or red lion and sun or of other protective signs;
- the transfer by the Occupying Power of parts of its own civilian population into the territory it occupies, or the deportation or transfer of all or parts of the population of the occupied territory within or outside this territory;
- unjustifiable delay in the repatriation of prisoners of war or civilians;
- practices of apartheid;
- making the clearly-recognized historic monuments, works of art or places of worship the object of attack;
- depriving a person protected by the Conventions or referred to in paragraph 2 of this Article of the rights of fair and regular trial.

As we see from this long list, grave breaches now included some new issues such as apartheid, in addition to some less severe issues (if compared to rape), such as making historic monuments and art the object of attack. Note that the list excluded rape.

The Process. Like the Geneva Conventions of 1949, the Additional Protocols do not mention rape as a grave breach of humanitarian law. How were these new grave breaches added to the Protocol, and did the parties just forget to add rape? According to Bothe et al., during the conference the delegations had a near consensus that a clear distinction must be drawn between grave breaches and other breaches and that only certain acts should become grave breaches, but there was a big disagreement on which acts should qualify.[98] Some Eastern European states, along with some countries from the Third World and certain individual delegates from Western Europe, wanted to follow the model of war crime tribunals and to include breaches committed on the battlefield (Parts III and IV of the Protocol, which includes Article 76 related to the protection of women). The majority of Western European states and other countries, however, wanted to be very careful about including breaches committed on the battlefield. Their argument was that "such breaches were only loosely formulated in the basic provisions of the Protocol concerned and that it would also be difficult to produce proof of such acts. In any event a much stricter definition of such acts would be necessary."[99]

One would think that if the formulation of the acts was the problem, reformulating them would be the next step—instead of leaving them loosely formulated in the articles and ignoring them altogether when it came to enforcement. That is what happened, however, with the new grave breaches created in Article 85, which combined the grave breaches of the Geneva Conventions (1949) and the law of the Hague, and which was very controversial at first. Since many delegations were opposed to this combination, they decided to define each individual item in the list with great caution—concrete and strictly clear definitions with a solid basis in the protocol.[100] Rape, of course, was not on the list and did not receive a clear definition. Some attempts to add other items on the list failed, but no delegation tried to include rape.

Examining some of these attempts, however, gives us an idea about the degree of diligence the delegations showed in writing this new article, which sheds light, once again, on the exclusion of rape and that the delegates could not have thought it was implied by any one of the grave breaches. The Philippines delegation introduced an amendment to add a new sub-paragraph (g) to paragraph 3 of Article 74 (CDDH/418) making the use of weapons prohibited under the Hague Declaration of 1899 and the Geneva Protocol of 1925 a grave breach. Mr. Aldrich, the U.S. delegate, criticized this attempt by arguing:

> At the present stage of international legal development, the criminal law [is] not the proper vehicle for dealing with the problem of weapons. Grave breaches [are] meant to be the most serious type of crime; Parties [have] an obligation to punish or extradite those guilty of them. Such crimes should therefore be clearly specified, so that a

soldier would know if he was about to commit an illegal act for which he could be punished. The amendment, however, [is] vague and imprecise.[101]

The Australian delegation also had problems with the new grave breaches, as it explained with its vote on Article 74 of draft Protocol I (Article 85 in the final text). The Australians' argument was that Article 74 was both "vague and impracticable" and "inconsistent with the basic tenets of criminal law." The reason for these flaws was that

> Any behavior which could give rise to punishment on the basis of universal jurisdiction should, among other things, be carefully identified. Not only should the nature of the offence be clear but the subject and object of the offence should also be clearly identifiable. It is essential that those who engage in warfare should not be confronted with accusations and criminal proceedings for matters which they could not reasonably expect to be a grave breach.

Therefore, Australia demanded greater precision in Article 74 to ensure better implementation of the article and greater justice for all.[102]

It is clear that these states chose the items in the list of grave breaches selectively, ensured that they were defined in the law very clearly, and emphasized that these acts and only these acts would be treated as grave breaches. Bothe et al. illustrate this situation when they discuss Norway and Sweden's attempt to add breaches of Article 54 of the final text of Protocol I (Annex B to CDDH/I/324 and CDDH/I/SR. 64, para. 8) to the list of grave breaches. Article 54 deals with the protection of objects indispensable to the survival of civilian populations. In the discussion of whether an attack against the natural environment (covered by Article 55, which also prohibits attacking the natural environment by way of reprisals) qualifies as an attack on objects indispensable to the survival of the civilian population, the ICRC argued that the natural environment was not an "object" (CDDH/III/SR.20, para.7). Bothe et al. say,

> But why then does Art. 55 form part of Chapter III on civilian objects and why are reprisals against the natural environment prohibited if it is not an object? In the course of the discussion it was also argued that the question whether such attacks should be regarded as grave

breaches was not correctly put: this question belonged to the problem of whether reprisals were legitimate or not (US, CDDH/III/SR.24,
para.39). This leads to the question of the relationship between grave
breaches and reprisals. Both are forms of implementation. Under a
system where grave breaches are prosecuted not by an international
institution but by States Parties both are unilateral measures. There
are, however, no general rules which would generally prohibit reprisals in cases where a prosecution of grave breaches is possible, nor
any which provide that all acts which are prohibited as reprisals are
automatically also grave breaches. There may be a presumption that
an act which is prohibited as reprisal should also be a grave breach (in
view of its gravity), but it is not more than a presumption and it is up
to the legislator whether he is willing to follow it or not.[103]

There is no way to presume an act, because of its relationship to another
act that is on the list of grave breaches or because of its gravity, is an implicit
grave breach of the Geneva Conventions and then to expect state parties to
act accordingly—not only because there is no international institution to interpret the law, but because the law was written as such.

An International Criminal Court. Some of the experts that the ICRC consulted
for writing the draft Additional Protocols envisaged an international criminal
court on the model of the Nuremberg Tribunal, despite the ICRC's resistance
to the idea.[104] With the proposal of the Philippines delegation (CDDH/56,
Add.1 with Rev.1), they added a new section (New Section III- Draft Code
of International Crimes in Violation of the Geneva Conventions of 1949 and
the Additional Protocols[105]) to the Draft Protocol I outlining an international
criminal court or tribunal, although it would never be part of the actual protocol. According to Article 12 of this new section,

> There is established an International Criminal Court or Tribunal to
> try persons accused of grave breaches of or crimes under interna-
> tional law, or the law of war, as may be provided in conventions or
> special agreements among States Parties to the present Convention.[106]

What grave breaches would this court handle? Article 2 ("Classification of
crimes against humanity") and Article 4 ("Classification of crimes against
the laws and customs of war," listing grave breaches) mention many acts that

the Court would try, among which we do not find rape. Anything that can come close to it would be Article 4 (a): "Any act perpetrated against, and causing bodily harm to, women, children, the sick, and the aged," which is very imprecise and unclear. Pillage is, interestingly, prohibited five times in various forms, four of which (Article 4) are considered to be grave breaches: "plunder of populations" (Article 2 (n)), "the destruction or seizure of the enemy's property" (Article 4 (l)), "pillage of any town or place" (Article 4 (n)), "confiscation of private property" (Article 4 (o)) and "forcible requisitions" (Article 4 (p)).[107] States did not want to deal with rape even in the context of debating over an international criminal court that did not have a chance of coming into being in the political context of the time. Yet they found it necessary to reemphasize the protection of private property forcefully at every opportunity.

What was the normative context that made some improvements in international law regarding women possible, but could not take them far enough?

The Normative Context and the Main Actors

After World War II two new developments increased the pace of change (which had started in the nineteenth century) in the normative context that regarded women as property of men: the emergence of human rights as a central concept in world politics, and later the emergence of women's movements on a global scale. Women's struggles during the 1950s, '60s, and '70s for political, legal, and economic rights, especially their activism at the UN, would lead to an increase in the visibility of women in the international arena as full candidates for human rights. These changes ultimately problematized the treatment of rape by international law.

Before I turn to the global women's movement and rape's appearance on the movement's agenda, however, I will look at the anti-rape movement in order to understand the emergence of rape as a central topic for feminists. I begin with a look at second wave feminism, which emerged in the Western world in the 1960s and continued into the '70s before it spread into the ranks of international feminism in the late '70s and early '80s.

Second wave feminism developed in the 1960s (particularly in the United States) when women's frustration in the workplace and in their homes began to radicalize from the discrimination or exclusion from the public sphere after the end of World War II. The motto of the second wave was equality, not only in political rights (as first wave feminism had accomplished with suffrage), but also in economic and social rights. Western feminism's demands for "true equal partnership with men" and an end to "the relationship of dominance and subordination" would lead to feminist concerns over the female body. In 1968 and 1969, feminists protested the Miss America contest for objectifying and diminishing women.[108] In 1971 Juliet Mitchell wrote that for the liberation of women, four areas of women's lives needed to be transformed: production, reproduction, sexuality, and socialization of children.[109] Women began consciousness-raising groups, where they gathered to "share, recognize and name" their oppression, for "speaking the unspoken." One of these "unspokens" was rape, and some second wave feminists took on the issue as emblematic of women's oppression and vulnerability.[110] An anti-rape movement developed in the 1970s, parallel to the second wave of the feminist movement. It would eventually spread to the rest of the world starting in the mid-1970s and continuing through the 1980s.

Speaking out about rape broke the taboo of silence on the part of women. This silence had been imposed on women (as we saw in the nineteenth-century cases) and not only prevented prosecution and punishment of perpetrators over the centuries, but also reinforced the view that rape is a form of sex (hence inevitable) that one needs to be discreet about.

The act of speaking out also helped women to learn that rape is not necessarily the product of the diseased minds of perverts which happens to some unfortunate women; instead, it is a pervasive tool of oppression that makes its presence felt in every woman's life. In 1971, the New York Radical Feminists organized a "rape speak-out" and a rape conference, and the first rape crisis center in the United States, the Bay Area Women Against Rape, was formed.[111] That same year, a leading radical feminist, Susan Griffin, published a landmark article, "Rape: The All American Crime," which questioned why women had always had to live with the fear of being raped. As the issue of rape was gaining more space on the radical feminist agenda, it was also accelerating the divergence of radical feminists from the mainstream liberal women's movement in the United States—which wanted to retain a "respectable" image and societal approval and thought "offensive" or "taboo" concepts like sexuality and rape could damage that image. Liberal feminists, however, would eventually start anti-rape work in 1973.[112]

Rape was different from the other topics on feminists' agenda in that there seemed to be no place for controversy in it. While there could be deep divisions not only among feminists but also within society on the issue of abortion, for instance, it is hard to imagine anyone to be pro-rape (although whether feminists needed to put it on the agenda caused some stir among them). The legal treatment of rape throughout much of history seemed to be confirming the historical double standard, since on paper rape has always been a crime. Feminists would help expose the fact that behind this façade there was an underlying "rape culture" where "sexual assault is tolerated, violent and sexual images are intertwined, women are blamed for being raped, sexist attitudes prevail, and male sexual privilege goes unquestioned."[113] They had to address the problem of the dismissal of rape's seriousness as a crime by legal and medical authorities as well as the society at large. They also had to challenge the rape myths—such as that "inappropriate behavior" brings on rape or that uncontrollable male sexual drive or passion, especially sex starvation, causes rape. Feminists also had to develop a "pro-woman understanding of rape" in order to make lawmakers take rape seriously.[114]

As the anti-rape movement started to emerge within the feminist movement, one of the most important books of the movement appeared in 1975, providing the basis of the feminist anti-rape ideology. In her groundbreaking book *Against Our Will*, Susan Brownmiller argued that rape has historically played the critical function of holding women under male dominance by means of "a conscious process of intimidation," and that all political and legal systems are created to perpetuate that fear and to hold women "in their place."[115] Her claim that rape is not about sex or passion but about violence would be one of the basic tenets of the anti-rape movement. By using research and victims' testimonies, anti-rape activists tackled the myth about the sex-starved man raping to fulfill his sexual needs, as well as other myths. Instead, they maintained that what triggered rape had always been the desire for power, control, brutalization, and humiliation.[116]

Starting in the 1970s in the United States, the anti-rape movement managed to create a new awareness of rape both at the societal level and at the public policy level by forming coalitions among different women's groups, holding media campaigns, and lobbying legislatures for new rape laws. Many women in the legal profession joined the anti-rape movement, providing legal expertise for the push for legal reform and adding legitimacy to the anti-rape cause through their "appeal to law-and-order sensibility."[117] The rape cases around which feminists organized—and rulings and statements by the courts belittling rape and rape victims, which were widely publicized by the media— also helped to raise public consciousness and sympathy for victims and eventually helped promote legal changes by proving feminists' points about rape myths and women's victimization. Women legislators also played a crucial role in terms of introducing and furthering anti-rape legislation, particularly at the federal level.[118] Through achieving changes in the "redefinition of rape in laws, evidentiary rules, statutory age offenses and penalties," anti-rape activists aimed to "increase[e] the reporting of rape, . . . prosecution and conviction rates, improving the treatment of rape victims in the criminal justice system, achieving comparability between the legal treatment of rape and other violent crimes, prohibiting a wider range of coercive sexual conduct, [and] expanding the range of persons protected by law."[119]

As a result, rape stopped being a taboo or something women should blame themselves for. Feminists also were able to push for new policies on issues like marital rape, rape-shield laws (to prevent the admittance of victim's sexual history in court), and corroboration requirement (the necessity of independent evidence for rape prosecution to corroborate the identity of the assailant, penetration, and victim's non-consent), among others.

In addition to these legal changes, rape crisis centers became widespread, providing support for the victims and collaborating with law enforcement and medical professionals to ensure justice for the victims. These centers also helped the campaign for rape law reform by locating weaknesses in the law through their proximity to the legal process.[120] By achieving considerable change in public opinion about women (like the recognition of women as free individuals entitled to determine their own lifestyles and plans), feminists managed to break the silence about women's oppression through customs and law pertaining to rape. By 1996, all states in the United States had reformed their rape laws, including marital rape laws.[121] Eventually, the anti-rape movement spread in the Western world, and as a result, rape laws in most Western countries were changed to respond to women's demands for sexual integrity.[122]

One other important development that accompanied the social activism of women against rape and rape myths was the new academic work into the causes of rape that started to deconstruct the idea of rape's inevitability. Besides the previously mentioned feminist theorizing with its emphasis on the sexual inequality and power relations as the sources of rape,[123] scholars in the late 1970s and early 1980s applied the social learning theory from psychology to rape.[124]

According to social learning theory, proposed by a leading psychologist in the 1960s and 1970s, Albert Bandura, people learn behavior through observation and imitation or through the interaction of cognition and environment.[125] The implications of this theory for the theorization of rape was an understanding of the sexual behavior manifested in rape as a behavior learned, transmitted, and reinforced through repeated exposure to social interpretations of sex roles. These socially constructed sex roles portray women as the passive sex that is to be dominated, and they cultivate an aggressive and forceful masculinity for men. Social attitudes that excuse or justify rape act as further negative reinforcements, eliminating the idea that rape is unacceptable behavior.[126] In other words, men learn sexual aggression through their exposure to violent pornographic materials, various rape myths like "no means yes," or through sex role scripts. The fact that society does not effectively discourage it as inexcusable behavior perpetuates the social learning process.[127]

This theory was obviously in stark contrast with the widely held social beliefs about the cause and nature of rape that produced the idea of "inevitability." In combination with feminist theories on rape, social learning theory also started to shape the way feminists framed their arguments about rape, exposing lawmakers, policymakers, and the wider public to the idea that rape is not inevitable, and that it is instead a learned behavior that has been reinforced by the lack of adequate social and legal emphasis on its illegitimacy. In the case of wartime rape, the idea that the militarized culture of "enemy," "soldiering," "victory," and "defeat" enables the practice of rape would ultimately become another important point.[128] Furthermore, the feminists argued, if rape is learned, it can be unlearned, especially if reporting and prosecuting rape becomes easier (in addition to changes in education and control over pornography).[129] Once these achievements in changing domestic rape laws began, the women's movement turned its attention to the issue of international law's treatment of rape.

The Global Women's Movement and Rape

In the 1970s, women's groups were very much divided at the international level (just as they had been within national boundaries) over issues such as race, class, ethnicity, sexual orientation, geographic location (the North-South gap in particular), religion, and ideology. The number of women in key international institutions such as the UN, however, was increasing rapidly and they were forming alliances both among themselves and with other movements at the time—the human rights and anti-colonial movements. The UN became an important forum for these new alliances. The traditional women's organizations that pioneered the establishment of the Commission on the Status of Women (CSW) in the UN[130] in 1946 also participated in the commission's work with consultative status. One of these organizations was the International Alliance of Women (IAW).

In 1972, with the initiative of the women's organizations, a woman delegate from Romania introduced a resolution calling for the designation of an
international women's year with a World Women's Conference the same year.
While the idea met opposition from some states, it was ultimately accepted.[131]
As a result, 1975 became International Women's Year (with the three themes
of equality, development, and peace) and the beginning of the UN Women's
Decade. Women's NGOs proliferated, and three world conferences were held,
at which NGOs brought their concerns about the issue of violence against
women before the mainstream CSW and the Committee on the Elimination
of Discrimination against Women (CEDAW). Neither the CSW, established
(1946) in the Economic and Social Council (ECOSOC) of the UN for advis-
ing on problems related to women's rights, nor CEDAW, established (1981)
to oversee the implementation of the Convention on the Elimination of All
Forms of Discrimination against Women by state parties, had focused on violence against women, let alone rape. Moreover, the International Covenant
on Civil and Political Rights (ICCPR), created in 1966 (entered into force in
1976) to make the UDHR into a binding law, did not mention rape or sexual
violence. Therefore, raising awareness about violence against women in these
mainstream UN institutions with close ties to the states was an important
task for women's organizations.[132]

The first women's conference of the UN Decade for Women was held
in Mexico in 1975. The focus of the conference was "equal legal capacity,
education, economic means, access to family planning and [more] women
in decision-making positions,"[133] and the issue of violence against women
did not come up. Was this absence because of the women delegates' lack
of confidence to bring up a controversial topic, or was it the fact that the
agenda of the conference was ultimately controlled by men?[134] Although a
large number of the delegates were women, the president of the conference
was a man. Most women delegates were chosen because of their personal
relationships to powerful (male) political figures, rather than their expertise or interest in women's issues.[135] Additionally, women faced difficulties
in terms of controlling the conference's agenda. For example, when women's
NGOs prepared a proposal for revisions to the official text of the program
of action, they learned that they could not present it to the delegates of
the conference because official rules prevented "unaccredited individuals
or groups" from submitting proposals. The secretary of the conference told
them "to go home and work on implementing the World Plan of Action"
instead.[136]

According to Jutta Joachim, there were four reasons for the silence of the conference on violence. First, the rivalry among the three blocs of UN members—the North/West, the East, and the South with the corresponding agendas of equality, peace, and development (the themes of the conference)—did not leave any space for the subject of gender violence. The blocs politicized the Mexico City Conference (as well as the Copenhagen Conference in 1980), which then became a battleground for the conflicts between the blocs. The media also paid more attention to the inter-bloc conflict than women. Second, the alignments to these blocs stripped the women's groups from the women allies within state delegations because the women delegates preferred their blocs' causes over women's causes. Third, women's organizations were divided not only over North-South/East-West conflicts, but also over their feminisms. While liberal feminists supported the UN and the Women's Conferences to further their agenda, radical feminists saw these conferences as window dressing for patriarchal governments' interests (until the 1995 Beijing Conference). Last, women's organizations did not have sufficient experience in the agenda-setting and lobbying processes in these settings. They also did not have much expertise on the issue of violence against women, since the subject was still taboo and information was still unavailable in most countries.[137]

In 1976, as a counteraction to the Mexico City Conference, some feminists organized the International Tribunal on Crimes against Women in Brussels to disassociate themselves from what they saw as the establishment of the oppressors. Women from around the world testified about the gender violence they experienced in order to politicize the issue. In the midst of many contestations, conflicts, and disruptions, the tribunal managed to create a "we-feeling" among the (predominantly Western and some Third World) women, and it stimulated both national and international actions against violence against women.[138]

In 1979 the UN General Assembly adopted the Convention on the Elimination of All Forms of Discrimination against Women, which came into force in 1981. Although CEDAW addressed many forms of discrimination, violence against women was not one of them.[139] A participant in the writing of the convention attributes this silence to the fact that violence against women—domestic violence and rape in particular—was the "world's dirty little secret," something that happened but was not talked about publicly. The drafters considered including provisions against violence, but they ended up covering it obliquely with the articles on prostitution and penal provisions that discriminated against women (Articles 6 and 2 (g)), rather than mentioning it openly.[140] Still, what is particularly striking about the exclusion of violence against women from the CEDAW is that women drafted it. According to Arvonne Fraser, the CSW gave its women members, women's NGOs, and female UN staff "a free space" in the drafting process.[141] Free space, however, did not mean no constraints. As Fraser also explains on the issue of reservations and ratification,[142] among all international human rights treaties, CEDAW has the highest number of reservations that were entered with ratifications, due to the changes it required in "the most basic legal and cultural assumptions about women."[143] This situation illustrates, one more time, the role of a strongly entrenched gender ideology in international lawmaking and its resistance to change even after women's involvement in the process as important political actors.

Rape in War

The assumption about the inevitability of rape and its connection to the nature of masculinity even found ways into the feminist movement. Especially during the early phases of the anti-rape campaign in the early 1970s, feminism could not come up with a theory of rape because it did not challenge the definition of masculinity as inherent or biologically determined.[144] Even in 1992, a self-proclaimed feminist and an opponent of the anti-rape movement wrote, "Hunt, pursuit, and capture are biologically programmed into male sexuality" in her attempt to "teach" women what rape is about—a biological reality that one needs to accept in order to protect one's self from it.[145] Of course, this was a marginalized view within feminism and by the 1990s it would be even more marginalized (at least politically incorrect) in Western societies at large, but it would not be a smooth process for feminists to come to that point. The rape myths were well entrenched in social, political, and legal systems.

In 1979, for example, a Connecticut judge said, "You cannot blame somebody for trying," in his remarks about a case of attempted rape.[146] In a 1983 Michigan court case, the prosecutor argued that the rapist's marital problems leading to unsatisfied sexual desires justified his actions (raping two thirteen-year-old girls).[147]

After Bangladesh's war of independence against Pakistan (1971), a Bengali politician's answer to the question of why rape happens in war is striking in terms of understanding this kind of mentality: "What do soldiers talk about in barracks? Women and sex. Put a gun in their hands and tell them to go out and frighten the wits out of a population and what will be the first thing that leaps to their mind?"[148]

Along similar lines, we find an American squad leader in the Vietnam War, John Smail, commenting about the rapes in Mai Lai: "That's an every-day affair. . . . [Y]ou can nail just about everybody on that—at least once. The guys are human, man."[149] "The guys are human," rather human males with a pressure-cooker inside that may explode at any moment. This line of thinking was why the American military allowed the establishment of brothels on army base camps in Vietnam and controlled their operations for health and security reasons.[150] The military emphasized the control of venereal disease in particular through official brothels and even giving daily penicillin shots to prostitutes. They also used anti-VD training films and merit ratings where a high VD count would be charged against the merit rating of a battalion. Yet they provided no training to prevent rape, and given the fact that "you can nail just about everybody on that at least once," the number of prosecutions and convictions for rape were quite small. During the eight-year period between 1965 and 1973, only 86 U.S. soldiers (in Vietnam) were court-martialed for sexual crimes; 50 were convicted, and they received very light sentences.[151]

Even when people try to explain why rape did not happen in a particular war (which is a rare occurrence), they could not refrain from appealing to the idea that men need sex, especially in a war when they lack access to women for long periods of time. Hence, men rape when they have the opportunity to satisfy this need. Peter Arnett, the Associated Press correspondent in Vietnam during the Vietnam War, thought that one of the reasons the Vietcong forces did not rape was their "sense of dedication to their revolutionary mission." According to Arnett, just like the few American officers who did not use the brothels during their stay in Vietnam because of their dedication to victory, the Vietcong "literally did not need sex" and they "could control their lust from . . . [their] sense of dedication."[152]

In 1972, some feminist groups organized around the issue of rape in war for the first time, as a reaction to the rape of 200,000 Bengali women by Pakistani soldiers during Bangladesh's war of independence in 1971. Although the organizations restricted themselves to providing aid to the victims, they convinced the Western press to show interest in the misfortune of the Bengali women.[153] Western media started paying attention to the brutalities of some "uncivilized" people somewhere in Asia, but it quickly forgot about them. When asked about the rapes, "Pakistani officers [would] maintain that their men were too disciplined 'for that sort of thing,' "[154] and it seemed the rest of the world was more than willing to accept their word for it.

As we see in the case of both Bangladesh and the Vietnam War and the loss of the voices of thousands of women who were raped, by the mid-1970s the women's movement was not yet able to call large-scale attention to rape in war. "The time was not right."[155]

Chapter 5

The Prohibition of Rape in War:
Success: The Rome Statute

Through their decisions in 1990s, the International Criminal Tribunal for the Former Yugoslavia (ICTY) and the International Criminal Tribunal for Rwanda (ICTR) set the precedents for prosecution of rape as a crime against humanity, a grave breach, a form of genocide, and, finally, a war crime. For the next legal step in the prohibition of rape, however, I examine the inclusion of rape in the Rome Statute of the International Criminal Court (ICC). Although the ICTY and the ICTR indicted[1] individuals for rape before 1998, I do not focus primarily on their work as the next steps of the legal change. I concentrate on the Rome Statute, because the rape-related judgments of both courts (the ICTR *Akayesu* case, September 2, 1998, and the ICTY *Celebici* case, November 16, 1998) came after the Rome Statute was signed (July 17, 1998), and both judgments refer to the Rome Statute.[2]

The Law

The Rome Statute (1998), establishing the ICC, is one of the legalization examples that rank the highest on the hard-soft law spectrum.[3] It puts the highest degree of obligation on the state parties by requiring them to prevent, investigate, and prosecute the violations or turn the violators over to the ICC for prosecution for all crimes under its jurisdiction.[4] With regard to rape, obligation is clear, too. Article 8, which defines war crimes explicitly, mentions

rape, sexual slavery, enforced prostitution, forced pregnancy, enforced sterilization, or any other form of sexual violence.[5]

The Rome Statute is on the highest end of the precision scale as well, since
detailed explanations of what exactly is prohibited can lead to "only narrow
issues of interpretation."[6] Both Article 7 concerning Crimes against Humanity and Article 8 on War Crimes include not only rape but also other forms
of sexual violence: "Rape, sexual slavery, enforced prostitution, forced pregnancy, enforced sterilization, or any other form of sexual violence" are declared to constitute grave breaches of the Geneva Conventions. And because
the ICC has jurisdiction over all the crimes mentioned in the Rome Statute,
delegation is at the highest point for everything prohibited by the statute.[7] We
can conclude that with very high degrees of obligation, precision, and delegation, the Rome Statute created the prohibition regime against rape in war.

The Normative Context and the Main Actors

The idea of an international criminal court had been around since the end of
World War II. In 1948, through Resolution 260, the UN General Assembly
(GA) asked the International Law Commission (ILC) "to study the desirabil-
ity and possibility of establishing an international judicial organ for the trial
of persons charged with genocide."[8] Although the UN prepared a draft statute
in 1951, and revisited the idea in the 1970s and again in 1989, it would not
be realized until the 1990s. The preparations for the establishment of an international criminal court started again in the post-Cold War period, in the
context of civil and ethnic conflicts around the world, widespread violence
targeting civilian populations, and the enormous publicity these events had
gained due to the advancements in communications technology.[9] The arguments for a permanent international criminal court gained power especially
after the atrocities in the former Yugoslavia (1992–1995, 1999) and the genocide in Rwanda (1994). In 1993, the UN Security Council established an ad
hoc tribunal for the war crimes committed in the former Yugoslavia. Then,
with the awareness of the atrocities in the former Yugoslavia and Rwanda,
the International Law Commission at the UN prepared a draft statute for a
permanent international criminal court and presented it to the General Assembly.[10] While the Security Council established another ad hoc tribunal,
this time for the genocide in Rwanda (1994), the General Assembly decided
to create a preparatory committee (PrepCom) to develop the draft statute

for the ICC into a finalized text that could be submitted to an international conference.

By this time, NGOs had already started their work to push for establishment of an international criminal court. Twenty-five NGOs formed a coalition, "a vanguard model type of coalition,"[11] in 1995, and by the time of the Rome Conference, the coalition included around 450 participants.[12] According to one of the members of the Coalition for the International Criminal Court (CICC), ICC negotiations would never have happened without the impetus of the tragedies in former Yugoslavia and Rwanda. "Nations, NGOs, and UN people alike were motivated by very powerful emotions and psychology having to do with the very recent atrocities of this kind," and it became much easier for them to bond as legitimate participants in the process with a clear motivation to turn the "never again" idea (also thought after World War II) into a reality.[13] The outrage and the sense of urgency pushed the process forward.[14]

According to *International Criminal Court Monitor*, the resolution for the establishment of the ICC (A/RES/51/207) the UN General Assembly eventually passed in 1996 is a major victory, because the governments who argued against the ICC or who had argued just two years previously that an international criminal court could not be established for another 50 to 100 years were unable to express public opposition.[15] In the face of these tragedies, it became more difficult to say no to an institution that could potentially prevent them from happening again. As a result, the atrocities in former Yugoslavia and Rwanda became major referral points for all advocates of the ICC; they were mentioned again and again during the process in order to show that the world needed an international criminal court. We see many examples when we look at the publications and speeches of the time by prominent actors:

> Time and again, we have been helpless in the face of the failure of national criminal-law systems to punish the perpetrators of atrocities and those behind them. Genocide, mass executions of political opponents, "ethnic cleansing," systematic rape as a means of "warfare" — the shocking TV reports from Cambodia, Vukovar and Srebrenica, Rwanda and elsewhere are still fresh in our minds.[16]

The horrors of the Balkans and Africa's Great Lake district will not be the last of their kind. In conflicts the world over, civilians are increasingly being used as military targets. This tide of barbarism must be stemmed. The world may not be able to deter war; it is capable, however, to more effectively deter war crimes. To do so the world needs to set up an International Criminal Court—a permanent tribunal, with global jurisdiction, with the power to indict and try individuals for war crimes, crimes against humanity and genocide.[17]

The Making of the ICC: The Role of the NGOs

The UN Diplomatic Conference of Plenipotentiaries in Rome (June 15–July 17, 1998) wrote the Rome Statute based on the draft prepared by the International Law Commission and revised by the Preparatory Committee meetings (PrepComs) between 1996 and 1998. One of the most striking features of this process that gave birth to the ICC was the huge impact of NGOs, particularly on the Rome Statute. For the first time in history, they played an important role in writing international law.[18] What publicists of the nineteenth century did for the Hague Regulations and government experts (with the leadership of the ICRC) for the most part did for the Geneva Conventions, the human rights NGOs did for the Rome Statute. As a result of the greater access NGOs gained to the international conferences after the end of the Cold War, they managed to influence events, unlike in previous decades when they were mostly excluded from the negotiation process.[19]

In addition to this new opportunity of access, the fact that so many NGOs came together under a very well organized and concerted effort[20] (plus the degree of expertise[21] within the coalition, particularly on international criminal law) helped them gain credibility in the eyes of the states. As one of the CICC members put it: "The CICC early on realized that if its views, lobbying was to be accepted as appropriate, useful and listened to, it would be necessary to show that lobbying and presentation of views and pushing for objectives came from a strong body of expertise."[22]

The members of the coalition were broken into thirteen teams and several caucuses, each responsible for a certain section of the statute. They each monitored their section's respective debates and then negotiated with the state representatives. Later they discussed those negotiations and their results at the coalition meetings, which led to new arrangements to meet with different delegations for further lobbying efforts.[23] Their publications, particularly the high-quality papers and documents examining the arguments both for and against the position of the NGO that was publishing the paper, as well as the daily newsletters explaining what was happening in the negotiations, were very instrumental in informing delegates about different issues. These activities gained much respect and appreciation among the state delegations for the NGOs.[24] These excerpts from CICC's newsletter, the *ICC Monitor*, depict the array of their activities during the writing of the statute:

> Twenty participating organizations of the NGO Coalition were able to attend the second session of the PrepCom, including representatives of NGOs in Africa, Asia and Eastern Europe, thanks to the generous support of funders including the European Communities, the Ford Foundation and the governments of Denmark, the Netherlands and Sweden. The sizable NGO presence allowed the Coalition to conduct numerous meetings and discussions with delegations and PrepCom officers. Luncheon meetings between the Coalition and members of the like-minded group were hosted by Germany, Finland and Denmark, and the Coalition held additional meetings with members of the delegations from France, China, the United States, Russia, India, the Nordic states and countries in Latin America, Africa and Southeast Asia. Useful meetings were also conducted with members of the Bureau of the Preparatory Committee.[25]

> Not content to merely monitor the negotiations, NGO (nongovernmental organization) representatives engaged in a flurry of activities during the Rome Conference—from gala receptions in elegant Rome nightclubs to dense policy papers on issues before the Rome delegations. The Sudan Room, a large meeting space assigned to NGOs at the conference, was the site of frenetic activity as NGO representatives debated with each other, drafted text, faxed and emailed reports to their headquarters, and tried to follow the official meetings broadcast on close circuit television from two monitors in the room.[26]

According to the *ICC Monitor*, "lobbying involved chatting with members of national delegations, usually at the beginning and end of sessions and during intermissions" which they did very carefully to avoid any offense to national sensitivities.[27]

The CICC as a whole contributed to the entrance of the prohibition against rape into the Rome Statute. One of the reasons that the whole NGO community was involved in the initiative to include rape and other forms of sexual violence in the ICC Statute was the fact that the rapes in the conflict in the former Yugoslavia came to the forefront of the public understanding of what had happened there. Widespread publicity on the so-called "rape camps" in the context of an ethnic cleansing campaign made the advocates for an international criminal court concentrate on the issue of sexual violence against women in war. The fact that the initial draft statute prepared by the ILC in 1994 did not include rape among the war crimes (although it did so in the list of crimes against humanity), even after all these tragedies, further increased the need for advocacy. Rape and other forms of sexual violence therefore became central in the debate, as found in various documents and publications of the coalition. Several NGOs within the coalition were working for express jurisdiction over gender-related crimes as one of the top issues on their agenda. They were actively supporting the women's groups in their efforts to make icrimes against women be expressly mentioned as distinct subcategories rather than as subclasses of humiliating or degrading treatment or outrages upon personal dignity.[28]

In a working paper submitted to the PrepCom in 1997, the ICRC also proposed to specify the crimes under grave breaches with explicit attention given to rape:

> We have divided our list of war crimes into three categories. Under the first category, we have listed grave breaches of humanitarian law committed in international armed conflicts. We would like here to draw your attention to sub-paragraph (a)(iii) which specifically mentions rape, thus making unambiguous its being a grave breach.[29]

Several documents published during the process of the writing of the Rome Statute—such as the Dakar Declaration for the Establishment of the International Criminal Court by twenty-five African states and several NGOs (February 6, 1998) and the letters by various mainstream NGOs participating in the CICC—called for making rape a war crime and a crime against humanity as precisely as possible. These documents proposed that rape reside in a separate section from the prohibition of outrages upon personal dignity, in order to make it clear that it is a crime of sexual and gender violence.[30]

Another example for the same demands can be found in the speech given by the Amnesty International observer at the Rome Conference:

> Abuses against women had been widespread in the conflict in Bosnia and Herzegovina. To combat rape as a weapon of war and crimes against humanity, Amnesty International called for the establishment

of a permanent international criminal court. . . . The Statute expressly recognized that rape and other forms of sexual abuse were war crimes and crimes against humanity. However, Amnesty International was disappointed that a few powerful countries appeared to hold justice hostage and seemed to be more concerned with shielding possible criminals from trial than with introducing a charter for the victims.[31]

Rape, its centrality in the ethnic cleansing campaign in the former Yugoslavia, and the necessity to prevent it were emphasized numerous times at every platform for the ICC. Human Rights Watch, for instance, issued an action alert just before the Rome Conference, stressing these facts one more time:

Women are commonly the targets and victims of egregious international crimes and have frequently been denied access to justice at both national and international levels. The conflicts in Rwanda and the former Yugoslavia are only the most recent examples of horrifying levels of violence against women, including acts of rape, sexual slavery, enforced prostitution and other forms of sexual assault. The ICC must be fully empowered to prosecute sexual and gender violence if it is to fulfill its mandate to end impunity for the most serious violations of international law. Toward this end, the ICC Statute should explicitly recognize the court's jurisdiction over these crimes against women and adopt legal principles and procedures that would facilitate the prosecution of these crimes without prejudice to the accused.[32]

What former Nuremberg prosecutor Benjamin Ferencz said during an interview is particularly illustrative of the effect of the conflict in the former Yugoslavia on the public conscience and, in turn, on the conference:

There were Pol Pots and mass killings around the world. The world paid no attention. I cried and I wrote books and I screamed and nothing happened. Until Yugoslavia. The crimes were so outrageous there. The mass rapes of Muslim women, "ethnic cleansing" as genocide (such a terrible term, there's nothing clean about that process at all), so outraged the public community that they finally created an ad hoc international criminal tribunal to try those special crimes for that special time. And as you know they followed through with the same thing in Rwanda. This was a great step forward, but was totally inadequate. Justice does not depend on a particular time and place. Justice is universal and should apply to everywhere. That's why I'm so excited about the prospect of an international criminal court and about the progress that's been made.[33]

This effect is further illustrated by the fact that most participants, including many state delegates and in particular the members of what became known as "the like-minded group,"[34] were very vocal about the necessity to include rape in the statute and very effective in helping the NGO agenda.[35] The like-minded group was a group of states committed to some of the principles also represented by the NGO community—such as an independent prosecutor for the court, independence of the court from the Security Council, prohibition of reservations, and an inherent jurisdiction of the court over the core crimes. These principles were mostly at odds with the premises supported by other states, yet these 60 like-minded states dominated the organization of the Rome Conference as the critical allies of the NGOs, providing a political opportunity structure for influencing the agenda.[36] We see several delegates from the like-minded group raising gender issues during the plenary meetings:[37]

Ethnic cleansing and systematic rape and torture were of such gravity that they must be included in the ambit of the Court's jurisdiction.—Mr. Downer (Australia)

Rape, sexual slavery and other forms of sexual violence must be recognized as war crimes in the Statute, reflecting the landmark decision made at the United Nations Conference on Women.—Mr. Axworthy (Canada)

As a party to the Geneva Conventions of 1949, Lithuania endorsed the list of crimes set out in those Conventions. In negotiations on the laws applying to armed conflicts and the definition of serious violations, it was in favor of recognizing a deliberate change in the demographic situation of occupied territories as a crime. Moreover, rape, sexual abuse and other forms of sexual violations should be recognized as war crimes and crimes against humanity.—Mr. Pakalniskis (Lithuania)

Speaking as a woman and as Minister of Justice of her country, stressed the need to give the International Criminal Court full powers to deal with all crimes in which the dignity of women was violated. The Statute must therefore include the crimes of rape, sexual slavery, prostitution and forced sterilization, as well as the recruitment of minors into the armed forces.—Ms. Nagel Berger (Costa Rica)

The sexual abuse of women committed as an act of war or in a way that constituted a crime against humanity should be deemed particularly reprehensible. The crime of rape should be gender-neutral and classified as a crime against persons.—Mr. Baja (Philippines)

A gender perspective had to be incorporated into the Statute and the crimes of rape and sexual violence enumerated in the Statute needed to be retained without change.—Ms. Trotter (New Zealand)

Rape and other crimes of sexual violence committed in armed conflicts should be properly defined and explicitly listed as war crimes in the Statute.—Mr. Jensen (Denmark)

Some states that were not part of the like-minded group also felt the need to mention rape at least once during their speeches in order to show that they cared about the issue:[38]

The prosecution of abduction, rape, enslavement and other forms of child abuse should be prominently reflected in the Statute. Gender concerns should also be taken into account.—Mr. Kirabokyamaria (Uganda)

His delegation endorsed the views of the speakers who had called for the inclusion of sexual violence, including acts of aggression against women in the course of war crimes, rape, sexual slavery and pedophilia in the Court's terms of reference.—Mr. Al Kulaib (Kuwait)

The jurisdiction of the Court must extend to internal armed conflicts and crimes against humanity, including rape and other grave sexual violence.—Mr. Richardson (United States of America)

Even when they wanted to challenge some part of the articles related to sexual violence, the states seemed to feel the need to first put forward their support for the prohibition of rape. It is also interesting to note that for the most part the objections were presented through female members of the delegations:

> Regarding *(p bis)*, rape was a punishable crime under Libyan legisla-tion. Enforced pregnancy was the result of rape and it was the act it-self that should constitute a crime. Under Libyan legislation, abortion, too, was a crime. That paragraph therefore warranted further consid-eration. Under *(t)*, her delegation preferred option 1.—Ms. Shahen (Libyan Arab Jamahiriya)[39]

> On subparagraph *(p bis)*, she agreed with previous speakers that en-forced pregnancy should be mentioned in the context of rape. She ac-cepted subparagraphs *(q)*, *(r)* and *(s)* as drafted and preferred option 1 of subparagraph *(t)*.—Ms. Mekhemar (Egypt)[40]

This picture is clearly different from what we found during the preceding conferences that wrote the Hague and the Geneva Conventions, specifically in terms of the emphasis on the crimes against women during wars. NGOs played a big role in terms of creating the atmosphere where rape became one of the most important items on the agenda. After all, no state would support rape, but making it an unavoidable discussion topic that was taken seriously as a legal issue was the success of the NGOs. And women's NGOs played the biggest role in this success, as we shall see. My next step, then, is to turn to the long struggle (since the writing of the Additional Protocols in 1977) through which women's organizations managed to create the prohibition against rape in war—first by preparing the normative basis, the core norms over which all NGOs could build, and then making the final push for the legal change through the ICC.

Women's NGOs and the ICC

This section traces the steps through which women's NGOs gradually cre-ated the normative context in which women's rights came to be considered as human rights, one of the most important core norms of the post-World War II period. The next point will be on the way they helped create a norma-tive shock out of the horrendous violations in the former Yugoslavia (and to a certain extent in Rwanda) by not only building on the normative context that was being created, but also by associating these events with other already existing core norms (such as the norm against genocide) in order to produce legal change from the shock. In other words, my focus will be on the efforts to develop a norm against the use of rape as a weapon in wartime, as well as the legalization of the norm in the context of the 1990s, as they gained pace and force, although the basis of the issue, the recognition of women's rights as human rights, had been prepared over long decades of struggle by the feminist movement.

The war in the former Yugoslavia (particularly in Bosnia-Herzegovina) and to a lesser extent the genocide in Rwanda was the shock that made the efforts of the women's groups possible, and caused a huge jump in the norm development process itself. As former president of the ICTY Theodor Meron put it: "Indescribable abuse of thousands of women in the territory of former Yugoslavia was needed to shock the international community into rethinking the prohibition of rape as a crime under the laws of war."[41]

In the post-World War II period, particularly the post-Holocaust world, the protection of human rights emerged as one of the most powerful international norms. The integration (or attempted integration) of women's rights into this human rights framework was not a new phenomenon when news about widespread abuse of women's human rights was coming out of the former Yugoslavia in the early 1990s, but the movement had only just started gaining momentum. Between 1945 and 1991, core norms such as the sanctity of human rights and, thanks to the work of women's organizations, women's status as human beings evolved and were reinforced, preparing the basis for the norm change on rape.[42]

At the Copenhagen Women's Conference in 1980, the radical feminist groups (or women's liberation movement) that had been working to bring attention to the role of violence and constructions of female sexuality in the domination and subordination of women joined other women's groups to bring attention to sexual violence against women.[43] One of these feminist groups was ISIS, a group based in Rome, which raised violence against women as an issue in the international arena for the first time.[44] The final platform for action at the Copenhagen Conference stated that "Legislation should also be enacted and implemented in order to prevent domestic and sexual violence against women. All appropriate measures, including legislative ones, should be taken to allow victims to be fairly treated in all criminal procedures."[45] This statement was groundbreaking in that domestic and sexual violence had not previously been pronounced explicitly in any of the official UN documents, due to the cultural sensitivities on the topic. The rest of the decade would be different as a result of the "activities, research and publicity" created by various women's groups.[46]

In Western countries, feminist criticisms against domestic rape laws were at last producing results in the 1970s and 1980s. Rape laws started to move from being mainly preoccupied with protecting men from false accusations toward protecting women from being raped.[47] Women's groups were finally bringing the issue of violence against women to the international arena after almost two decades of struggles over it in the domestic sphere. The groups attending the Women's Conferences had a chance to find common ground and transcend the political differences that had divided the women's movement.[48] One of the sources of common ground would be rape, which became a central backdrop for unification for feminists worldwide.[49]

In the 1985 Nairobi Women's Conference, the issues of peace and conflict emerged as mainstream concerns on the agenda, with violence against women situated in a human rights context.[50] This conference was the beginning of the real fight about rape because a major change in the debates was happening. Up until then, the subject of women and war had been treated only in terms of women's roles as mothers and caregivers, but now the focus was shifting to a better recognition of how armed conflicts affect women in their own right.[51]

In Nairobi, women were also better organized and focused than at previous women's conferences. They learned to overcome their differences and agree on common ground, to work together and become a global social movement. This new ability to overcome the North-South and East-West conflicts that divided women in conferences at Mexico City and Copenhagen, as well as the new strategies women developed during these conferences, would ultimately be the basis of women's NGOs' achievements in the 1990s.[52]

In 1986, social scientists and members of women's NGOs met in Vienna at the meetings of the UN Division for the Advancement of Women. These meetings began the work that would produce the basis of the recognition of violence against women as an international problem and states as being responsible to stop it through legal practices, hence formulating the issue within a criminal justice frame.[53]

In 1991, NGO activists decided to make violence against women a primary subject in the efforts for "women's rights as human rights." Upon their demands on the UN bodies, the CSW, ECOSOC and CEDAW took some steps to address the issue.[54] These agenda-setting efforts by the women's groups within the UN were critical in terms of preparing the basis of the normative change, since the UN serves a "collective legitimization function" slowly redefining the ideas, interests, and identities of its member states.[55]

Violence against women became the master framework that not only brought together women from all over the world, but also attracted allies from mainstream human rights organizations.[56] By 1992, a normative context where human rights (including individual security and bodily integrity) are important and where women are included in this circle of humans with rights emerged. It is also significant that war—and therefore rape in war—had been absent in Europe for almost 50 years, and the outbreak of war in the former Yugoslavia changed this situation. The real movement began in 1992, as the news about mass rapes and rape camps had begun to emerge.

In April 1992, a war of ethnic conflict started in the middle of European civilization, in Bosnia-Herzegovina. This war became a stage for murders, concentration camps, torture, and rapes—all part of an ethnic-cleansing strategy by the Serbs.[57] The first refugees who fled to Croatia reported the rapes for the first time in June 1992 and later, in August, an American journalist, Roy Gutman provided a complete report about them.[58] In September 1992, the International Human Rights Law Group launched its Women in the Law Project and published a report in 1993, *No Justice, No Peace: Accountability for Rape and Gender-Based Violence in the Former Yugoslavia*.[59] This was the first serious consideration of gender-based violence in war by human rights NGOs.

After almost fifty years of "progress"—that is, the absence of horrific human rights violations like genocide and mass rape in war in Europe—Europeans were witnessing a "regress." People were being subjected to the ruthless practices of war in the middle of "civilized" Europe. Things that Europeans thought belonged to either the era of medieval cruelty or to a different world and different culture were happening to white people in Europe.[60] This situation was indeed a potential normative shock. Not every tragedy, however, becomes a normative shock, especially a normative shock strong enough to change particular norms, as we learned in the example of hundreds of thousands of women that were raped both in Europe and Asia throughout World War II.[61] These events did not even produce any indictments in Nuremberg.[62] In fact, even after all that happened in the former Yugoslavia, the original draft statute for the ICC prepared by the ILC in 1994 did not include rape among war crimes—although it was on the list of crimes against humanity.[63]

How did the tragedy in the former Yugoslavia become a shock that led to the creation of the prohibition regime against rape in war with the ICC? As mentioned previously, "what counts as a shock, how shocking must shocks be and what will we say about the shocks that reinforce rather than change existing collective beliefs"[64] are critical questions about shocks. In the prohibition of rape in war, the "shockingness" of the shock and the direction of the development of a new norm and policies as a result of the shock were determined by the norm entrepreneurs, particularly women's NGOs. Once the shock occurred, they provided the alternative policy prescriptions, which derived from or built on their previous work for putting women's rights on the international agenda. A shock will not be a shock without the agitation of norm entrepreneurs, but at the same time norm entrepreneurs cannot agitate successfully without an event that has the potential to become a shock. In other words, "norm entrepreneurship is necessary but it is never sufficient."[65] The relationship we find between the shocking events in the former Yugoslavia and the establishment of rape as a war crime proved once again that "calamitous circumstances are needed to shock the public conscience into focusing on important, but neglected, areas of law, process and institutions."[66] Yet there have to be people agitating in order to put the issue on the agenda and present it in a way that will ensure that it will be taken seriously.[67]

Since human rights shocks, especially on an international scale, are often not that obvious until certain people make them so, the women's NGOs employed the tactic of working on the existing norms and associating the new issue to these existing norms to ensure coherence. The grafting of the new norm with existing ones was a very important part of women's advocacy. In the case of norm creation against the use of rape as a weapon of war, the background norm was the norm and laws against genocide,[68] and the norm entrepreneurs built their arguments on the ethnic cleansing campaign in former Yugoslavia (as well as the genocide in Rwanda.) How exactly did this process of shock creation work?

In February 1993, the UN Security Council (SC Res. 808) called for the establishment of an international tribunal for the crimes that had been occurring since 1991 in the territories of former Yugoslavia. And on May 25, 1993, the Security Council adopted the Statute of the International Tribunal (ICTY). The statute did not mention rape among grave breaches, violations of the laws and customs of war, or acts of genocide, but as a result of the struggles of women's groups, it included rape as a crime against humanity.[69]

The next important event was one of the most critical steps in the process of creating the normative shock, and was very illustrative of the impact of the war in former Yugoslavia on the normative context: the UN World Conference on Human Rights in Vienna (1993). Up until that point, the division between women's rights and human rights had been causing problems for women's groups in terms of accessing the human rights agenda. Under the leadership of the Center for Women's Global Leadership, a U.S.-based women's organization, a campaign started in preparation for the conference. The three-year campaign established "women's rights as human rights" as a powerful framework, which not only helped bring together women from different cultures and solved many problems of division among women, but also resonated with the global constituency in general.[70]

In Vienna, women's NGOs had followed various strategies in order to influence the agenda of the conference. First, they held an NGO Forum before the conference and prepared a unified NGO document to present at the conference.[71] The forum meeting in Vienna (200 miles from former Yugoslavia) "at a time when [the] international community was reeling from testimony on the rape of Bosnian women as a tactic of war" added the demand for "the establishment of an international penal court with jurisdiction over all kinds of crimes, including gender-specific abuses such as rape, sexual slavery, forced sterilization, and forced pregnancy" among its conclusions.[72]

Second, as part of the NGO Forum, they held a Global Tribunal on Violations of Women's Human Rights, in which testimonies of 33 women from 25 countries were heard to protest the failures of the existing human rights laws and mechanisms vis-à-vis women. The forum also included a worldwide petition campaign calling for the conference to address violence against women, which was quickly becoming the unifying issue for global feminism.[73]

Third, a professionally staffed and financed media campaign was held to make women's rights visible and legitimate in the eyes of the world as human rights.[74] Over 1,500 NGOs were present at the conference, inside and outside the halls, keeping pressure on delegates to recognize violence against women as a violation of human rights.[75]

The UN Development Fund for Women (UNIFEM)[76] organized a caucus in the area in which government delegates were meeting. Through these efforts NGOs negotiated and brought suggestions to the official drafting process.[77] These strategies, consequently, created an atmosphere in which almost every government delegation felt obligated to make a speech during the conference denouncing violence against women.[78]

The end product of the conference—the Vienna Declaration and

Programme of Action—was a success for women on the issue of violence. Violence against women in armed conflict (among other things) became explicitly recognized as a violation of human rights and of humanitarian law. As Jane Connors puts it:

> This was a direct result of NGO activism which had identified the issue as of immense significance to women in all areas of the world. This view was undoubtedly reinforced by evidence of the sexual violence perpetrated against women in the conflict in the former Yugoslavia, which had been the subject of eighteen NGO submissions to the Human Rights Commission at its 49th session in 1993.[79]

Though there was no explicit reference to the ICTY statute's exclusion of rape from the list of grave breaches, violations of the laws and customs of war, and acts of genocide, we see the issue emphasized strongly and explicitly in the Vienna Declaration and Programme of Action:

> The World Conference on Human Rights expresses its dismay at massive violations of human rights especially in the form of genocide, "ethnic cleansing" and systematic rape of women in war situations, creating mass exodus of refugees and displaced persons. While strongly condemning such abhorrent practices it reiterates the call that perpetrators of such crimes be punished and such practices immediately stopped.[80]

Similarly, it called for "the elimination of gender bias in the administration of justice" as well as the declaration that

> Violations of the human rights of women in situations of armed conflict are violations of the fundamental principles of international human rights and humanitarian law. All violations of this kind, including in particular murder, systematic rape, sexual slavery, and forced pregnancy, require a particularly effective response.[81]

In the aftermath of the conference, the UN Commission on Human Rights appointed a Special Rapporteur on Violence against Women, a very significant development. The Commission requested the Special Rapporteur to

(a) Seek and receive information on violence against women, its causes and consequences from Governments, treaty bodies, specialized agencies, other special rapporteurs responsible for various human rights questions and intergovernmental and non-governmental organizations, including women's organizations, and to respond effectively to such information;

(b) Recommend measures, ways and means, at the national, regional and international levels, to eliminate violence against women and its causes, and to remedy its consequences;

(c) Work closely with other special rapporteurs, special representatives, working groups and independent experts of the Commission on Human Rights and the Sub-Commission on Prevention of Discrimination and Protection of Minorities and with the treaty bodies, taking into account the Commission's request that they regularly and systematically include in their reports available information on human rights violations affecting women, and cooperate closely with the Commission on the Status of Women in the discharge of its functions.[82]

These requests meant the rapporteur would be in a position to expose states for engaging in, sponsoring, or allowing violence against women and hold them responsible before the international community.[83] The UN General Assembly adopted the Declaration on the Elimination of Violence against Women (GA Res. 48/103, December 20, 1993), the first international human rights instrument dealing with the issue of violence against women explicitly and exclusively as a political issue (rather than a private matter).[84] It basically repeated the Vienna Declaration.

In October 1994, a preparatory meeting was held in Vienna for Beijing, the next scheduled World Conference on Women. The war in former Yugoslavia was still going on, and during the preparatory meeting women's NGOs introduced a resolution about rape as a war crime—at which point the meeting erupted. The Yugoslav delegation argued that by turning the conference's attention to rape and sexual violence, women's groups were "picking on them" and that it was not just Muslim women who were being raped. The Yugoslav delegation did not find an ally, however, and the resolution was passed. According to one of the leaders of the women's groups at the meeting, that resolution was another watershed in making "rape as a war crime a public issue.[85]

On November 8, 1994, with SC Res. 955, the Security Council established the International Criminal Tribunal for Rwanda (ICTR). The call by women's organizations (documented in the Vienna Declaration and the UN Declaration) for recognition of sexual violence against women, particularly rape, in armed conflict found response in the adoption of the Statute of the ICTR. The statute included within the jurisdiction of the court the prosecution of rape (among other things) as a crime against humanity (Article 3) and as a serious violation of Article 3 common to the Geneva Conventions (1949) for the Protection of War Victims and of Additional Protocol II (1977) (Article 4). However, getting indictments and sentences for rape was not a smooth process. Not only would there not be a sentence for rape until 1998, but the first indictment would take another two years.[86]

In 1995, the fourth World Conference on Women in Beijing produced the first document that calls for accountability for rape. The Beijing Declaration and Platform for Action committed governments to investigate and punish perpetrators, and it reaffirmed that rape in armed conflict constitutes a war crime, under certain circumstances a crime against humanity, and an act of genocide, as defined in the Convention on the Prevention and Punishment of the Crime of Genocide. An argument arose during the conference over the use of "systematic rape" in UN resolutions as the only way to refer to the subject of rape because of the prevalence of systematic rape in the former Yugoslavia at the time. Women's NGOs protested against this usage since it gives the impression that rape is a serious offense only when it is systematic. As a result of their efforts, the Platform for Action (paragraph 132) said "rape, including systematic rape."[87]

For women's groups, the next significant step was the ICC. According to Gassoumis et al., during the early stages of the PrepCom meetings (March–April, August 1996), that is, before women's groups started their work—it was apparent that women would once again escape the attention of the states as major targets of human rights abuses. No delegate spoke about the need for discussing women's issues in the context of the new law the ICC would be creating.[88]

The Women's Caucus for Gender Justice was founded in January 1997 for the purpose of integrating gender issues in the ICC preparatory process by lobbying government delegations writing the ICC Statute.[89] By tapping into the networks that emerged during the Women's Decade Conferences, women established the Caucus, and by being part of the CICC, they organized themselves better than they had ever done before in similar negotiations.[90] Only after the Women's Caucus prepared and distributed a draft text integrating women's concerns into the draft statute during the February 1997 PrepCom did the delegations start mentioning gender issues.[91] As a result, the February PrepCom increased the precision of the proposed statute by expanding the language and scope of the article prohibiting rape as a crime against humanity: the words "other sexual abuse and enforced prostitution" were included with rape as a result of the advocacy of the Women's Caucus.[92] A proposal by the delegations of New Zealand and Switzerland (based on an ICRC paper) to include rape on the list of war crimes, however, was rejected by the February PrepCom, with the excuse that the list of war crimes should replicate the language of grave breaches of the Geneva Conventions (1949).[93]

Setbacks continued during the August PrepCom (August 4–15, 1997). Some delegates and some NGO participants told the Women's Caucus that the proposal for "the incorporation of a gender perspective throughout the ICC Statute is too 'specific' to be dealt with in all areas and aspects of the ICC." Those delegates and NGO participants also said that, "although they understood the need for the incorporation of 'gender issues' into the definition of the 'core crimes,' the issues at hand during the August PrepCom had nothing to do with gender." According to them, "if the statute were to deal with 'gender concerns,' then, in all fairness, it would also have to deal with the concerns of other disadvantaged groups, such as children, the disabled, etc."[94] Hence, in preparation for the December PrepCom, the Women's Caucus started distributing working drafts of recommendations, commentary, and draft text in order to engage in dialogue with delegates and to make their voices better heard.[95] In these documents, the caucus specifically demanded that the definition of war crimes include sexual and gender violence as part of the most serious violations of international criminal law. Addressing the December PrepCom, the Women's Caucus included the following recommendations and comments (among others):[96]

1. The Statute should clearly reject the prior treatment of rape and other sexual violence as simply "humiliating and degrading treatment" or as linked to a particular offense by eliminating the reference to rape and other sexual violence in this regard.

2. Following the approach of the article on crimes against humanity, the enumeration of war crimes in both internal and international armed conflict should include a subparagraph identifying rape, sexual slavery, enforced prostitution, forced sterilization and other forms of sexual and gender violence as war crimes in themselves.

3. One of the essential and defining characteristics of criminal law is gradation in the characterization or naming and punishment of crimes. In this way, society differentially condemns the perpetrator and recognizes the suffering of the victim. This is why, as discussed below, the Geneva Convention's treatment of rape and other forms of sexual violence as simply "attacks against honor" and "degrading and humiliating treatment" and not as forms of the gravest violence is discriminatory as well as a profound insult to women. While the ICRC has made a partial advance in linking rape solely to "wilfully causing great suffering or serious injury to body or health," this still underestimates the severity and character of various forms of sexual and gender violence.

4. While the line between torture and inhuman treatment is not a sharp one, it exists to encompass cases of sexual and gender violence which may not rise to the level of torture. The Women's Caucus cautions, however, that it is inappropriate to substitute these categories for rape and other sexual and gender violence which does and should properly be recognized and prosecuted as torture. For this reason, Recommendation 6 calls for deletion of the exclusive linkage of rape and other sexual violence to "willfully causing great suffering . . ." in paragraph A(c) of the grave breaches section of the Chair's text.

5. The Women's Caucus recommends following the precedent set in the definition provided by ICTY, and ICTR Art. 5(g) of Crimes Against Humanity where sexual violence is identified in a separate paragraph as well as potentially chargeable as other enumerated crimes. It is necessary to add this paragraph enumerating forms of sexual and gender violence as well as to mainstream sexual violence for a number of reasons. Sexual and gender violence are severe and particular and their particularities should not be lost by mainstreaming. Where not explicit, they are too often ignored, even today. Moreover, even while sexual violence can meet the elements of the other enumerated crimes, criminal law provides definitions of rape, enforced prostitution, and forced sterilization and other forms of violence and abuse that are different from that of the enumerated crimes.

Since the draft text included "reference to rape and sexual violence as an affront to personal dignity," the Women's Caucus successfully advocated that "rape and sexual violence should be prosecuted separately as forms of the most serious crimes such as genocide, torture, enslavement and mutilation" and that a separate section that would specify that rape and sexual violence should be prosecuted as serious forms of violence in themselves should be put into the statute.[97] In the end, the December PrepCom came up with a draft that was very comprehensive in terms of defining war crimes. According to the *ICC Monitor*, there was near unanimous agreement about referring "to the crime of rape, sexual slavery, enforced prostitution, enforced pregnancy, enforced sterilization and other forms of sexual violence not merely associated with the crime of committing outrages upon personal dignity."[98]

Once the Rome Conference had started, the process would not get easier for women. The fact that the delegates were predominantly lawyers and military people with no particular expertise in gender issues made the negotiation process difficult for the Women's Caucus.[99] When a controversy erupted during the conference because of the inclusion of "enforced pregnancy" among war crimes and the use of the concept "gender balance," the Women's Caucus focused its lobbying efforts on these issues.[100] The Holy See delegation, some Catholic states, some Arab states, and a group of anti-choice organizations were against the enforced pregnancy section, arguing that it could be used against anti-abortion laws.[101] They thought that once states ratified the statute, it would become part of their national laws; that is, someone might challenge the national laws prohibiting abortion by using the enforced pregnancy article in the ICC Statute and arguing that not having access to abortion is enforced pregnancy. They proposed to delete the provision on enforced pregnancy, arguing that since rape and unlawful detention were covered by the statute, enforced pregnancy would be covered, too. Bosnia-Herzegovina, Australia, Canada, New Zealand, Azerbaijan, Rwanda, Turkey, Nigeria, Solomon Islands, and India opposed this proposal by declaring that it would mean denying a "distinct and terrible crime."[102]

The most contentious issue, however, arose over the selection criterion for judges that included "gender balance" in the draft. As a selection criterion, it means using a quota system to ensure the election of women judges to the Court. The word *gender* was highly problematic for some delegations wherever it appeared—including Article 7 (2) h, which mentions persecution on gender grounds, among others, as a crime against humanity. An Arab delegate said "'gender balance' was unacceptable to his delegation as it could mean 'equality.'" Also, many Arab (and some other)[103] delegates had been convinced by anti-choice lobbyists that use of the word "gender" in the Statute would mean the state parties would have to permit same-sex marriages.[104]

According to one of the NGO observers of the conference, this situation not only stalled the negotiations but also caused problems within the coalition between mainstream human rights NGOs and the Women's Caucus. At times, mainstream NGOs felt uneasy about women's NGOs' insistence on the use of the word *gender* or the concept of enforced pregnancy, believing they could jeopardize the ICC.[105] One of the members of the CICC agrees that some tension occasionally arose between the Women's Caucus and other members of the CICC, especially having to do with their styles. From time to time, the leaders of the CICC felt that the Women's Caucus's approach, particularly in dealing with the officials of the negotiations and governments, were "unnecessarily strident and intrusive." The danger with this style of strident insistence and extreme persistence was that it might make it more difficult for other CICC members to work with the same people.[106] The problem became so complicated that some believed it started to jeopardize the effort to make rape a war crime: "A dispute between women's groups and the Vatican over a legal term has broadened into a battle of religion and gender politics that could jeopardize agreement on whether rape will be declared a war crime by an international criminal court."[107]

In the end, the two sides negotiated a compromise. Though *gender* was the term they used in the Statute, a special definition was included: "For the purpose of this Statute, it is understood that the term 'gender' refers to the two sexes, male and female, within the context of society. The term 'gender' does not indicate any meaning different from the above" (Art.7 (3)). Also a definition for "forced pregnancy" was included as a footnote, which states: " 'Forced pregnancy' means the unlawful confinement of a woman forcibly made pregnant, with the intent of affecting the ethnic composition of any population or carrying out other grave violations of international law. This definition shall not in any way be interpreted as affecting national laws relating to pregnancy" (Article 7 (2)f).

The solution of the stalemate was possible partly thanks to the forceful style of Committee of the Whole chairman Philippe Kirsch (Canada).[108] The major actors were NGOs and some government delegations, though, interestingly enough, not women's NGOs. One CICC leader indicated:

> It was necessary to show understanding and respect for the concerns of the Arab countries and some members of the Women's Caucus found it very difficult to do that because of the attitudes toward women within those Arab countries. It is significant therefore that

much of the negotiation which resolved into these two compromises was carried out by NGOs other than members of the Women's Caucus and by the government delegations especially the delegation of Norway, whose chief Mr. Fife was a fluent Arabic speaker.[109]

Hence, while women's work was central to the integration of women's issues into the ICC Statute, the fact that they had influential allies within the mainstream NGO community and the government delegations proved to be critical, too.

The Normative Shock

The atrocities reported in the former Yugoslavia and Rwanda appear to be at the forefront of the efforts of women's NGOs both before and during the Rome Conference. First, given that these atrocities were portrayed as major violations of human rights, women's organizations needed to describe what women had gone through during these conflicts in terms of human rights violations to make the case more effective. In other words, activists used the existing framework to make their point that women's human rights were violated. Second, since these organizations were going to push for legal change, these cases were used as evidence of the flaws in the existing body of law. In order to do this, they applied what Keck and Sikkink call "human rights methodology," which is "promoting change by reporting facts."[110] Some of these kinds of actions taken by women's groups during the PrepComs included inviting victims and witnesses from Bosnia and Rwanda as well as experts who had worked with the ICTY and the ICTR to share the failures and achievements of the institutions,[111] as well as reminding the delegates—every time they tended to surpass gender issues—of the horrific crimes committed against women in those conflicts. For them "it [was] critical that the stories of survivors and those working with them continue to influence the negotiations so that once the ICC is set up it will be well-positioned to do justice, having taken fully into account the lessons from past efforts at achieving justice in the international arena."[112]

The importance of framing is widely emphasized in the literature on agenda-setting geared toward norm and law change. Identifying the problems with the existing order, presenting them in a way that will convince the important actors and the general public that there is a problem, and that there is a particular solution to that problem have been the key components of framing.[113] "What is at issue" and "what is to be done" are determined by "the naming and framing" of policies.[114] Women's NGOs working to get rape to be included in the Rome Statute named and framed the issue in such a way that rape emerged as a major humanitarian problem and international law as the remedy for that problem. In order to push for immediate legal change, women's NGOs needed to create a sense of urgency for showing that the creation of the ICC was *the* opportunity to stop the horrific things that were happening. Hence, they needed to demonstrate that the existing legal framework was a burden on the conscience of the world by showing what was happening to women during wars from a shocking perspective.

As Bedont and Martinez argue, women's NGOs received support from most states on the basis of what had happened in former Yugoslavia and Rwanda in the absence of adequate treatment of sexual violence.[115] Their argument was that horrific human rights violations, including massive violation of women, which people believed belonged to history,[116] had returned to the "civilized world," which was a direct result of the inattention paid to legal arrangements to prevent them. Their argument had an implicit assumption that legal change would prevent these crimes from happening: if the reason that violence is happening is the past impunity enjoyed by the perpetrators (as well as the perpetrator states), then, if we create and enforce laws, they will not happen again (or will be minimized). Law reform, therefore, was identified as the key objective to further gender advances.[117]

Women "viewed the negotiations for the ICC as an historic opportunity to address the failures of earlier international treaties and tribunals to properly delineate, investigate, and prosecute wartime violence against women."[118] In other words, the claim about the "absence of adequate (legal) treatment of sexual violence" as the cause of the evil led to the claim that these events had happened because of previous impunity and flaws in the law. The underlying assumption was that "the historic failure of States and the international community to recognize and effectively punish serious gender violence as a grave human rights violation," as well as "the invisibility of sexual and gender violence and the presence of sex-stereotyped assumptions in these areas . . . historically insulate[d] perpetrators of that violence from accountability" and brought us to this point.[119] As the director of the Women's Caucus Alda Facio puts it, "It is precisely because the vast majority of laws, legal instruments and institutions have been created without a gender perspective that the everyday violations of women's human rights are invisible to the law and the most atrocious violations have been rendered trivial."[120]

Besides the reminder of past events where the abusers of women escaped from punishment, there is, again, the emphasis on former Yugoslavia and Rwanda. "Building on their successes in drawing attention to atrocities suffered by women in recent conflicts in Bosnia and Rwanda, [they] ensured that history did not pass women by again."[121] Yugoslavia and Rwanda were mentioned repeatedly as examples where women's human rights were violated during wars due to the international community's inability to make the necessary laws that would insure accountability and prevention. Even the very first publication of the CICC included an article emphasizing this point. Written by Beverly Allen, whose previous work, *Rape Warfare: The Hidden Genocide in Bosnia-Herzegovina and Croatia*, introduced the idea of "genocidal rape" in the context of former Yugoslavia, the article stated:

> Adequate legal, jurisprudential, and jurisdictional recognition of crimes not previously enumerated by international conventions and protocols is of the utmost urgency if we wish the ICC to be strong. Recent knowledge of sex-based crimes such as genocidal rape demonstrates that, while sex-based crimes are not by any means limited to female victims, they are perpetrated in overwhelming numbers of cases on women and girls. Therefore, by maintaining a strong and constant awareness of sex and gender-based crimes against humanity and developing legal instruments for the ICC that will address these, we shall assure that the Court will be a viable institution for present-day atrocities and a strong tool for the coming century.[122]

The recommendations the Women's Caucus submitted to the PrepComs also underlined the importance of former Yugoslavia and Rwanda for our thinking of what constitutes a war crime or a crime against humanity. In former Yugoslavia and Rwanda, women were the victims of sexual slavery in prisons, occupied towns, and rape camps, where they were detained and raped repeatedly.[123] So, the question the Women's Caucus presented to delegates was, How will we prevent them from happening ever again?

The efforts of women's NGOs to show the extent of tragedies caused by the inadequacy of the law prohibiting rape were not limited to publishing articles on the topic or emphasizing the point in their recommendations to the PrepComs or the Conference. They also made sure that the public as well as the state delegates saw and heard what these atrocities really entailed. For example, producing and showing films and documentaries with testimonials from victims was part of the campaign, too. The documentary *Calling the Ghosts* is the story of two women who were beaten and raped by Serbian soldiers at the Omarska detention camp in the former Yugoslavia and who fought to get rape classified as a war crime by the ICTY[124]; the documentary *If Hope Were Enough* documents the struggle of women to convince the ICC to address violation of women's human rights.[125] By producing or showing these films at every opportunity, women's organizations focused on promotion of legal change to ensure the protection of women's human rights.

During their advocacy for the ICC, women's NGOs relied heavily on the discourse of "women's rights as human rights." Their human rights-framed approach—that is, bringing human rights discourse and feminist goals together within the framework of violence issues as the basic violation of human rights—had two facets: legitimizing their agenda within a legitimate discourse (human rights discourse)[126] and "transforming the human rights concept from a feminist perspective."[127] While emphasis on gender and women's rights is prevalent in their documents, it is also possible to detect endeavors to use more neutral language. Some examples include

> Gender violence is violence that is targeted at women and men because of their sex and/or their socially constructed gender roles. . . .
> The recent conflicts in the former Yugoslavia and Rwanda have seen many examples of gender violence. Examples include: the forcible recruitment of young boys into the army who are put through violent indoctrination, and then made to perform suicidal missions in order to prove their masculinity; and the killing of pregnant women by the slashing of their wombs and removal of their fetuses. . . . Women's bodies, security or livelihood may be targeted because of their role as guardians of cultural traditions and because of their reproductive capacity. Men and boys may be targeted because they are identified as powerful or prominent, or as potential leaders or soldiers.[128]

> Expertise in gender and sexual violence is . . . necessary at all levels of the ICC because of the complex gender issues that are often part of genocide, war crimes, and crimes against humanity. Lack of expertise at any stage could prevent the Court from achieving justice.[129]

> Gender balance ... refers to a balanced composition of women and
> men in order to bring equality to the current male-dominated inter-
> national institutions.[130]

It is obvious that women's organizations needed this language, particularly in hard cases, such as the demand by eleven Arab countries for excluding crimes of sexual and gender violence when committed within the family
or as part of a religious or cultural concern.[131] Even after all the atrocities that
had happened to women, whether in former Yugoslavia or Rwanda or many
other places, after all the publicity that these events attracted, after all the
advocacy and work women's groups had done for decades to ensure the recognition of equality for women, and at a time when no one could say "raping
women is normal" or "we should not prohibit rape,"[132] women's organizations
still did not have an easy case. Some of the most intense controversies happened over the articles dealing with violence against women.

An incident that happened at the ICC negotiations illustrates the difficulty women faced. In a session discussing gender issues, NGO participants
were ordered to leave the room on the request of several delegations.[133] Even
at Beijing (1995), which was a platform rather than a conference writing a
binding international treaty, negotiations over the issues of abortion and gay
rights were so tense that they went on until 4:00 a.m.[134]

During this rough process of lobbying for legal change on rape, the Women's
Caucus linked rape with genocide, something that had already been rejected by
the world public opinion. Their tactic strengthened the women's human rights
discourse and thereby paved the way for the creation of a normative shock.[135]
What would ultimately turn out to be shocking for the public conscience and
the conscience of the writers of the ICC Statute more than the suffering of hundreds of thousands of women (which is basically the violation of noncombatant
immunity and causing unnecessary suffering) was that rape could be a tool for
genocide. It was a portrayal of rapes in Bosnia as "worse than 'normal' oppression."[136] Emphasizing this association was a major tactic for criminalizing rape
(and to a certain extent for creating the shock that facilitated this change). The
feminists' primary claim was that these systematic mass rapes in Bosnia were
part of the general policy of genocide: "This is ethnic rape as an official policy
of war in a genocidal campaign for political control."[137]

The talk of genocide was a purposeful reminder of the Holocaust.[138] Rape
and death camps in Bosnia were the parallels of the concentration camps in
World War II. For the public, the view was a "shocking reminder of Nazism,"

which people believed belonged to history;[139] and rape was presented as an alternative way of conducting genocide—made possible by the weakness of international law dealing with women.[140]

Of course, the way these arguments would reach the public and governments, galvanize them, and make legal action possible would be through the media.[141] As Stiglmayer puts it: "It was the pressure of publicity caused by press reports that led to this mysterious turnaround. Thus one of the war crimes has been exposed, at least, triggering worldwide outrage."[142] The fact that what was happening in the former Yugoslavia was happening in Europe, to white women, after Europe believed it would never see the type of atrocities that happened during World War II again, is significant in understanding why the case drew so much attention from Western media.

We have to also acknowledge the role of human rights organizations in using the media successfully. Research shows that the more international NGOs, especially on the issue of human rights, get involved with an issue, the more media coverage that issue gets.[143] This certainly proved true when it came to keeping the atrocities and rapes in former Yugoslavia on the agenda. Whenever the issue dropped from the front pages, a book, a medical report, or a statement by the human rights organizations helped it to surface again.[144] This method of keeping the public eye open to push for change was apparent during the ICC negotiations, too. In Rome, the NGOs organized many press conferences to brief the media on the progress of the negotiations (since almost all of the conference was closed to the press). The CICC experts met with the members of the press to provide analyses of debates and progress during the conference. The e-mail newsletters, constant updates on their websites, and the daily conference newspapers were other means of communication they employed to keep the media attention and awareness intact.[145]

Because of these efforts, the Rome Statute emerged as a "revolutionary document . . . [that] codifies a mandate for the Court to adopt specific investigative, procedural, and evidentiary mechanisms that are essential to ensure gender justice."[146] Rape was included in the statute as a grave breach, along with an extra success: the recognition of other forms of sexual violence such as forced pregnancy, sexual slavery, enforced prostitution, and enforced sterilization as war crimes despite opposition from certain governments.[147] According to Bedont and Martinez:

> Few, if any, government delegations would have been willing to expend the political capital needed to secure the [gender-related]

provisions . . . without the persistent lobbying efforts of the Women's Caucus. Indeed, even the few willing to do so would not have been successful without the pressure exerted by the Women's Caucus members on governments.[148]

As a result, Article 7 (1) (g) of the Rome Statute says that "Rape, sexual slavery, enforced prostitution, forced pregnancy, enforced sterilization, or any other form of sexual violence of comparable gravity" are crimes against humanity "when committed as part of a widespread or systematic attack directed against any civilian population, with knowledge of the attack." Article 8 (2) (e) (vi) states that "Committing rape, sexual slavery, enforced prostitution, forced pregnancy, as defined in article 7, paragraph 2 (f), enforced sterilization, or any other form of sexual violence also constituting a grave breach of the Geneva Conventions" are war crimes.[149] And "imposing measures intended to prevent births within the group," "committed with intent to destroy, in whole or in part, a national, ethnical, racial or religious group," constitutes genocide (Art. 6 (d)).

Besides the achievement of the inclusion of rape and other forms of sexual violence in international law under ICC jurisdiction, the Women's Caucus and other NGOs also managed to infuse a gender perspective into the structure of the ICC. Some states voiced strong opposition to a requirement of nominating judges with expertise on sexual and gender violence, and ultimately, a compromise emerged by making the obligation of states more vague.[150] Article 36 (8) b said that "States Parties shall also take into account the need to include judges with legal expertise on specific issues, including, but not limited to, violence against women or children." Article 42 (9) was accepted as "The Prosecutor shall appoint advisers with legal expertise on specific issues, including, but not limited to, sexual and gender violence and violence against children."[151]

The witness protection measures (Articles 43 (6), 54, and 68) also passed without much opposition (except the use of the word *gender*) during the conference, although the Women's Caucus and other NGOs played very important roles in formulating the exact language.[152]

After Rome

Since the ICC had not taken any cases between 1998 and 2003, and since the crimes committed against women in the ethnic conflicts in former Yugoslavia and the genocide in Rwanda were not fully punished, advocacy at the ICTY and the ICTR continued. In the programs of women's organizations, we find committees that, for example, worked for "the production of a memorandum to the Office of the Prosecutor of the ICTR and the ICTY on how rape should be charged in the indictments and [to] examine the issue of command responsibility with regard to crimes of sexual violence."[153] Women's human rights NGOs also filed *amicus curiae* briefs (legal opinions or information given to a court by volunteers) with the ICTY and the ICTR, which produced "discretionary reconsideration, resulting in revision of the investigations and indictments at issue."[154] For instance, in the ICTR Akayesu trial, "rampant sexual violence would not even have been charged but for the consistent and expensive monitoring, documentation and interventions, ultimately as *amicus curiae*, by women's human rights NGOs."[155]

The first ICTR judgment in a rape case came on September 2, 1998: *The Akayesu Judgment*.[156] Paragraph (d) of part 6.3.1 states that "Imposing measures intended to prevent births within the group, [which includes] rape" is included in the Statute's definition of genocide. Akayesu was found guilty of genocide, which included "rapes [that] resulted in physical and psychological destruction of Tutsi women, their families and communities. [S]exual violence was an integral part of the process of destruction, specifically targeting Tutsi women and specifically contributing to their destruction and to the destruction of the Tutsi group as a whole."[157]

Two months later, the ICTY handed down another important decision: the *Celebici Judgment*[158] (November 16, 1998). This judgment was the first conviction for rape as torture. The conviction is significant because in the basic documents of international humanitarian law (Geneva Conventions (1949) being the most prominent), torture is explicitly mentioned as a grave breach—a violation of the laws and customs of war.

The next important case also came from the ICTY: the *Furundzija Judgment*, issued on December 10, 1998.[159] Besides reiterating the standard for torture the court adopted in *Celebici*, the ICTY noted that "International case law . . . evinces a momentum towards addressing through the legal process, the use of rape in the course of detention and interrogation as a means of torture." In concluding that the "elements of torture were met" in *Furundzija*, the ICTY explained, "the physical attacks as well as the threats to inflict severe injury, caused severe physical and mental suffering to [the victim] . . . The intention of the accused . . . was to obtain information." Although Furundzija did not personally commit the rapes in this case, the ICTY found that "the accused is a co-perpetrator of torture [so] he is individually responsible for torture." As such, he is "guilty of a violation of the law or customs of war (torture)," in violation of Article 3 of the ICTY Statute. This case also advanced international jurisprudence on rape by expanding the legal definition of rape by drawing on the basic ICTR definition in *Akayesu*, which meant broadening the scope of rape crimes to include forced oral and anal sex.[160]

Meanwhile, rape returned to Europe with the Kosovo conflict in 1999, which resulted in the "re-doubling [of human rights advocates'] campaign for the strict enforcement of international laws against rape and other sexual crimes."[161] In June 1999 a conference was held in Vienna,[162] which issued a report, "Rape Is a War Crime: How to Support the Survivors." The report repeatedly asserted that these crimes were happening again because rape was not being punished appropriately. It identified rape as a war crime and emphasized the need to recognize "rape and sexual violence as a crime against humanity under national and international law."[163] A pressing need for clearer and more specific laws is one of the report's focal points.[164]

In June 2000, the UN General Assembly held a special session, "Women 2000: Gender Equality, Development, and Peace for the 21st Century," known as "Beijing Plus 5" to evaluate the five years since the Fourth Women's World Conference. This session brought the issue of "women's rights as human rights" on the world agenda once more.

After the reappearance of widespread sexual violence in the Balkans and women's groups' efforts to put the issue back on the agenda, the last important judgment on this issue came from the ICTY: the *Kunarac, Kovac and Vukovic Judgment* (February 22, 2001).[165] Kunarac, Kovac, and Vukovic, three Bosnian Serb soldiers, were charged with rape, as a crime against humanity and as a violation of the laws or customs of war. This judgment clearly established rape as a war crime in a judgment for the first time in history. In addition, the three were convicted of sexual enslavement, and thus the definition of slavery was expanded to include sexual abuse. This judgment became the first recognition of sexual slavery as a crime against humanity.[166] Another important point about the decision is that the charges were made both on the basis of command responsibility and individual criminal responsibility (which is in a way responding to the demand of the Beijing Declaration for accountability in all respects). As Julie Mertus puts it:

> This case represents a significant advance in the international law pertaining to the treatment of sexual violence in wartime. First, the decision demonstrates that rape will not be accepted as an intrinsic part

of war. . . . The Tribunal sent a message that it would prosecute cases of sexual violence vigorously. That the accused were low-level soldiers was of no consequence. Judge Mumba made clear that "lawless op-portunists should expect no mercy, no matter how low their position in the chain of command may be." Second, although this Tribunal, as well as the International Criminal Tribunal for Rwanda (ICTR), has dealt with rape in the past, this was the first to focus entirely on wartime crimes of sexual violence. It was also the first decision by the ICTY to issue convictions for rape as a crime against humanity. The detailed discussion of the elements of rape in the decision, including a broad survey of domestic legal systems, will serve as an important guide in future cases (see paragraphs 436–64). Third, while other in-ternational tribunals have considered the crime of torture, the Tribu-nal's authoritative discussion of the law of torture and its application to sexual violence cases is groundbreaking. . . . Fourth, the decision recognized the instrumental nature of rape in wartime. . . . [The] un-derstanding of rape as an instrument of terror can be applied in other cases where the evidence does not prove the existence of a direct order to rape. Finally, this decision was the first by an international tribunal to result in convictions for enslavement as a crime against humanity.[167]

In the end, rape (as well as other forms of sexual violence) in armed con-flict became a crime against humanity, a form of genocide, a grave breach, and a war crime. The ICTY and the ICTR set the precedents for prosecution of rape as a crime against humanity, grave breach, a form of genocide, and, fi-nally, a war crime through their decisions. These results could not have come without the women's groups' work to reshape state interests by changing the normative context and by using (and to a certain extent creating) a normative shock—depicting rape as a repulsive, uncivilized practice that should be re-jected by all civilized nations. If one wants to be a civilized nation, one needs to reject the practice of rape in war and participate in a prohibition regime to prevent it.

The next item on the agenda of the Women's Caucus and the other mem-bers of the CICC was to ensure ratification and entry into force of the Rome Statute and the completion of the annexes to the Statute, particularly the sec-tions on Elements of Crimes and Rules of Procedure and Evidence by the Preparatory Commission meetings.[168] Investigation, prosecution, and trial of rape and other related crimes were as important as their inclusion in the statute, so these issues became the next focus for the Women's Caucus, principally the nomination of women judges.[169]

ICTR judge Navanethem Pillay—who paved the way for the prosecution for rape in the Akayesu case by evoking testimonies during the trial—had shown the Women's Caucus one vital way in which women judges contributed to the prosecution of the perpetrators of sexual violence. As discussed previously, during the Rome Conference, the Women's Caucus, with the support of some states,[170] wanted the inclusion of "gender balance" as a condition for the presence of women judges. The term had encountered serious opposition, and, as a result, another language, "fair representation of female and male judges," had been adopted as Article 36 (8) a-iii. To make sure that there would really be fair representation, the Women's Caucus and its allies within the CICC started a campaign to ensure transparent nomination processes. States reached an agreement on the nomination process at the September 2002 Preparatory Commission meeting, and, taking a proposal by Liechtenstein and Hungary as the basis, they decided to require states to vote for a minimum of six male and six female candidates for the Court for the first four rounds of voting. If states could not elect the judges by that point, they would give up the requirement. In 2002 eight male judges and one female judge were nominated, an imbalance that triggered intensive campaigning from the Women's Caucus. As a result, the first ICC started its work with seven women judges (of eighteen total) on its bench.[171]

Interestingly, two paradoxical processes happened after Rome. First, some delegations attempted to at least partially reverse the gains women had made. Second, the inclusion of rape in the Rome Statute played a role for gathering support for ratifications. In the first case, problems erupted when it came to overarching gender integration into the Annex of the Statute (for making sexual violence a crime charged as other crimes were), as well as the definition of crimes against humanity. Some delegations found gender integration unnecessary since the ICTY and the ICTR already charged sexual crimes as torture and genocide. With respect to the definition of crimes against humanity, eleven Arab countries wanted to exclude crimes of sexual violence from the jurisdiction of the ICC when committed within the family, by inserting a definition into the Annex saying that "the state or non-state entity 'actively promote or encourage' the criminal conduct" for it to be a crime against humanity.[172]

During the road to ratification, the Women's Caucus continued organizing events, such as a public hearing in Tokyo (December 2000) in order to "reinforce public attention on the fact that it is partly because the crimes committed fifty years ago [against the use of "comfort women" for Japanese soldiers during World War II] remained unpunished that similar crimes continue to be perpetrated today."[173] Thus, they "urge all to join the larger campaign for the establishment of the ICC and help end impunity for crimes against women. It is in the interest of the world and community at large to ensure that crimes against women and men are adequately recognized and that the different ways these crimes are committed against women are reflected in [the] lawmaking process."[174]

In his address to the 56th Session of the General Assembly, UN Secretary General Kofi Annan called for the ratification of the Rome Statute, and in encouraging ratification, he stressed the historic nature of the Statute in advancing the rule of law by defining rape clearly as a war crime and a crime against humanity.[175] NGOs organized meetings to raise awareness about the ICC, with special focus on gender crimes.[176]

What is remarkable is that the fact of "rape in war"—along with all other horrendous crimes it evokes, including genocide—not only helped the push for ratification but also started to be the catch-phrases for any other tragedy in the world that needs the attention of the world public. When it came to gathering support to end the atrocities in places like Darfur, Uganda, the Central African Republic, Congo, or Côte d'Ivoire, rape was one of the first items mentioned to describe the gravity of the situation and the need for intervention.[177] Even U.S. actions—signing bilateral agreements with the state parties to prevent any American from being prosecuted by the ICC, which undermined the Court—were interpreted from a gender perspective:

> In responding to "Spoils of War No More," an editorial published on February 26, the writer points out that the ruling on rape and sexual slavery by the ad hoc tribunal for the former Yugoslavia constitutes a "precedent" for the permanent ICC, "with or without the United States on board." He further argues that by "seeking exemption for American armed services members and attempting to weaken the new court, [U.S. Senator] Helms and his followers are standing in opposition to women's rights and in support of good old days when a sovereign nation could rape, pillage and plunder enthusiastically."[178]

As a result, the required 60 states ratified the Rome Statute and it went into force April 11, 2002. The ICC started its work in 2003 and, since then, it has issued several indictments for rape both as a war crime and a crime against humanity.[179] As of 2012, there have been no convictions.

Chapter 6

Conclusions

Rape and pillage have been part of war throughout human history. Victors in wars had free rein with regard to property, and they pillaged women and goods accordingly. For General Andrew Jackson, "booty and beauty"[1] were the rewards of war. When it came to prohibiting rape and pillage, however, the sequence of rape and pillage was reversed: pillage and, a century later, rape. The puzzle that drove this project came out of this historical fact: rape and pillage were closely associated and similarly justified as weapons of war, yet delegitimized and prohibited a century apart. Why did the prohibition regime that regulated pillage of property not include "pillage" of women, and why did the prohibition regime against rape develop almost one hundred years later than the prohibition regime against pillage?

I addressed these historical questions using both knowledge-based and interest-based theories of regime development. I argued that three sets of conditions are necessary for the emergence of a global prohibition regime: As interest-based theories contend, *material factors* are important and states do make cost-benefit calculations when they agree to international commitments such as creating international regimes on the basis of these factors. Another very important calculation related to compliance is that states do not want to make international commitments with which they believe they cannot comply, because noncompliance is costly. International treaties are "a public signal that a state accepts a standard"[2] and, once accepted, the public (other states) expects compliance. However, as knowledge-based theories demonstrate, states are not just utility maximizers acting on the basis of the "logic of consequences"; they are also social beings affected by the social system surrounding them and their own beliefs about their place or identity in that social system. What behavior is "appropriate" for a "civilized" European nation-state can be as important as the costs and benefits of behaving in a certain way. Underneath the cost-benefit calculations lie ideational factors, too, such as beliefs about the possibility of compliance and the social costs of non-compliance.[3] Ultimately, besides a belief, on the part of the states, in the preventability of the practice, hence the possibility of compliance, a normative context conducive to the ideas at hand and a normative shock to give the final push for the normative change are necessary for the development of a global prohibition regime. Third, state and/or non-state actors actively propagating these ideas to promote the creation of a particular regime should exist.

Chapter 2 provided an overview of the historical development of the norm against pillage in war. Pillage was a normal part of war until the eighteenth century, when the rise of the conscripted armies ended the need for booty as a payment for the mercenary armies of the previous centuries. Even before that change, however, various states attempted to prohibit pillaging by their own armies through military codes. The reason for these attempts was purely interest-based: states did not want their soldiers' focus diverted by pillaging instead of concentrating on winning the war. States also did not want the local populations to become embittered by their conquerors. Beginning in the seventeenth century, states also wanted to keep the riches of the conquered land to themselves.[4] By the eighteenth century, it is apparent that state interests slowly changed the way states regarded and regulated pillage, but these regulations took the form of self-imposed military codes, not international treaties or conventions. From the perspective of a state, its own army pillaging during a war was more harmful to military objectives than pillage on its own territory by enemy soldiers. In fact, by that logic a state would want its rivals to continue pillaging since it would hurt their discipline as well as their relationship with the local population, which could lead to the loss of the war. Therefore, an interest-based approach to the prohibition of pillage does not work by itself. If states wanted to prohibit pillage on the basis of these material or security interests, they would have prohibited it (and in some cases they did) unilaterally for their own armies, and they would have refrained from ever creating a global prohibition regime.

Then why did the prohibition regime eventually emerge? Ideational factors provide the answer. The first of these factors is the normative context that emerged between eighteenth and nineteenth centuries. The major ideological changes of the eighteenth century, the Age of Enlightenment—especially with respect to the concepts of private property, civilization, and progress—are key in understanding the new normative context. This normative context paved the way for the emergence of a prevalent norm that considered pillage an uncivilized practice. After a whole century (the 1700s) without major wars and pillage, the Napoleonic Wars turned Europe's self-image upside down. Widespread violations of the customary rules of war, including pillage, during these wars in the early nineteenth century instigated the idea that the customs and rules of warfare should be codified and that a prohibition of pillage should be included in this codification. For the next eighty-four years (1815–1899), therefore, European jurists and publicists worked to give the "civilized" world's wars a "civilized" face. Inspired by the Lieber Code's achievement of being accepted by a state as the legitimate guideline for the conduct of war, these publicists began agitating for codification. Among others, jurists of the Russian and German emperors and publicists of the laws of war in Britain and other parts of Europe would not accept failure on this subject. These jurists were undeterred by the failure of the Brussels Conference, and they continued their work of writing and rewriting drafts for a possible code to be submitted to a future international conference under the Institute of International Law.[5] States vehemently opposed these efforts to produce multilateral codes and renounced the texts (like the Oxford Code of 1880). Despite these hurdles, however, the works of these publicists (or norm entrepreneurs)—with the backing of certain states such as Russia, the Netherlands, and Belgium—would bear fruit with the Hague Conventions, which included a prohibition against pillage.[6]

Chapter 3 addressed the main question of this project: Why did the Hague Conventions not prohibit rape alongside pillage? Looking at the normative context of the nineteenth century, it is not surprising that rape was not prohibited as an outrage on women's bodily integrity or a violation of their basic rights—because no one thought of women in these terms. Yet it is puzzling that the fact that women were considered part of men's property did not spur the prohibition of rape for the same reasons. One can argue that the drafters of the Brussels Declaration, which would become the Hague Regulations (with minor changes in the article that was supposed to include rape), thought that mentioning a vulgar word like *rape* in the context of the nineteenth-century Europe would give the states (already suspicious of the idea of codifying the laws of war) an excuse to repudiate the project because of its lack of decency. One can also argue that the drafters themselves thought the word was improper for a diplomatic document. Yet they made no attempts to include a more veiled or vague description of the term by mentioning women or a prohibition (or even protection for that matter), so decency was not the major problem. We must turn to other possible explanations for why women were not property enough to be protected by a regime that protects other property.

For pillage, we can find all the conditions necessary to instigate a prohibition regime. Pillage had become costly, and the benefit of feeding the army off the land had disappeared by the nineteenth century. A favorable normative context, valuing private property, progress, and civilization, existed. The publicists served as the actors who helped develop and reinforce that normative context. Finally, a normative shock occurred when the Napoleonic Wars showed states the need for new arrangements to protect private property. Besides, states believed that they could comply with a regime against pillage by strict discipline and by providing troops with sufficient food, clothing, and other basic needs to obliterate the motive for pillage.[7] Moreover, if war conditions brought about some pillage, "military necessity" could always be used to justify it, as long as the violations were proportional and owners could be compensated later.

In the case of rape, some of the material conditions that existed for pillage were valid as well. For instance, rape was as costly as pillage (if not more so) in terms of upsetting army discipline and local populations. Neither of the ideational conditions for the emergence of a prohibition regime, however, was present. First, states did not believe they could prevent rape in war because they believed rape in war was inevitable; the standard drill sergeant's ditty illustrated the military's attitude toward that inevitability: "This is my weapon, this is my gun; This is for business, this is for fun."[8] The common belief was that in the "most exclusive male-only club,"[9] the soldiers become "famished tigers"[10] who could not be prevented from satisfying their "hunger" with the spoils of war. This gendered assumption about male sexuality that goes out of control when unsatisfied for a period of time is apparent in the fact that military regulations always allowed and usually even encouraged access to prostitutes for soldiers when in military camps.[11]

Societies (and militaries) interpreted the biological makeup of the male and female bodies in a way that constructed rape as an inevitable byproduct of nature. Because men have penises that can erect and interlock into the female body by force, as opposed to women whose "lacking" genitalia cannot perform such a function, men are gendered as "the able" and women as "the rapeable."[12] Rape was understood as something that a man, as the active sex, does to a woman, the passive sex, which also ignores the fact that men can be raped by other men or women, as well. Since penises erect for sexual purposes, they had to find their release by fulfilling their natural purpose—that is, by entering a vagina.[13]

According to this "pressure-cooker theory of male nature," as the involuntary victims of their sexual instincts, men cannot control their actions, and their uncontrollable drive "has to run its course in a manner that is unfortunate, to be sure, but also unavoidable."[14] This line of thinking even continued into the twentieth century. For instance, when Soviet soldiers were raping German women by the thousands in 1945, "Stalin was merely amused by the idea of Red Army soldiers having 'some fun' after a hard war."[15] The Japanese forced around 200,000 women from all over East Asia into sexual slavery to give "comfort" to Japanese soldiers during World War II. Hence, when it came to making a commitment to stop wartime rape for the state parties at The Hague, in a context where women were considered not only property but also inevitable objects of male lust, writing a vague article was the desirable option. States believed they could not prevent soldiers from satisfying their "needs," so making a commitment to stop rape did not seem sensible. When "boys get out of control," it is not possible to justify it with "military necessity," nor is it possible to compensate the "owners" of the raped women properly.[16] Therefore, it would be costly for a state to make a commitment simply to stop rape and then be in a position in which the state was unable to comply with its commitment.

The second set of ideational factors for the emergence of a prohibition regime, which could trigger a regime protecting women as human beings, was not present for rape either. The normative context was not conducive to regarding rape as an attack on women; rather, it was regarded as an attack on the honor of the men who owned the women. By looking at the major marriage, adultery, and rape laws in nineteenth-century Europe, we found that when it came to the female body, the major concern was protecting the lineages of gentlemen (because inheritances and property must go to the rightful heirs), and international law reflected that mentality. Stipulation to protect the honor of the family meant that the "property" of the propertied class should be respected, but there is no reason to punish a soldier for not "respecting" the "property" (only women) of the lower classes. Although women from all classes and backgrounds are vulnerable to rape in war, it is common knowledge that well-off people have the resources to protect themselves or escape from war zones and the poor are disproportionately affected by wars.[17] Rape victims during wars were predominantly lower-class

women, and the domestic rape laws in England and France show that rape of
a lower-class woman was not even considered rape. Even when the proximity
of war reached upper-class women, they had usually been protected against
the common soldiers by knights and squires; in the exceptional cases where
noblemen did not protect women of rank, the incidents were reported with
shock and horror.[18] From the perspective of European states, then, lower-
class women, the major victims of wartime rape, were not "property enough"
to be protected, because their bodies were not the sites for the protection and
rightful transfer of other property.

The actors necessary to help the development of a normative context in
which rape is as undesirable and preventable as pillage were not effective on
the international stage. The publicists who pushed for the codification of the
laws of war did not include rape in the drafts they prepared, because they did
not want to jeopardize their projects by putting potentially unacceptable articles in them. Friedrich Martens's draft for the Brussels Declaration and later
the Hague Regulations, therefore, purposefully excluded rape even though
his inspiration, the Lieber Code, included it. Women's groups, on the other
hand, were just beginning to organize around suffrage. Even though international feminism started to emerge in the mid-nineteenth century, and even
though some of these feminists started to talk about sexual violence against
women as an important part of women's oppression in their individual countries, the force of the movement was not powerful enough to reach The Hague
in 1899 or 1907. There were no women delegates at the conferences. The only
women who played any role during the conferences were peace activists, such
Baroness Bertha von Suttner.[19] Although she was known to have influenced
Russian tsar Nicholas II, and indirectly contributed to the Hague Conventions,[20] von Suttner's influence—and that of her fellow peace activists—was
mostly limited to the peace movement. As a result, the normative context
that could make rape in war shocking for the public conscience—by presenting women as human beings who are brutally violated or as property that is
universally valuable (as opposed to class and rank determining value)—did
not emerge in the nineteenth century.

In concluding Chapter 3, we found that a prohibition regime could not
develop against rape with The Hague Conventions because of the lack of advocates for change in the process and the lack of the ideational conditions
necessary for the development of a prohibition regime.

Chapter 4 examined the next important legal documents, the Geneva
Conventions. Since they were written on account of the horrific human rights

violations during World War II, which included widespread sexual violence against women, one might expect that a prohibition regime against rape would develop here. However, despite mentioning rape, the Geneva Conventions fell short of creating a hard law against it. By using the language of protection rather than prohibition, and by excluding rape from the list of grave breaches, they failed to provide the precision, obligation, and delegation required for a prohibition regime. We saw that a mention of rape had escaped the Hague Conventions, but why the Geneva Conventions, too? In fact, if it were not for the intervention of a women's organization, the Geneva Conventions would not have even mentioned the word *rape*. While the women's movements had gained enough ground to convince the lawmakers to at least mention rape in the Geneva Conventions, they could not erase the idea about rape's inevitability in war, and the weakness of the provisions against rape in the Geneva Conventions were the result. The fact that lawmakers mentioned the word *rape* in the document but failed to prohibit it or to include it among the grave breaches shows that this failure was not about decency and propriety either.

The relative absence of women's voices during the international law creation process contributed to this failure as well. During the Conferences nobody pushed for further change. The percentage of women state delegates in the 1949 Conference was 5.8 percent, which was very low, although a big improvement over the percentage at the Hague Peace Conferences, with 0 percent. We do know that Article 27 was changed to include rape at the proposal of the International Alliance of Women, but there were no women's organizations participating directly at the conference. Similarly, the conferences between 1974 and 1977 that prepared the Additional Protocols included some women among the state delegates, yet the percentage of women was 6.1 percent, still a dismal percentage, considering the advances women's movements had achieved between the 1940s and 1970s.

Chapter 5 outlined the triumph of women's organizations in the creation of a prohibition regime against rape with the Rome Statute after the 99-year-old international law had ignored it. Starting in the late 1970s and early 1980s, and building on the mostly successful battle to change domestic rape laws in individual (particularly Western) countries, women's movements turned their attention to the international law dealing with sexual violence against women. The long struggle of the women's movements to move women out of the category of property and into the category of humanity, and to move rape into the category of crimes against human beings, was bearing fruit and the new norm of "women's rights as human rights" was taking root. Women had been agitating to change domestic rape laws since the 1970s—with success in the Western world. These improvements were thanks to the social, political, and economic advances, both domestic and international (as in the UN), that women's organizations all over the world had made over the last century. Western feminists had also been networking around the issue of violence against women since the 1970s, although not on a scale that could have a transformative effect yet. CEDAW (adopted in 1979, came into force in 1981), for instance, did not mention rape or violence against women among the forms of discrimination that should be eliminated. Starting with the 1980 Copenhagen Conference, however, women would carry the subject to the global agenda, with particular attention to building it within the human rights framework. Not only did that approach bring women from all countries together around the issue, but, as an already legitimate framework on the global agenda, it also worked to legitimize the agitation of feminists over violence against women. The 1993 UN Human Rights Conference in Vienna would be the ground for proving the success of this framing.

Meanwhile, an unexpected narrow window opened for the women's movement. This was the decade of opportunity between the end of the Cold War and the War on Terror. The "no accountability" system for human rights abuses, put in place because of the strategic considerations of the Cold War, had collapsed with the Berlin Wall, and governments turned to international institutions in this euphoria of the "new world order."[21]

The idea of creating an International Criminal Court, which had been on the international agenda off and on for almost half a century, was revived in this context. People thought that freedom and human rights had triumphed over autocracy, and the great power rivalry at the barrel of nuclear weapons had ended. Under such conditions, international cooperation and international institutions continuing their mission where they had left off seemed realistic for the first time since the beginning of the Cold War.

At the same time, the normative context of the 1990s, in which women had been categorized as human for a few decades (at least in the Western world) and with the belief that human civilization (especially for Europe) was at the height of its existence, no longer allowed states to dismiss rape as inevitable, unpleasant to talk about, or a property crime that could be selectively punished. Two centuries of feminist work to make women "human," three decades of which saw active campaigning against sexual violence, changed the terms of the debate on rape. Even if some people still believed in the "pressure-cooker theory" of male sexuality as the source of rape, it was no longer possible to defend it. For example, when three U.S. marines gang-raped a twelve-year-old schoolgirl on the Japanese island of Okinawa in 1995 their commander, Admiral Richard Macke, commented: "I think it was absolutely stupid. I have said several times: for the price they paid to rent the car, they could have had a girl [prostitute]." The reaction was surprising, considering the trivialization of rape in the past. The United States handed over the perpetrators to Japanese authorities for prosecution, and Admiral Macke was not only condemned, but forced into early retirement with reduced rank.[22] "Boys may get out of control" was no longer an option as a defense, and states could no longer afford to regard rape as inevitable, even for sex-starved soldiers who could not satisfy their hunger with a prostitute.

It was also not possible to ignore the issue of rape in international law and sweep it under the rug without explanations, since women were present for questioning it. At the 1998 Rome Conference, 19 percent of the state delegates were women, and 16 of the 267 women delegates were head or deputy heads of their delegations. NGO participation and influence in the conference in general was at a previously unseen level, and women's NGOs were present in full force. The major feminist actor in the negotiations, the Women's Caucus for Gender Justice, alone included more than 200 women's organizations.[23]

This normative context, along with the outbreak of the ethnic-cleansing campaign in the former Yugoslavia (and later the genocide in Rwanda), with widespread and widely publicized sexual violence against women, and the historic opportunity to write new international law regarding the laws of war (the Rome Statute), gave the women's cause the necessary boost. During the ICC negotiations, women's NGOs could point to the mass rapes in former Yugoslavia as evidence that when international law fails, this kind of savagery happens. The scenes were shocking for the self-image of the "civilized" world (particularly Europe), which had never expected to see them again, believing in their post-World War II slogan, "Never again." If women had not been working to establish women's rights as human rights, however, these images of rape and violence would not have been so shocking. After all, the rapes of the Napoleonic Wars[24] or World War II were not. If the tragedies in former Yugoslavia had not happened, would the Rome Statute still prohibit rape, including it in both crimes against humanity and war crimes? Probably not, since there is no reason to believe women would have been successful in persuading states that the provisions in the Geneva Conventions were insufficient to prevent rape.

By tracing the development of the prohibition regimes against pillage and rape and exploring the temporal disparity between their development, we can conclude that for a prohibition regime to emerge, three sets of conditions need to be satisfied. First, the prohibition of the practice should not be materially costly for the states. Second, two ideational conditions need to be fulfilled: states need to believe that they can comply with the regime; and there must be a normative context responsive to a possible change and a potentially shocking event. Third, actors who promote the new norms and change should emerge alongside it. In order to support these actors' work to attract policymakers' attention and provide the final push for legal change, the potentially shocking event must be turned into a normative shock.

The premises of this book are twofold. First, the events leading to prohibition regimes do not happen independently. The shocking events that ultimately set the legal changes in motion were not independent of the normative context. Neither the Napoleonic Wars nor the ethnic conflict in former Yugoslavia was unique and unprecedented. The pillaging armies of Napoleon and the perpetrators of the rapes in former Yugoslavia did not do anything novel that would have a particularly shocking effect on the rest of the world in and of themselves; the world had already seen these kinds of events. But they did happen in the right normative context, partly created, partly reinforced, and partly used by the norm entrepreneurs who promoted change.

The second premise arises from the particular cases that I examined. The fact that international law failed to prohibit "pillage" of women for almost one hundred years after it prohibited pillage of private property illustrates the deep impact gender has on international relations, both as an ideology (meaning the way people think about men and women and what they should or should not do) and as an institutional obstacle to exclude women from politics. Therefore, this study provides an example of the way the gendered structure of international relations works by illustrating the role of gender as a category on international regime change.

"Hard Laws" and Change?

Telford Taylor, chief counsel prosecutor at the Nuremberg trials, pointed out in 1970 that "Violated or ignored as they are, enough of the rules are observed enough of the time so that mankind is very much better off with them than without them."[25] Is that so? Why is the creation of prohibition regimes, particularly through legalization, important? Does more legalization bring more change on the ground?

In the context of international law, we can search for answers by addressing three issues. First, is international law an effective tool or just window dressing that states ignore at will? Second, does enforcement, which is one of the key features of legalization, matter in terms of making law "matter"? And third, what is the record of compliance for the two cases at hand?

Law Matters

Signing and ratifying an international treaty is a sign that a state promises to abide by the rules in that treaty. More legalization may lead to more compliance by increasing the clarity (the precision and obligation components of legalization) of the commitments and by making noncompliance easier to detect, thereby increasing its costs.[26] Although the scholars who contributed to the *International Organization* volume on legalization show that the record of legalization leading to more compliance is mixed, they conclude that a positive relationship exists between norms and more legalized institutions, especially in the area of laws of war.[27] In other words, legal restraints serve to change the meanings of the expected behavior from the subjects of the law. As a result, the organizational culture and public opinion—the norms— change as well. This, in turn, increases the drive to comply, both by imposing a "sense of obligation"[28] or powerfully constituting states' identities, interests, and actions[29] and by creating a watchful domestic audience. Without a precise regime that entails clear obligations, contestations and more widespread violations are likely to occur.[30]

Although this book is about the emergence of regimes and not compliance with them, many scholars believe that having a hard law in place is a necessary (although not a sufficient) step for compliance. Precision and obligation are very important factors in "hardening" a law and inducing compliance through the creation of costs of non-compliance (reputation or reciprocity) and a sense of obligation to follow the law or audience pressure. The last component of legalization, delegation, is a significant factor as well. Especially for the cases at hand, enforcement makes a difference.

Enforcement Matters

Enforcement is a key factor for compliance with international law, especially for those laws whose effectiveness depends on the behavior of individuals (in this case, individuals on the battlefield).[31] Some laws of war, specifically the

ones that depend on the obedience of individual soldiers, are relatively difficult for states to comply with because they cannot always control the behavior
of individual soldiers.[32] Both pillage and rape are in this category. State policy
and military manuals may prohibit these practices, but in the end it comes
down to the behavior of the soldiers on the battlefield.

Lack of enforcement does not necessarily lead to an ineffective regime,
but it may lead to a less effective one. Scholars with different perspectives
have studied the role of enforcement in explaining compliance with international laws and regimes. Realists argue that states comply with international regimes and laws only if it is in their national interests to do so. In
other words, law does not have a force of its own. Realists assume there is no
genuine enforcement in an anarchical world, so when states act according to
the requirements of international law, realists argue that these states would
have acted the same way if the law did not exist.[33] Neoliberals argue that enforcement is a significant mechanism (among others) to ensure compliance
because cheating and free-rider problems may result in its absence.[34] For constructivists, compliance is about the internalization of the appropriate behavior by the states.[35] Thomas Franck, for instance, describes this phenomenon
as laws having a "compliance pull of their own" and therefore not requiring strong enforcement.[36] But enforcement may help increase compliance by
communicating or teaching the new norms and rules.

Laws of war, especially the ones that require adherence by individuals,
require enforcement for better compliance, because most of the other incentives and processes that ensure state compliance (reputation and reciprocity
costs at the state level, sense of obligation or audience pressure) do not impose the same restraint on individuals on the battlefield. James Morrow argues that all militaries (although there are some exceptions) try to control the
behavior of their soldiers to prevent violations of the treaties they signed and
ratified, but the success of control depends on factors such as military training and the opportunities soldiers have to commit violations.[37] According to
Morrow, two of the important factors that lead to the hierarchy of compliance
among different types of laws are the possibility of retaliation and reciprocity that the violation will bring about, and whether compliance depends on
the behavior of individuals rather than the centralized decision making of
the state. In other words, if the violation of a certain law of war can potentially produce immediate retaliation and the decision to violate it is made
at the state level (for example, the use of chemical or biological weapons),
compliance will be high. When, on the other hand, the threats of immediate

retaliation and reciprocity from the enemy are absent or low and when the soldiers on the ground are making the decision to comply, compliance is less likely. This puts the treatment of civilians at the bottom on Morrow's scale of compliance, because civilians lack the ability to retaliate and soldiers decide to violate the laws.[38] Overall, it seems that soldiers on the ground need additional incentives to comply with the laws of war to which their governments have committed. They need to know that they may be prosecuted for their actions,[39] and enforcement—whether by governments as required by the Hague Conventions (1907) and the Geneva Conventions (1949) or by international bodies with significant powers of delegation like the ICC—seems to be the key to providing compliance.

With this idea in mind, the women's groups who organized around the issue of prohibition of rape by international law also turned their attention to enforcement after the establishment of the ICC. The Women's Caucus for Gender Justice moved to The Hague under its new name, "Women's Initiatives for Gender Justice," to perform a "gender watch" of the Court.[40]

Track Record for Pillage and Rape

Pillage

Seven years after the conclusion of the Hague Conventions, World War I began. Although the articles of the Conventions with regard to private property were violated at times, particularly by Germany in Belgium and France,[41] on the whole the law was obeyed.[42] During World War II, instances of pillage happened on a larger scale. Besides Germany confiscating private property on the territories it occupied, looting artwork and cultural heritage was commonplace. The Soviet Union, for instance, pillaged occupied Germany and Manchuria in 1945.[43]

All laws, domestic and international, are violated at times; it is therefore no surprise that the law against pillage was violated as well. How do we follow the process of compliance then? According to Richard Price, one important indicator to distinguish between a law that has broad enough acceptance (and compliance) and one that does not is a court ruling granting damages to a victim of a violation.[44] In the case of pillage, we find that, although it continued to occur in several wars after its prohibition, most of the time the government of the offenders took steps to punish the violators.[45] Although exceptions such as "military necessity" and "unknown ownership" (turning the private property into public property and therefore open to confiscation by the enemy government) were applied in many cases, there have also been cases where unlawful seizure of private property was compensated.[46]

Prosecutions by international bodies also occurred. A Germano-Greek Mixed Arbitral Tribunal after World War I, for instance, found Germany to be a violator of the Hague Regulations regarding requisition of private property and awarded compensation accordingly.[47] During World War II, the Allies reaffirmed the international laws protecting private property against pillage by issuing the London Declaration (1943) as "a formal warning to all concerned, and in particular to persons in neutral countries, that they intend to do their utmost to defeat the methods of dispossession practiced by the Governments with which they are at war against the countries and peoples who have been so wantonly assaulted and despoiled."[48] It established the concept of restitution, on the basis of which many governments demanded the return of looted property after the war. Even when contested property was not returned (because proof could not be made that the property had been looted), full investigations were conducted to find out exactly how these properties were acquired.[49]

The Nuremberg Tribunal Charter also included pillage, and charges were brought for it,[50] although the exact extent of pillage during the war was not clear. In 1949, Graber wrote that not enough data existed to evaluate occupation practices during World War II:

> Contemporary accounts in newspapers and periodicals consist largely of recitals of specific instances of alleged abuses in occupied regions, and a refutation or justification of these acts, both types of accounts usually written by persons partial to either the occupant or his adversary.[51]

While cases of widespread looting and destruction of public and private property by the Axis powers in occupied countries had been reported, belligerents made the Hague Regulations "the formal basis of their practice and their contentions in particular cases." The conditions of warfare had changed, yet nobody had denounced the rules as outdated, and the postwar "peace treaties . . . were based in part on the enforcement of these rules, and the governments of former occupants were held liable to make reparation for violations of them. Moreover, the tribunals established by those treaties in numerous cases made great efforts to uphold and apply the regulations."[52]

Furthermore, claims for pillaged property are still continuing after half a century. These efforts sometimes result in successful recoveries, which show the law had force even though it did not deter violations in the first place. Looted art and cultural property are the most common subjects of these claims. For example, during World War II the Nazis looted the Koenigs Collection from the Netherlands and the Soviet Union looted it from Germany. Parts of the collection were returned in 2004; for the rest, claims are continuing. Other examples include the Kandinsky painting settlement in 2002, the Tate Gallery settlement in 2001 for a Griffier painting, and a case won against the Hungarian state for holding on to art pillaged by the Nazis in 2000.[53]

Armed conflicts of the 1990s, including the war in the former Yugoslavia and the genocide in Rwanda, also witnessed some looting. As a result, the Statutes of the ICTY and the ICTR both included pillage, and both tribunals prosecuted individuals for it.[54]

In 2003, the war in Iraq brought the issue of pillage back into the spotlight— especially because it involved massive pillage of invaluable artwork and cultural property, which had not happened on a large scale since World War II.[55] After U.S. troops invaded Iraq in March 2003, news surfaced about the plunder of Iraqi museums and ancient sites by both Iraqis and U.S. troops.[56] The U.S. forces were blamed not only for participating in or encouraging looting, but also for not preventing it, as an occupying power is required to do according to international law.[57] The International Council on Monuments even described the events as a crime against humanity, and there was the talk of a war crimes trial against the commander of the U.S. troops, General Tommy Franks, for not preventing the postwar pillaging.[58] The chairman and several members of President George W. Bush's Advisory Committee on Cultural Property resigned over the issue, and the U.S. government initiated several measures to return the stolen property to Iraqi museums, including sending FBI agents to Iraq for recovery.[59] (Part of the looted property was recovered as a result.) Nevertheless, no prosecutions have been brought, and some of the U.S. officials defended their inaction during the looting as a "matter of priorities" (probably a reference to the military necessity issue) or simply as "stuff happens."[60] International reaction, on the other hand, was considerable and with the attention of major news outlets, the stories opened widespread discussion over the laws of war with respect to protection of property as well as responsibilities of occupying powers in general.

These historical examples indicate that although there have been violations, contestations, and challenges with respect to the prohibition against pillage, there have also been court cases, settlements, retributions, and

condemnations, as well as adherences and justifications that contributed to
the internalization of the norm protecting property, mostly by referring to
the law (the Hague Regulations in particular). It is significant that 110 years
after its prohibition by international law, pillage today is rather exceptional
in wars, and when it happens, as in the Iraq War, it is considered a surprising
mishap or a war crime that needs to be addressed, sometimes through retribution and sometimes through enforcement.[61]

Rape

Just after the Rome Statute was signed, another ethnic cleansing campaign,
which included rape as one of its tools, was launched in 1999 in the Kosovo
region of Yugoslavia. Though the conflict lasted only a short time because of
the early intervention of NATO, British foreign secretary Robin Cook stated
that the British government seized on evidence that young ethnic Albanian
women were being subjected to systematic rape by Serbian security forces,
information that had surfaced slowly because many of the victims were reluctant to admit the events. The British newspaper *The Guardian* said that
although there was no evidence of a similar pattern of Bosnian rape camps in
Kosovo, testimony from people at the scene, such as a gynecologist working
in the refugee camps in Albania, indicated that mass rape had returned to the
Balkans.[62] Human Rights Watch reported evidence of credible cases of rape,
but there was no evidence that rape camps existed[63] (which was the dominant
pattern in the Bosnian case). The rapes in Kosovo were in the form of gang
rapes, which sometimes resulted in pregnancies, but there was no proof of a
policy of forced pregnancy.

These facts, however, do not mean that systematic rape was not used as a
weapon for ethnic cleansing in Kosovo. The evidence suggests that rape was
used to force people to flee and never come back, as well as to destroy the
community through stigmatizing women. Victims and witnesses told human
rights organization investigators that rapes had been perpetrated mostly by
police or paramilitary forces, who attacked houses and gang-raped women
there or while refugees were fleeing.[64] We find significant differences between
the cases of wartime rape in Bosnia and Kosovo. The war in Kosovo lasted a
shorter time, and NATO intervention came much earlier than in Bosnia.

What does this mean in terms of the effectiveness of the prohibition regime created by the Rome Statute? First, although mass rapes occurred in
Kosovo, they were not done overtly in established camps. As Julie Mertus
puts it: "For the most part Serbian police, military and paramilitary groups

in Kosovo have been careful to avoid [or to hide] the kind of atrocities we see in Bosnia."[65] The fact that some of the perpetrators in Kosovo were trying to hide their identities by wearing ski masks is also noteworthy in terms of showing their fear of being detected and punished.[66] Second, the difference between the two communities—Bosnian Muslims and Kosovo Albanians—is significant in terms of the reaction two societies would have to these rapes. In the Kosovo Albanian society, women were far more silenced about what had happened to them because of their community's commitment to the traditional Code of Leke Dukajini,[67] which covers all aspects of social activity, particularly honor and reinforcing traditional patriarchal ideas about gender roles. Because of this extreme power of the rape stigma in Kosovo, it was less likely that Albanian victims would testify (and that indeed was the case).[68] Therefore, although specifically law and more generally the norm that had developed against the use of rape as a weapon seemed to force the offenders to hide what they were doing, the fact that the victims were reluctant to testify meant that the law could not be enforced and therefore prevented it from being effective.[69] Women's organizations' push for rigorous witness protection measures in the ICC Statute indicates their awareness of the problem.[70] Finally and most important, we need to recognize that when the Kosovo conflict happened, the prohibition regime against rape was only one year old (counting from the signing of the Rome Statute) and not even in force yet (counting from the statute's ratification).

Later conflicts, such as the ones in the Sudan and the Democratic Republic of Congo (DRC), also became stages for mass rapes. While the Sudanese army and the government-sponsored militia, Janjawid, have been responsible for the rapes of thousands of women in Darfur as part of a genocidal campaign since 2003, a senseless rape epidemic has also been going on in the DRC since the late 1990s perpetrated mainly by the militias who are after natural resources in the region.[71] Both cases are examples of the ineffectiveness of the new law to deter rape and impose compliance. Nevertheless, both cases have been brought to the ICC, and in both the Court indicted individuals for rape.[72]

In the case of the DRC, two of the ICC cases present interesting challenges to enforcement of the law, as well as the contribution of legalization toward better enforcement and perhaps better compliance in time. The first challenge came in the case of Germain Katanga and Mathieu Ngudjolo Chui. These former rebel leaders in the DRC were charged with various war crimes and crimes against humanity in 2008. When the ICC considered dropping the charges related to sexual violence, because of some internal conflict in the ICC over witness protection, victims and women's groups were outraged.[73] Ultimately, the Court confirmed charges of sexual violence as crimes against humanity and war crimes.[74]

The second case concerns Thomas Lubanga Dyilo.[75] Although Lubanga, another rebel leader, was accused of various counts of sexual violence, and most of the victims' testimony during his trial focused on rape, his indictment did not include any crimes of sexual violence. The representatives for the victims submitted a motion to amend the charges against him to include these crimes, but the Appeals Chamber reversed a decision of the Trial Chamber that would have allowed their inclusion.[76]

These examples provide us with a glimpse of the continuing struggles of international law prohibiting wartime rape. Courts are charging people with this crime, and whenever they fail to do so, a big public outcry often results in some adjustment. Yet thousands of women continue to suffer the horrors of rape in various conflicts around the world, and there does not seem to be a reduction in the occurrence of this particular war crime.

Some people also criticized the prohibition regime against rape in wartime as "a right development for wrong reasons," because it first began[77] in a general reaction to human rights violations during World War II, which resulted in selective prosecutions (Nuremberg and Tokyo), since rape was not considered a war crime per se. Additionally, women's movements found a real opportunity to fight against it only after the shocking, systematic rapes during the ethnic and civil conflicts in former Yugoslavia and Rwanda, and on the basis of the fact that these rapes were parts of the genocide. The developments that followed have depended largely on this argument about rape being a tool for genocide. Liz Philipose argues, for example, that the legalization of the issue occurred because the wars were considered unjust—as wars for ethnic cleansing attacking a community—not because of the violation of the human rights of women.[78]

The extension of this argument is that the prohibition regime will be ineffective because the attitude toward rape and the underlying assumption that had legitimized it for centuries has not changed, although the law against the use of rape as a weapon in war has developed. Similarly, some feminists criticize international law as a whole because they do not believe in its liberating potential due to its deeply gendered structure.[79]

These critics overlook three important elements for optimism about the prohibition regime for rape. First, the pattern of regime creation, with its normative shock and grafting onto an existing framework, is common to many international laws that are now internalized and with which many states now comply. Second, law can constitute meanings that accelerate the push for further normative change, which is necessary for better compliance.[80] The fact that after hundreds of years of impunity, perpetrators have finally been prosecuted (and in some cases convicted) of rape by international courts is a very important development. Having the law on paper, and thus the subject of a more legalized regime, helps the process along because it provides courts, norm entrepreneurs, states, and victims of violations a concrete reference point for enforcement (especially for the courts), a tool for retribution (for the victims), and a powerful way of denouncing, criticizing, and justifying (for norm entrepreneurs and states), all of which are necessary instruments of norm internalization.

Most important, it takes time for regimes and laws to become effective, and the regime against rape is too young to make definitive conclusions about its ultimate effectiveness. The fact that the law against pillage is a century older than the law against rape and has gone through some challenges should tell us something. Creation of a prohibition regime is an important benchmark in terms of providing the norm internalization process with a significant pillar and momentum, but it is neither a pinnacle nor a guarantee for compliance, which requires time above everything else.

Finally, the work scholars do by demonstrating the gendered nature of international politics and law in their research and the work that activists do by keeping laws, courts, and state practices under constant scrutiny are important and useful ways of deconstructing these gendered structures and minds and, ultimately, transforming them in a way to end oppression.[81] Change takes time and effort.

The Hague Conventions

(First Peace Conference at The Hague: Signed July 29, 1899)

Laws of War: Laws and Customs of War on Land (Hague II)

Article 1
The High Contracting Parties shall issue instructions to their armed land forces, which shall be in conformity with the "Regulations respecting the Laws and Customs of War on Land" annexed to the present Convention.

Article 2
The provisions contained in the Regulations mentioned in Article 1 are only binding on the Contracting Powers, in case of war between two or more of them.

These provisions shall cease to be binding from the time when, in a war between Contracting Powers, a non-Contracting Power joins one of the belligerents.

SECTION II— ON HOSTILITIES

Article 22
The right of belligerents to adopt means of injuring the enemy is not unlimited.

Article 23
Besides the prohibitions provided by special Conventions, it is especially prohibited:

(a) To employ poison or poisoned arms;
(b) To kill or wound treacherously individuals belonging to the hostile nation or army;
(c) To kill or wound an enemy who, having laid down arms, or having no longer means of defense, has surrendered at discretion;
(d) To declare that no quarter will be given;
(e) To employ arms, projectiles, or material of a nature to cause superfluous injury;
(f) To make improper use of a flag of truce, the national flag or military ensigns and uniform of the enemy, as well as the distinctive badges of the Geneva Convention;
(g) To destroy or seize the enemy's property, unless such destruction or seizure be imperatively demanded by the necessities of war.

Article 28
The pillage of a town or place, even when taken by assault, is prohibited.

SECTION III—ON MILITARY AUTHORITY
OVER HOSTILE TERRITORY

Article 42
Territory is considered occupied when it is actually placed under the authority of the hostile army.

The occupation applies only to the territory where such authority is established, and in a position to assert itself.

Article 43
The authority of the legitimate power having actually passed into the hands of the occupant, the latter shall take all steps in his power to re-establish and insure, as far as possible, public order and safety, while respecting, unless absolutely prevented, the laws in force in the country.

Article 44
Any compulsion of the population of occupied territory to take part in military operations against its own country is prohibited.

Article 45
Any pressure on the population of occupied territory to take the oath to the hostile Power is prohibited.

Article 46

Family honors and rights, individual lives and private property, as well as religious convictions and liberty, must be respected.

Private property cannot be confiscated.

Article 47

Pillage is formally prohibited.

Article 48

If, in the territory occupied, the occupant collects the taxes, dues, and tolls imposed for the benefit of the State, he shall do it, as far as possible, in accordance with the rules in existence and the assessment in force, and will in consequence be bound to defray the expenses of the administration of the occupied territory on the same scale as that by which the legitimate Government was bound.

Article 49

If, besides the taxes mentioned in the preceding Article, the occupant levies other money taxes in the occupied territory, this can only be for military necessities or the administration of such territory.

Article 50

No general penalty, pecuniary or otherwise, can be inflicted on the population on account of the acts of individuals for which it cannot be regarded as collectively responsible.

Article 51

No tax shall be collected except under a written order and on the responsibility of a Commander-in-Chief.

This collection shall only take place, as far as possible, in accordance with the rules in existence and the assessment of taxes in force.

For every payment a receipt shall be given to the taxpayer.

Article 52

Neither requisitions in kind nor services can be demanded from communes or inhabitants except for the necessities of the army of occupation. They must be in proportion to the resources of the country, and of such a nature as not to involve the population in the obligation of taking part in military operations against their country.

These requisitions and services shall only be demanded on the authority of the Commander in the locality occupied.

The contributions in kind shall, as far as possible, be paid for in ready money; if not, their receipt shall be acknowledged.

Article 53

An army of occupation can only take possession of the cash, funds, and property liable to requisition belonging strictly to the State, depots of arms, means of transport, stores and supplies, and, generally, all movable property of the State which may be used for military operations.

Railway plant, land telegraphs, telephones, steamers, and other ships, apart from cases governed by maritime law, as well as depots of arms and, generally, all kinds of war material, even though belonging to Companies or to private persons, are likewise material which may serve for military operations, but they must be restored at the conclusion of peace, and indemnities paid for them.

Article 54

The plant of railways coming from neutral States, whether the property of those States, or of Companies, or of private persons, shall be sent back to them as soon as possible.

Article 55

The occupying State shall only be regarded as administrator and usufructuary of the public buildings, real property, forests, and agricultural works belonging to the hostile State, and situated in the occupied country. It must protect the capital of these properties, and administer it according to the rules of usufruct.

Article 56

The property of the communes, that of religious, charitable, and educational institutions, and those of arts and science, even when State property, shall be treated as private property.

All seizure of, and destruction, or intentional damage done to such institutions, to historical monuments, works of art or science, is prohibited, and should be made the subject of proceedings.

(Second Peace Conference at The Hague:
Signed October 18, 1907) (Hague IV)

Article 3
A belligerent party which violates the provisions of the said Regulations shall, if the case demands, be liable to pay compensation. It shall be responsible for all acts committed by persons forming part of its armed forces.

Article 28
The pillage of a town or place, even when taken by assault, is prohibited.

Article 46
Family honour and rights, the lives of persons, and private property, as well as religious convictions and practice, must be respected.
Private property cannot be confiscated.

Article 47
Pillage is formally forbidden.

Article 52
Requisitions in kind and services shall not be demanded from municipalities or inhabitants except for the needs of the army of occupation. They shall be in proportion to the resources of the country, and of such a nature as not to involve the inhabitants in the obligation of taking part in military operations against their own country.

   Such requisitions and services shall only be demanded on the authority of the commander in the locality occupied.

   Contributions in kind shall as far as possible be paid for in cash; if not, a receipt shall be given and the payment of the amount due shall be made as soon as possible.

Article 56
The property of municipalities, that of institutions dedicated to religion, charity and education, the arts and sciences, even when State property, shall be treated as private property.

   All seizure of, destruction or willful damage done to institutions of this character, historic monuments, works of art and science, is forbidden, and should be made the subject of legal proceedings.

Charter of the International Military
Tribunal at Nuremberg, 1945

II. JURISDICTION AND GENERAL PRINCIPLES

Article 6

  (b) War Crimes: namely, violations of the laws or customs of war. Such violations shall include, but not be limited to, murder, ill-treatment or deportation to slave labor or for any other purpose of civilian population of or in occupied territory, murder or ill-treatment of prisoners of war or persons on the seas, killing of hostages, plunder of public or private property, wanton destruction of cities, towns or villages, or devastation not justified by military necessity;

  (c) Crimes Against Humanity: namely, murder, extermination, enslavement, deportation, and other inhumane acts committed against any civilian population, before or during the war; or persecutions on political, racial or religious grounds in execution of or in connection with any crime within the jurisdiction of the Tribunal, whether or not in violation of the domestic law of the country where perpetrated.

Leaders, organizers, instigators and accomplices participating in the formulation or execution of a common plan or conspiracy to commit any of the foregoing crimes are responsible for all acts performed by any persons in execution of such plan.

Convention (IV) Relative to the Protection of Civilian
Persons in Time of War, Geneva, 12 August 1949

PART III. STATUS AND TREATMENT OF PROTECTED PERSONS

Section I. Provisions common to the territories of the parties to the conflict and to occupied territories

Article 27

Protected persons are entitled, in all circumstances, to respect for their persons, their honor, their family rights, their religious convictions and practices, and their manners and customs. They shall at all times be humanely treated, and shall be protected especially against all acts of violence or threats thereof and against insults and public curiosity.

Women shall be especially protected against any attack on their honor, in particular against rape, enforced prostitution, or any form of indecent assault.

Article 33

No protected person may be punished for an offence he or she has not personally committed. Collective penalties and likewise all measures of intimidation or of terrorism are prohibited. Pillage is prohibited.

Reprisals against protected persons and their property are prohibited.

Article 53

Any destruction by the Occupying Power of real or personal property belonging individually or collectively to private persons, or to the State, or to other public authorities, or to social or cooperative organizations, is prohibited, except where such destruction is rendered absolutely necessary by military operations.

PART IV. EXECUTION OF THE CONVENTION

Section I. General Provisions

Article 146

The High Contracting Parties undertake to enact any legislation necessary to provide effective penal sanctions for persons committing, or ordering to be committed, any of the grave breaches of the present Convention defined in the following Article.

Each High Contracting Party shall be under the obligation to search for persons alleged to have committed, or to have ordered to be committed, such grave breaches, and shall bring such persons, regardless of their nationality, before its own courts. It may also, if it prefers, and in accordance with the provisions of its own legislation, hand such persons over for trial to another High Contracting Party concerned, provided such High Contracting Party has made out a prima facie case.

Each High Contracting Party shall take measures necessary for the suppression of all acts contrary to the provisions of the present Convention other than the grave breaches defined in the following Article.

In all circumstances, the accused persons shall benefit by safeguards of proper trial and defense, which shall not be less favorable than those provided by Article 105 and those following of the Geneva Convention relative to the Treatment of Prisoners of War of 12 August 1949.

Article 147

Grave breaches to which the preceding Article relates shall be those involving any of the following acts, if committed against persons or property protected by the present Convention: willful killing, torture or inhuman treatment, including biological experiments, willfully causing great suffering or serious injury to body or health, unlawful deportation or transfer or unlawful confinement of a protected person, compelling a protected person to serve in the forces of a hostile Power, or willfully depriving a protected person of the rights of fair and regular trial prescribed in the present Convention, taking of hostages and extensive destruction and appropriation of property, not justified by military necessity and carried out unlawfully and wantonly.

Protocol Additional to the Geneva Conventions of August 12, 1949, and Relating to the Protection of Victims of International Armed Conflicts (Protocol I), June 8, 1977

Article 11 Protection of persons

1. The physical or mental health and integrity of persons who are in the power of the adverse Party or who are interned, detained or otherwise deprived of liberty as a result of a situation referred to in Article I shall not be endangered by any unjustified act or omission. Accordingly, it is prohibited to subject the persons described in this Article to any medical procedure which is not indicated by the state of health of the person concerned and which is not consistent with generally accepted medical standards which would be applied under similar medical circumstances to persons who are nationals of the Party conducting the procedure and who are in no way deprived of liberty.

2. It is, in particular, prohibited to carry out on such persons, even with their consent:
   (a) Physical mutilations;
   (b) Medical or scientific experiments;
   (c) Removal of tissue or organs for transplantation, except where these acts are justified in conformity with the conditions provided for in paragraph 1.

3. Exceptions to the prohibition in paragraph 2 (c) may be made only in the case of donations of blood for transfusion or of skin for grafting, provided that they are given voluntarily and without any coercion or inducement,

and then only for therapeutic purposes, under conditions consistent with generally accepted medical standards and controls designed for the benefit of both the donor and the recipient.

4. Any wilful act or omission which seriously endangers the physical or mental health or integrity of any person who is in the power of a Party other than the one on which he depends and which either violates any of the prohibitions in paragraphs 1 and 2 or fails to comply with the requirements of paragraph 3 shall be a grave breach of this Protocol.

5. The persons described in paragraph I have the right to refuse any surgical operation. In case of refusal, medical personnel shall endeavor to obtain a written statement to that effect, signed or acknowledged by the patient.

6. Each Party to the conflict shall keep a medical record for every donation of blood for transfusion or skin for grafting by persons referred to in paragraph 1, if that donation is made under the responsibility of that Party. In addition, each Party to the conflict shall endeavour to keep a record of all medical procedures undertaken with respect to any person who is interned, detained or otherwise deprived of liberty as a result of a situation referred to in Article 1. These records shall be available at all times for inspection by the Protecting Power.

Article 75 Fundamental guarantees

1. In so far as they are affected by a situation referred to in Article 1 of this Protocol, persons who are in the power of a Party to the conflict and who do not benefit from more favourable treatment under the Conventions or under this Protocol shall be treated humanely in all circumstances and shall enjoy, as a minimum, the protection provided by this Article without any adverse distinction based upon race, colour, sex, language, religion or belief, political or other opinion, national or social origin, wealth, birth or other status, or on any other similar criteria. Each Party shall respect the person, honour, convictions and religious practices of all such persons.

2. The following acts are and shall remain prohibited at any time and in any place whatsoever, whether committed by civilian or by military agents:
   (a) Violence to the life, health, or physical or mental well-being of persons, in particular:
   (i) Murder;
   (ii) Torture of all kinds, whether physical or mental;
   (iii) Corporal punishment; and
   (iv) Mutilation;

(b) Outrages upon personal dignity, in particular humiliating and degrading treatment, enforced prostitution and any form of indecent assault;

(c) The taking of hostages;

(d) Collective punishments; and

(e) Threats to commit any of the foregoing acts.

3. Any person arrested, detained or interned for actions related to the armed conflict shall be informed promptly, in a language he understands, of the reasons why these measures have been taken. Except in cases of arrest or detention for penal offences, such persons shall be released with the minimum delay possible and in any event as soon as the circumstances justifying the arrest, detention or internment have ceased to exist.

4. No sentence may be passed and no penalty may be executed on a person found guilty of a penal offence related to the armed conflict except pursuant to a conviction pronounced by an impartial and regularly constituted court respecting the generally recognized principles of regular judicial procedure, which include the following:

(a) The procedure shall provide for an accused to be informed without delay of the particulars of the offence alleged against him and shall afford the accused before and during his trial all necessary rights and means of defence;

(b) No one shall be convicted of an offence except on the basis of individual penal responsibility;

(c) No one shall be accused or convicted of a criminal offence on account of any act or omission which did not constitute a criminal offence under the national or international law to which he was subject at the time when it was committed; nor shall a heavier penalty be imposed than that which was applicable at the time when the criminal offence was committed; if, after the commission of the offence, provision is made by law for the imposition of a lighter penalty, the offender shall benefit thereby;

(d) Anyone charged with an offence is presumed innocent until proved guilt according to law;

(e) Anyone charged with an offence shall have the right to be tried in his presence;

(f) No one shall be compelled to testify against himself or to confess guilt;

(g) Anyone charged with an offence shall have the right to examine, or have examined, the witnesses against him and to obtain the attendance and examination of witnesses on his behalf under the same conditions as witnesses against him;

(h) No one shall be prosecuted or punished by the same Party for an offence in respect of which a final judgement acquitting or convicting that person has been previously pronounced under the same law and judicial procedure;

(i) Anyone prosecuted for an offence shall have the right to have the judgement pronounced publicly; and

(j) A convicted person shall be advised on conviction of his judicial and other remedies and of the time-limits within which they may be exercised.

5. Women whose liberty has been restricted for reasons related to the armed conflict shall be held in quarters separated from men's quarters. They shall be under the immediate supervision of women. Nevertheless, in cases where families are detained or interned, they shall, whenever possible, be held in the same place and accommodated as family units.

6. Persons who are arrested, detained or interned for reasons related to the armed conflict shall enjoy the protection provided by this Article until their final release, repatriation or re-establishment, even after the end of the armed conflict.

7. In order to avoid any doubt concerning the prosecution and trial of persons accused of war crimes or crimes against humanity, the following principles shall apply:

(a) Persons who are accused of such crimes should be submitted for the purpose of prosecution and trial in accordance with the applicable rules of international law; and

(b) Any such persons who do not benefit from more favourable treatment under the Conventions or this Protocol shall be accorded the treatment provided by this Article, whether or not the crimes of which they are accused constitute grave breaches of the Conventions or of this Protocol.

8. No provision of this Article may be construed as limiting or infringing any other more favourable provision granting greater protection, under any applicable rules of international law, to persons covered by paragraph 1.

Article 76 Protection of women

1. Women shall be the object of special respect and shall be protected in particular against rape, forced prostitution and any other form of indecent assault.

2. Pregnant women and mothers having dependent infants who are arrested, detained or interned for reasons related to the armed conflict, shall have their cases considered with the utmost priority.

3. To the maximum extent feasible, the Parties to the conflict shall endeavour to avoid the pronouncement of the death penalty on pregnant women or mothers having dependent infants, for an offence related to the armed conflict. The death penalty for such offences shall not be executed on such women.

Article 85 Repression of breaches of this Protocol

1. The provisions of the Conventions relating to the repression of breaches and grave breaches, supplemented by this Section, shall apply to the repression of breaches and grave breaches of this Protocol.

2. Acts described as grave breaches in the Conventions are grave breaches of this Protocol if committed against persons in the power of an adverse Party protected by Articles 44, 45 and 73 of this Protocol, or against the wounded, sick and shipwrecked of the adverse Party who are protected by this Protocol, or against those medical or religious personnel, medical units or medical transports which are under the control of the adverse Party and are protected by this Protocol.

3. In addition to the grave breaches defined in Article 11, the following acts shall be regarded as grave breaches of this Protocol, when committed wilfully, in violation of the relevant provisions of this Protocol, and causing death or serious injury to body or health:

  (a) Making the civilian population or individual civilians the object of attack;

  (b) Launching an indiscriminate attack affecting the civilian population or civilian objects in the knowledge that such attack will cause excessive loss of life, injury to civilians or damage to civilian objects, as defined in Article 57, paragraph 2 (a) (iii);

  (c) Launching an attack against works or installations containing dangerous forces in the knowledge that such attack will cause excessive loss of life, injury to civilians or damage to civilian objects, as defined in Article 57, paragraph 2 (a) (iii);

  (d) Making non-defended localities and demilitarized zones the object of attack;

  (e) Making a person the object of attack in the knowledge that he is hors de combat;

(f) The perfidious use, in violation of Article 37, of the distinctive emblem of the red cross, red crescent or red lion and sun or of other protective signs recognized by the Conventions or this Protocol.

4. In addition to the grave breaches defined in the preceding paragraphs and in the Conventions, the following shall be regarded as grave breaches of this Protocol, when committed wilfully and in violation of the Conventions of the Protocol;

(a) The transfer by the Occupying Power of parts of its own civilian population into the territory it occupies, or the deportation or transfer of all or parts of the population of the occupied territory within or outside this territory, in violation of Article 49 of the Fourth Convention;

(b) Unjustifiable delay in the repatriation of prisoners of war or civilians;

(c) Practices of apartheid and other inhuman and degrading practices involving outrages upon personal dignity, based on racial discrimination;

(d) Making the clearly-recognized historic monuments, works of art or places of worship which constitute the cultural or spiritual heritage of peoples and to which special protection has been given by special arrangement, for example, within the framework of a competent international organization, the object of attack, causing as a result extensive destruction thereof, where there is no evidence of the violation by the adverse Party of Article 53, sub-paragraph (b), and when such historic monuments, works of art and places of worship are not located in the immediate proximity of military objectives:

(e) Depriving a person protected by the Conventions or referred to in paragraph 2 of this Article of the rights of fair and regular trial.

5. Without prejudice to the application of the Conventions and of this Protocol, grave breaches of these instruments shall be regarded as war crimes.

Protocol Additional to the Geneva Conventions of August 12, 1949, and Relating to the Protection of Victims of Non-International Armed Conflicts (Protocol II), June 8, 1977

PART II. HUMANE TREATMENT

Article 4 Fundamental guarantees

2. Without prejudice to the generality of the foregoing, the following acts against the persons referred to in paragraph I are and shall remain prohibited at any time and in any place whatsoever:
   (a) violence to the life, health and physical or mental well-being of persons, in particular murder as well as cruel treatment such as torture, mutilation or any form of corporal punishment;
   (b) collective punishments;
   (c) taking of hostages;
   (d) acts of terrorism;
   (e) outrages upon personal dignity, in particular humiliating and degrading treatment, rape, enforced prostitution and any form or indecent assault;
   (f) slavery and the slave trade in all their forms;
   (g) pillage;
   (h) threats to commit any or the foregoing acts

Statute of the International Criminal Tribunal for the Former Yugoslavia, May 25, 1993 (as Amended in 2003)

Article 2

Grave breaches of the Geneva Conventions of 1949

The International Tribunal shall have the power to prosecute persons committing or ordering to be committed grave breaches of the Geneva Conventions of 12 August 1949, namely the following acts against persons or property protected under the provisions of the relevant Geneva Convention:
   (a) wilful killing;
   (b) torture or inhuman treatment, including biological experiments;
   (c) wilfully causing great suffering or serious injury to body or health;
   (d) extensive destruction and appropriation of property, not justified by military necessity and carried out unlawfully and wantonly;

(e) compelling a prisoner of war or a civilian to serve in the forces of a hostile power;

(f) wilfully depriving a prisoner of war or a civilian of the rights of fair and regular trial;

(g) unlawful deportation or transfer or unlawful confinement of a civilian;

(h) taking civilians as hostages.

Article 3
Violations of the laws or customs of war

The International Tribunal shall have the power to prosecute persons violating the laws or customs of war. Such violations shall include, but not be limited to:

(a) employment of poisonous weapons or other weapons calculated to cause unnecessary suffering;

(b) wanton destruction of cities, towns or villages, or devastation not justified by military necessity;

(c) attack, or bombardment, by whatever means, of undefended towns, villages, dwellings, or buildings;

(d) seizure of, destruction or wilful damage done to institutions dedicated to religion, charity and education, the arts and sciences, historic monuments and works of art and science;

(e) plunder of public or private property.

Article 5
Crimes against humanity

The International Tribunal shall have the power to prosecute persons responsible for the following crimes when committed in armed conflict, whether international or internal in character, and directed against any civilian population:

(a) murder;

(b) extermination;

(c) enslavement;

(d) deportation;

(e) imprisonment;

(f) torture;

(g) rape;

(h) persecutions on political, racial and religious grounds;

(i) other inhumane acts.

Statute of the International Criminal Tribunal
for Rwanda, November 8, 1994

Article 3: Crimes against Humanity
The International Tribunal for Rwanda shall have the power to prosecute
persons responsible for the following crimes when committed as part of a
widespread or systematic attack against any civilian population on national,
political, ethnic, racial or religious grounds:
  (a) Murder;
  (b) Extermination;
  (c) Enslavement;
  (d) Deportation;
  (e) Imprisonment;
  (f) Torture;
  (g) Rape;
  (h) Persecutions on political, racial and religious grounds;
  (i) Other inhumane acts.

Article 4: Violations of Article 3 Common to the Geneva Conventions and of
Additional Protocol II
The International Tribunal for Rwanda shall have the power to prosecute persons committing or ordering to be committed serious violations of Article 3
common to the Geneva Conventions of 12 August 1949 for the Protection
of War Victims, and of Additional Protocol II thereto of 8 June 1977. These
violations shall include, but shall not be limited to:
  (a) Violence to life, health and physical or mental well-being of persons,
      in particular murder as well as cruel treatment such as torture, mutila-
      tion or any form of corporal punishment;
  (b) Collective punishments;
  (c) Taking of hostages;
  (d) Acts of terrorism;
  (e) Outrages upon personal dignity, in particular humiliating and de-
      grading treatment, rape, enforced prostitution and any form of inde-
      cent assault;
  (f) Pillage;
  (g) The passing of sentences and the carrying out of executions with-
      out previous judgment pronounced by a regularly constituted court,

affording all the judicial guarantees which are recognized as indispensable by civilized peoples;

(h) Threats to commit any of the foregoing acts.

Rome Statute of the International Criminal Court, Rome, July 17, 1998

Article 5

Crimes within the jurisdiction of the Court

1. The jurisdiction of the Court shall be limited to the most serious crimes of concern to the international community as a whole. The Court has jurisdiction in accordance with this Statute with respect to the following crimes:
   (a) The crime of genocide;
   (b) Crimes against humanity;
   (c) War crimes;
   (d) The crime of aggression.
2. The Court shall exercise jurisdiction over the crime of aggression once a provision is adopted in accordance with articles 121 and 123 defining the crime and setting out the conditions under which the Court shall exercise jurisdiction with respect to this crime. Such a provision shall be consistent with the relevant provisions of the Charter of the United Nations.

Article 7

Crimes against humanity

1. For the purpose of this Statute, "crime against humanity" means any of the following acts when committed as part of a widespread or systematic attack directed against any civilian population, with knowledge of the attack:
   (a) Murder;
   (b) Extermination;
   (c) Enslavement;
   (d) Deportation or forcible transfer of population;
   (e) Imprisonment or other severe deprivation of physical liberty in violation of fundamental rules of international law;
   (f) Torture;
   (g) Rape, sexual slavery, enforced prostitution, forced pregnancy,

enforced sterilization, or any other form of sexual violence of comparable gravity;

Article 8
War crimes
(b) Other serious violations of the laws and customs applicable in international armed conflict, within the established framework of international law, namely, any of the following acts:
(xvi) Pillaging a town or place, even when taken by assault
Committing rape, sexual slavery, enforced prostitution, forced pregnancy, as defined in article 7, paragraph 2 (f), enforced sterilization, or any other form of sexual violence also constituting a grave breach of the Geneva Convention
(e) Other serious violations of the laws and customs applicable in armed conflicts not of an international character, within the established framework of international law, namely, any of the following acts:
(v) Pillaging a town or place, even when taken by assault;
(vi) Committing rape, sexual slavery, enforced prostitution, forced pregnancy, as defined in article 7, paragraph 2 (f), enforced sterilization, and any other form of sexual violence also constituting a serious violation of article 3 common to the four Geneva Conventions.

Article 11
Jurisdiction ratione temporis
1. The Court has jurisdiction only with respect to crimes committed after the entry into force of this Statute.
2. If a State becomes a Party to this Statute after its entry into force, the Court may exercise its jurisdiction only with respect to crimes committed after the entry into force of this Statute for that State, unless that State has made a declaration under article 12, paragraph 3.

Article 12
Preconditions to the exercise of jurisdiction
1. A State which becomes a Party to this Statute thereby accepts the jurisdiction of the Court with respect to the crimes referred to in article 5.
2. In the case of article 13, paragraph (a) or (c), the Court may exercise its jurisdiction if one or more of the following States are Parties to this Statute or have accepted the jurisdiction of the Court in accordance with paragraph 3:

(a) The State on the territory of which the conduct in question occurred or, if the crime was committed on board a vessel or aircraft, the State of registration of that vessel or aircraft;

(b) The State of which the person accused of the crime is a national.

3. If the acceptance of a State which is not a Party to this Statute is required under paragraph 2, that State may, by declaration lodged with the Registrar, accept the exercise of jurisdiction by the Court with respect to the crime in question. The accepting State shall cooperate with the Court without any delay or exception in accordance with Part 9.

Article 36

Qualifications, nomination and election of judges

8. (a) The States Parties shall, in the selection of judges, take into account the need, within the membership of the Court, for:

(i) The representation of the principal legal systems of the world;

(ii) Equitable geographical representation; and

(iii) A fair representation of female and male judges.

(b) States Parties shall also take into account the need to include judges with legal expertise on specific issues, including, but not limited to, violence against women or children.

Article 42

The Office of the Prosecutor

9. The Prosecutor shall appoint advisers with legal expertise on specific issues, including, but not limited to, sexual and gender violence and violence against children.

Appendix B: Indicators of Legalization

Indicators of Obligation

High

Unconditional obligation; language and other indicia of intent to be legally bound
Political treaty; implicit conditions on obligation
National reservations on specific obligations; contingent obligations and escape clauses
Hortatory obligations
Norms adopted without law-making authority; recommendations and guidelines
Explicit negation of intent to be legally bound

Low

Indicators of Precision

High

Determinate rules; only narrow issues of interpretation
Substantial but limited issues of interpretation
Broad areas of discretion
"Standards"; only meaningful with reference to specific situations
Impossible to determine whether conduct complies

Low

Indicators of Delegation

a. Dispute Resolution

High

Courts: binding third-party decisions; general jurisdiction; direct private access; can interpret and supplement rules; domestic courts have jurisdiction
Courts: jurisdiction, access or normative authority limited or consensual
Binding arbitration
Nonbinding arbitration
Conciliation, mediation
Institutionalized bargaining
Pure political bargaining

Low

b. Rule Making and Implementation

High

Binding regulations; centralized enforcement
Binding regulations with consent or opt-out
Binding internal policies; legitimation of decentralized enforcement
Coordination standards
Draft conventions; monitoring and publicity
Recommendations; confidential monitoring
Normative statements
Forum for negotiation

Low

Notes

Chapter 1. Prohibition Regimes

1. Askin, *War Crimes Against Women*, 20–21. She gives the example of John of Salisbury, who attempted to regulate the conduct of justifiable wars in 1159 and considered "acts of theft and rapine-property crimes" together; 24. Also see Hirschon, *Women and Property*; Hecker, *A Short History*; Porter, "Does It Have"; Brownmiller, *Against Our Will*; Engels, *The Origin of the Family*. Charlesworth and Chinkin argue that widespread violence against women around the globe is an indication of the fact that society's concept of "women as property" still exists. Charlesworth and Chinkin, *The Boundaries*, 13. Unfortunately, clear examples of the direct association between women and property can still be found. In this respect, the fact that women are regularly bought and sold into marriage with a bride price (sometimes in the form of cattle) is striking. See Ilkkaracan, "Doğu Anadolu'da Kadın."

2. Askin, *War Crimes Against Women*, 27; Enloe, "Afterword," 220. Both rape and pillage were allowed as bonuses for soldiers.

3. Besides international relations scholars, some scholars in international law have also developed similar arguments. Charlesworth and Chinkin, for instance, argue that international law is "man-made" rather than universal and that women are on the margins of the international legal system not only because of their exclusion from the law-making process but also because it is "built on and operates to reinforce gendered and sexed assumptions." Charlesworth and Chinkin, *The Boundaries*, 18, 22, 48, 50, 312.

4. Krasner, *International Regimes*, 2.

5. Nadelmann, "Global," 479.

6. Ibid., 479.

7. Ibid., 480–81, 525.

8. Nabulsi, *Traditions*, 24.

9. See Appendix A.

10. *The Prosecutor v Akayesu.* From the twelve cases, in which the International Criminal Tribunal for the Former Yugoslavia and the International Criminal Tribunal for Rwanda dealt with the definition of rape, Anne-Marie de Brouwer derives three definitions. See de Brouwer, *Supranational Criminal Prosecution*, 105–126.

11. Krasner, *International Regimes*, 2.

12. Abbott and Snidal, "Hard and Soft Law," 421. They call highly legalized laws "hard laws."

13. Abbott et al., "The Concept of Legalization."

14. For a detailed explanation of formal versus behavioral and cognitive approaches, see Hasenclever et al., *Theories*.

15. Finnemore and Toope, "Alternatives to 'Legalization,'" 743. Customary international law results when states follow certain practices generally and consistently out of a sense of obligation that comes out of norms, which developed over time through customary exchanges among states.

16. Ibid., 745.

17. Askin traces some rare prohibitory measures on rape in war as far back as ancient times, but the most comprehensive customary law regarding this matter comes with Grotius's *On the Law of War and Peace* (1625) (or *The Rights of War and Peace*) and his laws' adoption by various nations (*War Crimes Against Women*, 22–30).

18. Abbott et al., "The Concept of Legalization," 401, 404.

19. Ibid.

20. Ibid., 406. See Table 1, "Forms of Legalization," where regimes may range from hard law to anarchy according to the degrees of obligation, precision, and delegation.

21. I use these indicators (obligation, precision, and delegation) to help determine where the prohibition regimes against pillage and rape should reside. For the indicators, see Appendix B.

22. March and Olsen, "The Institutional Dynamics," 943.

23. See Mearsheimer, "The False Promise"; Strange, "Cave!" For the distinction, see Hasenclever et al., *Theories*.

24. Finnemore, *National Interest*.

25. March and Olsen, *Rediscovering Institutions*.

26. Goldstein et al., "Introduction," 387.

27. For example, Goldstein and Keohane, *Ideas*.

28. Jervis, "Ideas."

29. March and Olsen, *Rediscovering Institutions*.

30. For example, Finnemore, *National Interest*.

31. For example, Finnemore, *National Interest*; Nadelmann, "Global"; Price, "Reversing."

32. Price, *The Chemical Weapons*.

33. Nadelmann, "Global," 480.

34. Ibid., 481–82.

35. Some examples include Adler and Haas, "Epistemic Communities"; Haas, "Epistemic Communities"; Goldstein and Keohane, *Ideas*; Young, "The Effectiveness."

36. Ashley, "The Poverty of Neorealism"; Kratochwil and Ruggie, "International Organization"; Wendt and Duvall, "Institutions"; Müller, "Arguing."

37. Von Glahn, *The Occupation*, 3.

38. I derived the definition by using Cass Sunstein's discussion on social norms, social meanings and self-conception. Sunstein, *Free Markets*, 38–50.

39. See Finnemore and Sikkink, "International Norm Dynamics," for constitutive and regulative norms.

40. I derive the concept from the shock hypothesis of Kowert and Legro, "Norms," 473.

41. Meron uses a similar understanding of shock to explain the emergence of new international laws. See Meron, *War Crimes*, 204.

42. Young, "The Politics," 371–72.

43. McNamara, *The Currency of Ideas*, 84. For the impact of the devastating experience of policy failure in the interwar period on this dramatic policy shift, she cites Gourevitch, *Politics*. Also see Ikenberry, "Creating Yesterday's New World Order," for the impact of the normative context or a "new thinking," as he calls it, on the emergence of Keynesianism as the alternative policy.

44. Legro, *Rethinking*, 11.

45. Kowert and Legro, "Norms," 473.

46. Berger, "Norms."

47. Meron, *War Crimes*, 143.

48. For example, the deportation of one million Russians to Siberia in the nineteenth century, Jews from Moscow and Rostov-on-Don (1891–92), or the entire Muslim population in the Black Sea region of Russia and the Caucasus (starting in the early nineteenth century). See Polian, *Making Women*.

49. Kowert and Legro, "Norms," 473–74. They give the example of the Japanese attack on Pearl Harbor as a shock reinforcing American identity.

50. We see a discussion of the relationship between exogenous shocks or crises and epistemic communities in Haas, "Introduction," 14.

51. I am not trying to suggest that in the case of exogenous shocks there is only one direction that the norm can take and that norm entrepreneurs and experts have no effect on it. For example, after the shock of the Great Depression, the direction of economic policy change was affected by what was available as an alternative. The Keynesian model was available as an alternative, and it was taken seriously only after the dramatic policy failures of the Depression. See Odell, *U.S. International Monetary Policy*, 371–72.

52. The invisibility of women's human rights abuses up to the present day is one example of the possibility of selectivity among policy makers about what counts as a shock. Mass rape in war is not a new phenomenon, but it was never able to provide the necessary shock until the 1990s. A similar pattern may be found in environmental issues: though there can be more obvious shocks, in many cases epistemic communities contribute to the creation of the shock with scientific advances or reports capturing public attention (Haas, "Introduction," 14). In the security area, shocks are usually obvious, for example, the Second World War's devastating effects on Germany and Japan, but the direction of norm change (or sustenance) is more indeterminate.

53. Florini, "The Evolution," 375.

54. Rochon, *Culture Moves.*

55. Legro, *Rethinking*, 28, 163.

56. Florini, "The Evolution," 376. This is what Florini calls "coherence."

57. Nadelmann, "Global," 493.

58. Florini, "The Evolution," 377.

59. Price, "Reversing," 628.

60. The reason I distinguish the cost-benefit structure as a separate level is purely analytical, since I argue that the cost-benefit considerations of states are not independent of the normative context they are situated in, which includes their identities. See, for example, Katzenstein, *The Culture*; Finnemore, *National Interest*; Wendt, *Social Theory.*

61. In the nineteenth century, the word *publicist* meant "those learned men, philosophers with a practical bent, who specialized in what we now call public international law and international relations." See Nabulsi, *Traditions*, 158.

62. Clark, *Women's Silence.*

63. Using women as a category to look at the gendered structure of the international system is sometimes criticized as essentializing. However, it is a necessary move because of its powerful theoretical and political potential. See Charlesworth and Chinkin, *The Boundaries*, 55.

64. Enloe, *Bananas*; Enloe, *The Morning After*; Grant and Newland, *Gender*; Pateman, *The Sexual Contract*; Peterson, *Gendered States*; Tickner, *Gender in International Relations*; Kenney, "New Research."

65. See Elshtain, *Women and War*; Tickner, *Gender in International Relations*. It is possible to see the exclusion of women particularly from international politics, even in the UN Women's Conferences. As late as 1980, during the Second World Conference on Women in Copenhagen, women delegates were pushed aside by their male counterparts whenever the introductory and international sections of the documents were being discussed. Fraser, *The UN Decade*, 48.

66. Kenney, "New Research."

67. Joachim, *Agenda Setting.*

68. Mallock, *Aristocracy*, 84. He describes Herbert Spencer's depiction of the Napoleonic Wars, but the list of disasters is his. For rape and pillage during some of the battles in the Napoleonic Wars, see Fletcher, *In Hell*; Fremont-Barnes, *The Napoleonic Wars.*

69. Mearsheimer, "The False Promise"; Strange, "Cave!"; Goldsmith and Posner, *The Limits.*

70. See Abbott and Snidal, "Hard and Soft Law," 447–48.

71. Scott, *The Proceedings, 1899*, 517.

72. Keohane, *After Hegemony.*

73. The argument here is about states' ability to abide by a treaty rather than their intention to do so, which is what is argued in Downs et al., "Is the Good News About Compliance."

74. The arguments about the reputation effects of regime violations are considered by both interest-based and knowledge-based approaches, though in different terms.

See Keohane, *After Hegemony*; Axelrod and Keohane, "Achieving Cooperation"; Stein, *Why Nations Cooperate*; Simmons, "International Law"; Bull, *The Anarchical Society*; Franck, *The Power of Legitimacy*; Hurrell, "International Society." While interest-based approaches see reputation concerns as rational investments for possible future cooperation and gains, knowledge-based approaches emphasize the normative aspects. I do not think the two are separable. In other words, a state not wanting to commit to a treaty it is bound to violate because it does not want to be known as a violator feel repelled not only by the idea of law-breaking as not "appropriate" behavior but also because it include the costs of this behavior on the regime and its future relations with others in its calculations, being aware of the "consequences." See Kelley, "Who Keeps," for the integration of these factors.

75. Abbott and Snidal, "Hard and Soft Law," 428.

76. Scott, *The Proceedings, 1899*, 351.

77. Axelrod and Keohane (1985) cited in Morrow, "When Do States Follow," 561.

78. Scott, *The Proceedings, 1899*, 506.

79. Ibid., 496.

80. Abbott and Snidal, "Hard and Soft Law," 445.

81. We need to realize that "military necessity" as an excuse to violate laws of war is related to states' national interests and the desire to leave an open door in the laws of war so that one can ignore them when "necessary." But in spite of the use of this obscure concept in many treaties, the bare need of any excuse or justification for violation indicates the normative force as a source for "distaste" among members of international society. See Kratochwil and Ruggie, "International Organization"; Kratochwil, *Rules*; Reus-Smith, "Introduction."

82. When a crime is called a "grave breach," states become obliged to search for persons alleged to have committed the crime and to bring them before courts if found in their territory.

83. The earliest known example of such a prohibition is English king Richard II's proclamation in 1385. Brownmiller also mentions a possible example from 546 A.D., a prohibition by the Ostrogoths who captured Rome, but the sources are insufficient to give the exact details. See Brownmiller, *Against Our Will*, 34.

84. Brownmiller, *Against Our Will*, 37–38.

85. For instance, in the eleventh century, William the Conqueror, king of England, reduced the sentence for rape from death to castration and loss of eyes—because the rapist's eyes, which "gave him the sight of the virgin's beauty for which he coveted her," and his testicles, which "excited his hot lust," had to be taken away as punishment. This shows how people understood rape as originating from passion for the beautiful woman rather than desire to dominate violently. Burgess-Jackson, "A History of Rape Law," 17.

86. This does not mean that understanding of rape as a sexual act disappeared after the nineteenth century. In the twentieth century, especially with the influence of Darwinism, the male-centric idea of "rape as an instinctual sexual act" gained a new perspective. In academia (and probably in the general public) there are still people who

advocate that rape is a sexual act with roots in the evolution of human species. For example, see Thornhill and Palmer, *A Natural History*. In their attempt to make a case for the evolutionary basis of rape, they also argue that rape in war is sexually motivated and that the vulnerability of women during wartime due to the absence of male protectors explains its prevalence (134). Also see Ellis, *Theories*, for different theories of rape; Burgess-Jackson, "A History of Rape Law," for different perspectives on rape laws; Burgess-Jackson, *Rape*, for the philosophical debate over whether rape is an act of violence or sex.

87. Donat and D'Emilio, "A Feminist Redefinition," 37–38.

88. Edwards, *Female Sexuality*, 107–8.

89. Ibid., 108.

90. Butler Committee Report, 1975, cited in ibid., 108.

91. Brownmiller, *Against Our Will*, 103. The statement was made at a court-martial by the superior officer of a sergeant who led his squad to gang-rape and murder a Vietnamese girl in 1966.

92. Morris, "By Force," 676.

93. Copelon, "Surfacing Gender," 197.

94. Barkan, "As Old as War Itself."

95. Enloe, *Maneuvers*, 108.

96. "Comfort women" is used to describe thousands of women (from various Asian countries under Japanese occupation) who were forced into prostitution by the Japanese military during World War II.

97. See Appendix A.

98. Feilchenfeld, *The International Economic Law*, 30.

99. See Appendix A.

100. Scott, *The Proceedings, 1907*, 3: 13, 140–43.

101. Renault, "The Work at The Hague," 152.

102. See Appendix B.

103. Renault, "The Work at The Hague," 152.

104. See Appendix B.

105. The Hague Conventions established a mechanism of international arbitration for settlement of disputes between states (through the Convention for the Pacific Settlement of International Disputes (Hague I)), but it was established for the purpose of settling disputes before war happens rather than prosecuting the violations of Laws and Customs of War on Land (Hague II).

106. See Appendix A.

107. Graber, *The Development*, 34–35. Also see Higgins, *The Hague*, 260–61.

108. See Appendix B.

109. See Appendix A.

110. As for a detailed description of what counts as pillage, the Geneva Conventions do not go into much detail, but since those descriptions had been put into international law previously by the Hague Conventions, there is no need to look for a repetition there.

111. See Appendix A.

112. See Appendix B.

113. Some scholars argue that this clause can be regarded as a prohibition on rape because by the time of the Hague Conventions, rape was already considered a violation of customary international law, and if the will to punish rape had been present, states could have brought rape charges at Nuremberg and Tokyo using this provision. See Askin, *War Crimes against Women*, 40. However, this is precisely the problem with imprecision: it leaves too much to the will of the states, which makes creating international laws pointless.

114. See Appendix A.

115. See Appendix B.

116. Gardam, "Women and Law," 57; Charlesworth and Chinkin, *The Boundaries*, 314.

117. See Appendix A.

118. See Appendix B.

119. See Appendix B.

120. There are many pre-1949 domestic documents, but no international legal ones, prohibiting rape.

121. See Appendix A.

122. See Appendix B.

123. See Appendix A for a list of grave breaches in Article 147. For the implications of the exclusion of rape from grave breaches, see Charlesworth and Chinkin, *The Boundaries*, 315–16.

124. See Appendix A.

125. See Appendix A.

126. See Appendix B.

127. See Appendix B.

128. See Appendix A.

Chapter 2. The Prohibition of Pillage in War

1. Redlich, *De Praeda Militari*, 3, 5, 19–20. Redlich talks about texts written as late as 1737 that deemed seizure of enemy property lawful.

2. Sutcliffe (1595) cited in Redlich, *De Praeda Militari*, 20.

3. Grotius, *The Rights*, Book III, Chapter 5.

4. Ibid., 1303–4.

5. Redlich, *De Praeda Militari*, 37.

6. Grotius, *The Rights*, 1300.

7. See Appendix A.

8. Hogue, "Lieber's Military Code," 52.

9. Freidel, *Francis Lieber*, 326–32.

10. Hogue, "Lieber's Military Code," 55; Raymond, "Lieber," 69; Glazier, "Ignorance," 148–49.

11. Graber, *The Development*, 19.

12. Hogue, "Lieber's Military Code," 51–52; Johnson, "Lieber," 66.

13. Johnson, "Lieber," 65.

14. Freidel, *Francis Lieber*, 318–19.

15. Freidel, *Francis Lieber*, 335–37; Hogue, "Lieber's Military Code," 55.

16. Raymond, "Lieber," 72.

17. *Actes de la Conférence de Bruxelles 1874*, 26. It is also known that some of the leading people involved in the Brussels Conference were friends of Lieber. See Glazier, "Ignorance," 160.

18. Graber, *The Development*, 20; Pustogarov, "Fyodor Fyodorovich Martens." The German delegate's impression at The Hague in 1899 was that Martens's vision of the laws of war derived comprehensively from Lieber's Code. See Nabulsi, *Traditions*, 161.

19. Pustogarov, "Fyodor Fyodorovich Martens"; Davis, *The United States and the First Hague*, 126.

20. Grabar, *The History*, 382; Pustogarov, "Fyodor Fyodorovich Martens."

21. Grabar, *The History*, 386.

22. Nabulsi, *Traditions*, 168. She also puts Lieber on the list of these publicists.

23. Pustogarov, "Fyodor Fyodorovich Martens." For more on the peace movement in nineteenth-century Europe, see Cooper, *Patriotic Pacifism*.

24. For a detailed account of each power's position, see Nabulsi, *Traditions*, 5–8.

25. Graber, *The Development*, 21.

26. Pustogarov, "Fyodor Fyodorovich Martens."

27. Graber, *The Development*, 199.

28. Article 17 of the draft code: "A city taken by assault should not be given over for pillage by the victorious troops." *Actes de la Conférence de Bruxelles 1874*, 15.

29. Ibid., 20 (my translation).

30. Ibid., 353 (my translation).

31. Ibid., 207 (my translation). The French words in the original document are "butin" versus "pillage" and "doit être" versus "est."

32. Ibid., 207–8.

33. Ibid., 274 (my translation).

34. Ibid., 58.

35. The original draft said "ne doit pas." He proposed "ne peut pas"; ibid., 249.

36. See Graber, *The Development*, 23–24.

37. Pustogarov, "Fyodor Fyodorovich Martens."

38. Graber, *The Development*, 24–25.

39. Scott, *The Proceedings, 1899*, 504.

40. Nabulsi, *Traditions*, 6.

41. Graber, *The Development*, 27.

42. Ibid., 28.

43. For example, in 1893 he advised on a dispute between Greece and Romania about the succession of immovable property in Romania. See Grabar, *The History*, 384.

44. Best, "Peace Conferences," 620, 622.

45. "Peace Conference at The Hague 1899: Russian Circular Note Proposing the Programme of the First Conference, January 11, 1899 (New Style) (December 30, 1898, Old Style)," in Rosenne, *The Hague*, 24–26.

46. Pustogarov, "Fyodor Fyodorovich Martens." Also see Nabulsi, *Traditions*, 7, 11 for an alternative view on Martens's motivations for contributing to the Brussels Declaration and the Hague Regulations, i.e., serving the needs of the Russian army. This position, however, is not well supported.

47. Scott, *The Proceedings, 1899,* 416–17.

48. Ibid., 417.

49. Ibid., 427.

50. In 2000, Bulgaria, the Republic of Korea, and Zambia and in 2001 Macedonia acceded to the 1907 Convention. Rosenne, *The Hague*.

51. Nabulsi, *Traditions*, 167.

52. Ibid., 8.

53. Ibid., 9.

54. Best, "Peace Conferences," 620.

55. Ibid., 620–21.

56. Nabulsi, *Traditions*, 10. It should also be noted that the Second Conference in 1907 was called due to the efforts of civil society groups in the United States. Peace societies, in particular, convinced President Theodore Roosevelt to convoke the conference. See Hull, *The Two Hague Conferences*, 4–5.

57. In 1907, the public would be allowed to participate in the conference, but their participation was still limited.

58. Best, "Peace Conferences," 623–25.

59. Ibid., 624, 627. Nabulsi argues that Martens plagiarized the Martens Clause from Baron Lambermont. See Nabulsi, *Traditions*, 161. This puts Martens's ethics into question, though it does not change the fact that the law was saved by the efforts of a publicist.

60. Feilchenfeld, *The International Economic Law*, 30.

61. See Appendix A.

62. See Appendix A.

63. Redlich, *De Praeda Militari*, 37.

64. Ibid., 2–3.

65. Ibid., 58–59.

66. Woloch, *Eighteenth-Century Europe*, 51; Redlich, *De Praeda Militari*, 59–62.

67. Redlich, *De Praeda Militari*, 6–7.

68. Some examples are the armies of the Holy Roman Empire and Spain in the sixteenth century, as well as the Polish army, English army, and Swedish army in the seventeenth century. See Redlich, *De Praeda Militari*, 9–10.

69. Redlich, *De Praeda Militari*, 14.

70. Ibid., 14.

71. Contributions are in money; requisitions are in goods and services. See Graber, *The Development*, 217.

72. Redlich, *De Praeda Militari*, 60.

73. Ibid., 61.

74. Jurists only debated whether the "justness" of the war affects the pillage practice. Some claimed pillage is only permissible if the war is "just," while others said they are unrelated things. See Redlich, *De Praeda Militari*, 20.

75. Johnson, "Lieber," 62; Spadafora, *The Idea of Progress*, 9.

76. Johnson, "Lieber," 62.

77. Griffith, *The Art of War*, 57–58.

78. Ibid., 58. Also see Duffy, *The Military Experience*, 10–13 for the physical, political, and ethical constraints imposed on eighteenth-century warfare. "Style and restraint" were at the foundation of the eighteenth century's characteristics, and they found their way into the conduct of war as well (3–4, 304–5).

79. Duffy, *The Military Experience*, 15.

80. According to Redlich, the first doubts about the legitimacy of pillage also appeared in the eighteenth century. Redlich, *De Praeda Militari*, 26.

81. Feilchenfeld, *The International Economic Law*, 10–13. Although the ideas legitimizing private property started to emerge in the sixteenth and seventeenth centuries, the process gained momentum in the eighteenth century.

82. See Higgins, *War*.

83. Graber, *The Development*, 14; Higgins, *War*, 11–12; Redlich, *De Praeda Militari*, 79. It is also significant that Europeans codified in international law a "standard of civilization" associating liberal ideals with legitimate statehood; protection of the individual by the state therefore became part of the definition of a civilized state. See Reus-Smith, "Introduction," 33–34.

84. Redlich, *De Praeda Militari*, 72–76.

85. Spadafora, *The Idea of Progress*, 297.

86. Ryan, *Property*, 32.

87. Smith, *An Inquiry*, 456–57. Smith discusses the behavior of slaves versus *métayers* here in order to show how being able to gain your own property as a result of your labor makes a difference in terms of increasing overall production. This kind of reasoning will become a dominant way of thinking in the nineteenth century utilitarianism. Utilitarianism also justifies private property on the basis of its contribution to economic efficiency, and therefore general happiness of the society. See Ryan, *Property*, 103.

88. Ryan, *Property*, 95, 98.

89. See Smith, *An Inquiry*, 158, 196.

90. Ryan, *Property*, 104.

91. Rousseau, *Discourse*, Part II.

92. Wagar, "Modern Views," 55.

93. Lovejoy and Boas (1935), cited in Wagar, "Modern Views," 55.

94. Bury, *The Idea of Progress*, 2.

95. Wagar, "Modern Views," 62.

96. Inge, *Outspoken Essays*, 161.

97. Wagar, *Good Tidings*, 4.

98. Bury, *The Idea of Progress*, 206.

99. Ibid., 220.

100. Inge, *Outspoken Essays*, 162.

101. Wagar, "Modern Views," 56–57.

102. Spadafora, *The Idea of Progress*, 2.

103. Woloch, *Eighteenth-Century Europe*, 8; Redlich, *De Praeda Militari*, 63–64.

104. Grotius, *The Rights*, 1531.

105. Redlich, *De Praeda Militari*, 63.

106. See, for example, Rousseau, *The Social Contract*, Book I, Chapter 4.

107. Redlich, *De Praeda Militari*, 64–65.

108. For pillage and contributions, see Graber, *The Development*, 235–36. By the late nineteenth century, although the majority opinion was that requisitions and contributions violate the principle of the sanctity of private property and should be abandoned, for practical reasons they were retained but strictly regulated by law. Graber, *The Development*, 256.

109. Redlich, *De Praeda Militari*, 65–67, 70–71. Looting was done by individual soldiers while contributions and foraging were collected by the state.

110. Ibid., 72, 75–76.

111. Ibid., 76.

112. Griffith, *The Art of War*, 55.

113. Ibid., 55–57. Also see Quynn, "The Art Confiscations," 438, 440–41, 443.

114. Griffith, *The Art of War*, 58; Blanning, *The French Revolution*, 318–19.

115. Von Müffling, *The Memoirs*, 22–23.

116. Ibid., 388.

117. Redlich, *De Praeda Militari*, 76–77.

118. Johnson, "Lieber," 62.

119. Redlich, *De Praeda Militari*, 78.

120. Griffith, *The Art of War*, 52.

121. Ibid., 58.

122. Magazines were the depots where goods and ammunition necessary for the army were stored.

123. Griffith, *The Art of War*, 55.

124. Nabulsi, *Traditions*, 22.

125. Griffith, *The Art of War*, 55.

126. Ibid., 55. See also Quynn, "The Art Confiscations," 440, for Napoleon's incitement for constant search for booty.

127. Griffith, *The Art of War*, 52.

128. Redlich, *De Praeda Militari*, 76–77.

129. Von Müffling, *The Memoirs*, 118.

130. Ibid., 470–71.

131. Ibid..

132. Ibid., 513.

133. "The League of Nations and the Laws of War," 844.

134. Ibid., 846. The pillage of artwork should also be mentioned in this context, since it was one of the most widespread forms of pillage during the Napoleonic Wars. Although artwork was taken by the state, it was pillage (not requisition) because it was not for meeting the needs of the army or the administration of the occupied territories, and there was no plan of returning it or providing restitution. In fact, Napoleon rationalized the pillage by saying that all great artists and minds are French; they just happened to be born elsewhere. Therefore, their works belonged in Paris. See Quynn, "The Art Confiscations," 439.

135. Redlich, *De Praeda Militari*, 78.

136. Bentwich, *The Law of Private Property*, 26–27.

137. Johnson, "Lieber," 62–63.

138. Ibid., 66.

139. The Concert of Europe was the Congress System established by the great powers in Europe. The idea was for the great powers to meet periodically to discuss the political situation in Europe so that they can prevent another widespread war like the Napoleonic Wars.

140. Feilchenfeld, *The International Economic Law*, 10.

141. See Graber, *The Development*.

142. The Hague Conventions (1899), Articles 28, 46, and 47. See Appendix A.

143. Graber, *The Development*, 290.

144. Ibid., 290.

145. Ibid., 291.

146. Ibid., 35.

147. White, *The Hague*, 6, 20. Also see Davis, *The United States and the First Hague*.

148. Ibid., 40–41.

149. Ibid., 68.

150. Scott, *The Proceedings, 1899*, 488. The article would be modified once again before it took its final form, but the double emphasis on private property, as well as the vagueness of family rights and honor, would stay the same. See Appendix A.

151. Scott, *The Proceedings, 1907*, v.III, 128.

152. Ibid., 128.

153. Graber, *The Development*, 214, 215.

154. Ibid., 216.

155. Spadafora, *The Idea of Progress*.

156. Inge, *Outspoken Essays*, 164.

157. Ibid., 169–70.

158. Ibid., 174.

159. Trustram, "Distasteful," 155–56.

160. Nabulsi, *Traditions*, 164.

161. Raymond, "Lieber," 70.

162. *Proceedings at the Laying of a Wreath on the Tomb of Hugo Grotius*, 13.

163. Ibid., 18.

164. Ibid., 15.

165. Ibid., 22.

166. Ibid., 22.

167. Ibid., 24.

168. Andrew White mentions Francis Lieber, who wrote the code for making American Civil War more humane, as the leading disciple of Grotius. Ibid., 17.

169. Ibid., 26–27.

170. President of the Institute of International Law and Netherlands delegate to the Conference T. M. C. Asser mentioned the United States as having the opportunity of establishing liberal and humane principles of international law on various occasions. Ibid., 42–43.

171. White, *The Hague*, 6.

172. *Proceedings at the Laying of a Wreath on the Tomb of Hugo Grotius*, 31–32.

173. Preamble of the Hague Conventions II (1899) in Scott, *The Hague Conventions*, 101–2.

174. Gregory Raymond makes this distinction between principles, norms, and rules, which may be helpful in clarifying how regimes develop. Raymond, "Problems and Prospects," 218–19.

175. See Appendix A.

176. The Geneva Conventions do not go into much detail about what counts as pillage, but since descriptions had been put into international law previously by the Hague Conventions, there is no need to look for a repetition in Geneva.

177. See Appendix B.

178. *Revised and New Draft Conventions for the Protection of War Victims*, Texts Approved and Amended by the XVIIth International Red Cross Conference, Geneva, August 1948, 118, 123 (ICRC-A). These two are not the only articles related to the protection of property. Articles 46, 97, and 98 are as well, although they deal with separate issues such as the property of internees or the restrictions on the use of property.

179. Diplomatic Conference of Geneva, *Committee III (Civilians Convention) meetings*, Twelfth meeting, May 10, 1949 (SFA).

180. *The Report of Committee III to the Plenary Assembly of the Diplomatic Conference of Geneva*, July 27, 1949, 23 (SFA).

181. Diplomatic Conference of Geneva, *Committee III (Civilians Convention) meetings*, Thirty-first meeting, June 16, 1949 (SFA).

182. *Fourth Report of the Special Committee of the Joint Committee*, Report on Penal Sanctions, July 12, 1949, 9 (SFA).

183. *The Report of Committee III*.

Chapter 3. The (Non) Prohibition of Rape in War: The Hague Conventions

1. Brownmiller, *Against Our Will*. Her history begins with the ancient Hebrews, works through the ancient Greeks, the Roman Empire, the Crusades, World War I and World War II, and ends with 1970s Bangladesh and Vietnam cases.

2. Patricia Sellars (the Office of the Prosecutor's Legal Office on Gender Issues in ICTY), cited in . . . *And the First on Rape and Sexual Assault Charges Since Tokyo*, 1.

3. See Card, "Rape as a Weapon of War."

4. Brownmiller, *Against Our Will*, 38.

5. For instance, rapes of German women by Soviet troops in 1945 were largely acts of revenge to counter the rapes of Russian women by the Germans earlier in the war. German women were also the easiest targets for the bitter Russian soldiers' humiliation by their own officers throughout the war. See Anonymous, *A Woman in Berlin*, xix. For other examples, see Card, "Rape as a Weapon of War"; Seifert, "War and Rape"; Tomaselli and Porter, *Rape*.

6. . . . *And the First on Rape and Sexual Assault Charges Since Tokyo*.

7. As will be seen in more detail in Chapter 4, the definition of rape as an outrage on women's honor in the Geneva Conventions (1949) was changed in 1977's Protocol Additional II, where rape was defined as an outrage upon personal dignity. See Appendix A.

8. Anonymous, *A Woman in Berlin*, xv.

9. That is why historically the expression "the rape of country/city X" is used to indicate not only the rapes of women during the conquest of that country or city but also the pillages or the conquest itself. For example "the rape of Nanking," "the rape of Europa," "the rape of Europe," "the rape of Russia," or "the rape of Iraq."

10. Ellis, *Theories*; Scheffer, "Rape as War Crime."

11. Especially in the case of rape, not mentioning the word *rape* in law codes is considered critical by some feminists because the word has a "unique indignity," and replacing it with other words, they believe, obscures the seriousness of the act. See Estrich, *Real Rape*, 81.

12. Askin, *War Crimes against Women*, 39. Davis says that the first Hague Peace Conference's (1899) discussions on the laws of war on land required relatively little effort because the commission revised the Brussels Declaration (1874) and practically turned it into a convention. Davis, *United States and the Second Hague*, 27. But given that the Declaration of Brussels, which also does not mention rape, was based on the Lieber Code (1863) (see Graber, *The Development*, 20; Carnahan, "Lincoln," 215), the question may be why did the drafters of the Brussels Declaration exclude rape?

13. Graber, *The Development*, 192–94.

14. Bugnion, "The Arrival."

15. Graber, *The Development*, 20; Pustogarov, "Fyodor Fyodorovich Martens."

16. *Actes de la Conférence de Bruxelles 1874*, 20 (my translation).

17. Ibid., 207.

18. Ibid., 20 (my translation).

19. Ibid., 20 (my translation).

20. Ibid., 274, 382 (my translation).

21. Hogue, "Lieber's Military Code," 58–59.

22. Scott, *The Proceedings, 1899*, 488.

23. Ibid.

24. Ibid.

25. Chevalier Descamps (Belgium) and Mr. Rolin (Siam) in particular opposed the amendment. Ibid.

26. Ibid. The article would be modified once again before it took its final form, but the double emphasis on private property, as well as the vagueness of family honor and rights, would stay the same. See Appendix A.

27. Graber, *The Development*, 215–16.

28. Scott, *The Proceedings, 1899*, 502.

29. Perrin, *Dr. Bowdler's*, 9–17. Also see Edwards, *Female Sexuality*, 27.

30. The words *violation* or *violate* are used three times in The Hague IV. See Articles 3, 40, and 41.

31. Scott, *The Proceedings, 1899*, 276.

32. Ibid., 276–78, 286–87. Also see 343–48 for the prior debates in the subcommission meeting.

33. Ibid., 278–79.

34. Ibid., 500.

35. Ibid., 500–502, 504.

36. Vogel, "Whose Property," 164.

37. Ibid., 149–50.

38. Mill, *The Subjection of Women*, 57.

39. Shanley, *Feminism*, 8.

40. Engels, *The Origin of the Family*, 128–35, 137–38.

41. Smart, "Disruptive Bodies," 8, 11, 13. This idea of women's powerlessness was used for much different legislation. In 1874, for the reinstitution of flogging, "Colonel Egerton Leigh rose in the House of Commons to ask the government to impose increased punishment for crimes of violence against women," and then he said, "he was merely seeking 'fair play for the fairer sex.'" Shanley, *Feminism*, 162.

42. Smart, "Disruptive Bodies," 24, 25.

43. Shanley, *Feminism*, 37–38.

44. Ibid., 40.

45. Vogel, "Whose Property," 159.

46. This understanding of the need to regulate the female rather than the male body is interesting in terms of understanding why the international laws on rape are so vague or nonexistent.

47. Mr. Justice Hawkins in *R v. Clarence* (1888), cited in Edwards, *Female Sexuality*, 34.

48. Shanley, *Feminism*, 185.

49. Ibid., 42.

50. See Desan, *The Family*.

51. Vigarello, *A History of Rape*, 126.

52. Mainardi, *Husbands*, 9.

53. Ibid., 2–3. Mainardi regards Dumas's description as oversimplified because of the regional differences in French inheritance laws, though she finds his analysis on the obsession about adultery accurate.

54. McBride, "Public Authority," *750*.

55. Offen, "The Theory," 341.

56. Perkin, *Women and Marriage*, 23.

57. Ibid., 24.

58. Vogel, "Whose Property," 149.

59. Perkin, *Women and Marriage*, 24.

60. Vogel, "Whose Property," 160; Shanley, *Feminism*, 24; Edwards, *Female Sexuality*, 32–33.

61. Vogel, "Whose Property," 148.

62. Susan Moller Okin focuses on Rousseau's writings regarding women as representative of the whole Western tradition, specifically his obsession with establishing paternity and the requirement of the subjugation of women as the unlimitedly powerful sex in the area of sexuality. Okin, *Women*, 99–101.

63. Vogel, "Whose Property," 151–53. Prussia also changed its civil code to the detriment of women after the Napoleonic Wars to secure the wife's special obligation of chastity and to insulate the bourgeois family against the consequences of men's sexual freedom. Vogel, "Whose Property," 154, 159.

64. Shanley, *Feminism*, 22–23. However, there was a loophole in common law that permitted the setting up of trusts that allowed women to own and govern their property by the laws and courts of equity. See Reiss, *Rights and Duties*.

65. Shanley, *Feminism*, 15–16.

66. Ibid., 108.

67. See, for example, Holcombe, *Wives*, for the role of the women's movement in the change of English laws regarding married women's property.

68. Shanley, *Feminism*, 163.

69. Clark, *Women's Silence*, 14.

70. Mill, "Enfranchisement of Women," 105.

71. Shanley, *Feminism*, 166–67.

72. Cobbe (1878) cited in Shanley, *Feminism*, 166.

73. Shanley, *Feminism*, 43.

74. Mainardi, *Husbands*, 7.

75. It is also necessary to consider the role race played in the issue of rape, especially in the cases of European colonies. Pamela Scully points out the fact that in the nineteenth century, both people of color and some working-class whites were classified under the racial classification of "the colored," and the color of the victim determined

the presence or the severity of the punishments in the cases of rape. Scully, *Liberating*, 154–56.

76. Smart, "Disruptive Bodies," 26.

77. Clark, *Women's Silence*, 59.

78. Ibid., 3.

79. Ibid., 3–4.

80. Smith, "Social Revolution," 33. She argues that although the idea that women are property started to change in nineteenth-century England with the influence of legal changes such as the Married Women's Property Act that allowed women to own property themselves, women were still viewed as "sex objects" and "prey."

81. Smith, "Social Revolution," 33; Clark, "Rape or Seduction," 14–16; Edwards, *Female Sexuality*, 35, 53–55.

82. Clark, "Rape or Seduction," 17–18.

83. Clark, *Women's Silence*, 5.

84. Clark, "Rape or Seduction," 19. Also see Clark, *Women's Silence*, 6, 88.

85. Clark, "Rape or Seduction," 17.

86. Clark, *Women's Silence*, 67–69.

87. Ibid., 6–7, 59, 61.

88. Ibid., 62.

89. Edwards, *Female Sexuality*, 27–28, 50.

90. Clark, *Women's Silence*, 8, 59–60, 63. Ignorance of sexual matters on the part of women was considered a characteristic of "civilized society." Edwards, *Female Sexuality*, 27.

91. Clark, "Rape or Seduction," 25.

92. Clark, *Women's Silence*, 80.

93. *Morning Chronicle*, August 3, 1826, cited in Clark, *Women's Silence*, 63.

94. Clark, *Women's Silence*, 64–66.

95. Edwards, *Female Sexuality*, 121–25; Clark, "Rape or Seduction," 17.

96. Clark, *Women's Silence*, 71–72.

97. Clark, "Rape or Seduction," 20.

98. Ibid., 20.

99. Ibid., 26. Also see Edwards, *Female Sexuality*, 136–48.

100. Clark, "Rape or Seduction," 23–24.

101. Vigarello, *A History of Rape*, 13.

102. Ibid., 14.

103. Ibid., 7, 9, 16, 18.

104. Ibid., 15–16.

105. Jousse, *Traité de la justice criminelle de France*, cited in Vigarello, *A History of Rape*, 17.

106. Vigarello, *A History of Rape*, 20–22.

107. Ibid., 30.

108. Ibid., 32–33.

109. Ibid., 112.

110. Ibid., 107–8.

111. Ibid., 105, 121–22. "Indecent assault" is another term that could have been used instead of "rape" in the Hague Regulations—if the real concern was delicate language.

112. Ibid., 116–18.

113. Ibid., 126.

114. Ibid., 148, 151, 154.

115. Ibid., 148–51.

116. Ibid., 177–78.

117. Ibid., 187.

118. Burgess-Jackson, "A History of Rape Law," 15.

119. Walters, *Feminism*, 41.

120. Shanley, *Feminism*, 10, 187.

121. Okin, *Women*, 202; Shanley, *Feminism*, 10–12. Also see Elshtain, *Public Man.*

122. Okin, *Women*, 233–47, 281.

123. Ibid., 282.

124. Mill, *The Subjection of Women*, 82, 193–94.

125. Ibid., 84–85.

126. Bevacqua, *Rape*, 19–20.

127. Ibid., 21–25.

128. Jeffreys, "'Free from All," 631–32.

129. Ibid., 636–39.

130. Moses, *French Feminism*, 84–85.

131. In 1840 American feminists, who had first organized under abolitionism (the anti-slavery movement), went to London to attend the World Anti-Slavery Conference, but they were not allowed to participate in the assembly. This situation motivated the American feminists to hold the Seneca Falls Convention eight years later. See Bolt, *The Women's Movements*, 68.

132. Anderson, "The Lid Comes Off."

133. See Rupp, *Worlds of Women.*

134. "The Hague Appeal for Peace."

135. The International Woman Suffrage Alliance would change its name to International Alliance of Women in the late 1920s.

136. Rupp, "Constructing Internationalism," 1584.

137. Oldfield, *International Woman Suffrage*, V.I, 213.

138. Ibid., 213.

139. Oldfield, *International Woman Suffrage*, V.II, 89.

140. Joachim, *Agenda Setting*, 45.

141. Brownmiller, *Against Our Will*, 40.

142. Donat and D'Emilio, "A Feminist Redefinition," 37. Even the language used in place of rape in the nineteenth century indicates the trivialization of the rapists' actions: "seduction, attempted ravishment and indecent or outrageous assault." See Edwards, *Female*

Sexuality, 121. The trivialization in the twentieth century is done through distinguishing between "ordinary rape" without "mitigating or aggravating features" and grave cases, which involve "violence" such as choking or using a knife. Edwards, *Female Sexuality*, 157.

143. Geddes and Thomson (1899) cited in Edwards, *Female Sexuality*, 24.

144. Edwards, *Female Sexuality*, 53.

145. At the same time, these assumptions raised expectations that women should defend themselves against that aggression, particularly by placing themselves under the protection of their fathers or husbands (thus the confinement in the private sphere), which all chaste women were expected to do.

146. Smith, "Social Revolution," 33–34.

147. Clark, *Women's Silence*, 6.

148. Nietzsche, *Thus Spake*, 50.

149. Krafft-Ebing (1886) cited in Sanday, "Rape-Free," 348.

150. Ellis (1897–1910) cited in Sanday, "Rape-Free," 348–49.

151. Sanday, "Rape-Free," 350.

152. Skelley, *The Victorian Army*, 54. As an extension of the same policy of "the alleviation of the evils of enforced celibacy in the forces, both at home and in India," short-service enlistment was also considered in 1870; see ibid.

153. Trustram, "Distasteful," 156–58, 163.

154. Fukumura and Matsuoka, "Redefining Security," 243–44.

155. Vigarello, *A History of Rape*, 15. In 1635, during the Flanders campaign, a group of soldiers actually turned their weapons against their colonel, who had prohibited pillage and rape.

Chapter 4. The Prohibition of Rape in War: First Steps: The Geneva Conventions and the Additional Protocols

1. Gardam, "Women and Law," 57.

2. Preliminary Conference of National Red Cross Societies for the Study of the Conventions and of Various Problems Relative to the Red Cross, Geneva, July 26 to August 3, 1946, Documents furnished by the International Committee of the Red Cross, Volume III, Situation and Protection of Civilians, Introduction (ICRC-A).

3. Rapport sur les travaux de la Conférence préliminaire des Sociétés nationales de la Croix-Rouge pour l'étude des Conventions et de divers problèmes ayant trait à la Croix-Rouge (Genève, 26 July 26–August 3, 1946), Geneva, January 1947, 97 (my translation) (ICRC-A).

4. Commission of Government Experts for the Study of Conventions for the Protection of War Victims (Geneva, April 14–26, 1947), Preliminary Documents Submitted by the International Committee of the Red Cross, Volume III, Condition and Protection of Civilians in Time of War, 41 (ICRC-A).

5. Ibid., 47 (ICRC-A).

6. Commission of Government Experts), Recommendations of Commission III, Chapter I, Definition of Protected Civilians, 3 (ICRC-A).

7. Ibid. Later in the documents, the Commission says that it "endorsed in general manner the ideas set forth by the ICRC in Vol. III of their reports regarding particular treaty guarantees that would be ensured to women and children of all nationalities. (Chapters II and III). The Commission considered these guarantees as a minimum, which it would be desirable to extend and specify." One might think that this meant a recommendation about the status of women; however, the Commission continued to say that the ICRC needed to further study the question in cooperation with other bodies, particularly with the International Union for Child Welfare. This recommendation gives the impression that the guarantees that they suggest to be specified are the ones related to children rather than women per se. Commission of Government Experts for the Study of Conventions, Recommendation of Commission III with regard to the Protection of Women and Children, 16 (ICRC-A).

8. XVIIe Conference Internationale de la Croix-Rouge, Stockholm, Août 1948, Résumes des Débats des Sous-Commissions de la Commission Juridique (December 1948), 91 (my translation) (ICRC-A).

9. Ibid.

10. Revised and New Draft Conventions for the Protection of War Victims, Texts Approved and Amended by the XVIIth International Red Cross Conference, Geneva, August 1948, 123 (ICRC-A). The article uses "especially" instead of "specially" in the previous draft prepared by the ICRC. See XVIIth International Red Cross Conference, Stockholm, August 1948, Draft Revised or New Conventions for the Protection of War Victims, International Committee of the Red Cross, Geneva, May 1948, 164–66 (ICRC-A).

11. Grave breaches put obligations on state parties to bring the violators of these crimes before domestic courts or hand over them for trial by other parties. See Article 146, Appendix A.

12. XVIIth International Red Cross Conference, Stockholm, August 1948, Repression of Infringements of the Humanitarian Conventions, Report by the International Committee of the Red Cross (Under Item III of the Agenda of the Legal Commission), Geneva, June 1948, 1 (ICRC-A).

13. Draft Revised or New Conventions for the Protection of War Victims, International Committee of the Red Cross, Geneva, May 1948, 211–12 (ICRC-A).

14. Revised and New Draft Conventions for the Protection of War Victims, Texts Approved and Amended by the XVIIth International Red Cross Conference, Geneva, August 1948, 159–60 (ICRC-A).

15. Projets de Conventions Revisées ou Nouvelles Protégeant les Victimes de la Guerre, Remarques et Propositions du Comité International de la Croix-Rouge, Document destine aux Gouvernements invites par le Conséil Fédéral Suisse à la Conférence diplomatique de Genève (21 Avril 1949), Geneva, February 1949, 88 (my translation) (ICRC-A).

16. International Alliance of Women, Report of the 15th Congress, Amsterdam, July 18–24, 1949, 12 (SSC).

17. Interview with a leader in the women's movement, September 11, 2007.

18. Balthazar, "Gender Crimes," 44. The prosecutor did ask about the "atrocious details" of Nazi torture.

19. IAW, Report of the 15th Congress, 13.

20. Ibid., 35.

21. Ibid., 51.

22. Ibid.

23. International Alliance of Women, Report of the 14th Congress, Interlaken, August 11–16, 1946 (SSC).

24. Diplomatic Conference of Geneva, Committee III (Civilians Convention) meetings, Ninth meeting (May 5, 1949) (SFA).

25. See Appendix B.

26. Diplomatic Conference of Geneva, Plenary Meetings, Twenty-Sixth meeting (August 3,1949), 8 (SFA).

27. Diplomatic Conference of Geneva, Committee III (Civilians Convention) meetings, Tenth meeting (May 6, 1949) (SFA).

28. Diplomatic Conference of Geneva, Committee III, Eleventh meeting (May 9, 1949) (SFA).

29. Report of Committee III to the Plenary Assembly of the Diplomatic Conference of Geneva (July 27, 1949), 20 (SFA).

30. Ibid., 22.

31. Ibid., 23. Also see Figure 4.1 showing what the prohibitions in the convention were, according to the Working Party.

32. Diplomatic Conference of Geneva, Committee III, Tenth meeting.

33. See Appendix A.

34. XVIIth International Red Cross Conference, Stockholm, August 1948, Repression of Infringements of the Humanitarian Conventions, Report by the International Committee of the Red Cross (Under Item III of the Agenda of the Legal Commission), Geneva, June 1948, 1 (ICRC-A).

35. XVIIth International Red Cross Conference, Draft Revised or New Conventions for the Protection of War Victims, International Committee of the Red Cross, Geneva, May 1948, 211–12; Revised and New Draft Conventions for the Protection of War Victims, Texts Approved and Amended by the XVIIth International Red Cross Conference, Geneva, August 1948, 159–60; Projets de Conventions Révisées ou Nouvelles Protégeant les Victimes de la Guerre, Remarques et Propositions du Comité International de la Croix-Rouge, Document destine aux Gouvernements invites par le Conséil fédéral Suisse à la Conférence diplomatique de Genève (21 Avril 1949), Geneva, February 1949, 88 (ICRC-A).

36. Commission III, Compte rendu en extense de la 30e séance tenue (15 Juin 1949); Special Committee of the Joint Committee, Twenty-ninth meeting (June 27, 1949), Thirtieth meeting (June 27, 1949); Joint Committee, Tenth meeting (July 16, 1949) (SFA).

37. Report of the Joint Committee to the Plenary Assembly, July 26, 1949: Article 40/44/119A/130A (SFA).

38. Commission III, Compte rendu in extense de la 30e séance tenue (15 Juin 1949). For instance Hungarian, Polish, and Romanian delegates (SFA).

39. Report of the Joint Committee to the Plenary Assembly, July 26, 1949: Article 40/44/119A/130A.

40. Special Committee of the Joint Committee, Thirty-first meeting, June 28, 1949 (SFA).

41. Fourth Report of the Special Committee of the Joint Committee, Report on Penal Sanctions, July 12, 1949 (SFA).

42. Some examples are the rapes during the independence war of Bangladesh (1971), the Vietnam War (1956–1975), the civil wars in various Latin American countries—in particularly high numbers in Guatemala, Colombia, Peru, and Haiti (1961–present)—the civil war in Sierra Leone (1991–2000), and the first Gulf War (1990–1991).

43. "Women 2000: Sexual Violence and Armed Conflict: United Nations Response," 4.

44. See Askin, War Crimes Against Women; Askin and Koenig, Women and International Human Rights Law, and Appendix A.

45. See Keck and Sikkink, Activists, 168.

46. Commission III, Compte rendu in extense de la 30e séance.

47. Gardam, "The Law," 178.

48. Connors, "NGOs," 152.

49. Herschberger, Adam's Rib, 21–22.

50. Whittick, Woman into Citizen, 163–64.

51. Joachim, Agenda Setting, 52–54.

52. The only official NGO participants of the Conference were the ICRC and the League of Red Cross Societies, both as experts.

53. Letter to Monsieur Ernest Gloor, Vice Président du Comité International de la Croix-Rouge from Helen Roberts, Secrétaire Générale d'Alliance Universelle des Unions Chrétiennes de Jeunes Filles, July 22, 1948 (my translation) (ICRC-A).

54. Ibid.

55. Letter to Miss Helen Roberts, Secrétaire Générale d'Alliance Universelle des Unions Chrétiennes de Jeunes Filles from Claude Pilloud, Chef de la Division Juridique du Comité International de la Croix-Rouge. August 5, 1948. (my translation) (ICRC-A).

56. Letter to Madame Jeanne Eder-Schwyzer, Présidente du Conseil International des Femmes from Robert Haas, Secrétaire Général du Comité International de la Croix-Rouge. July 13, 1948 (my translation) (ICRC-A).

57. Letter to Mr. Robert Haas, Secrétaire Général du Comité International de la Croix-Rouge from the International Federation of University Women, June 14, 1948 (ICRC-A).

58. Hillis, German Atrocities, 55–56.

59. Patton and Harkins, War, 23.

60. Ibid., 71–72.

61. Anonymous, A Woman in Berlin, xviii, 21. Despite this widespread expectation

that the rapes were bound to happen, the author of the diary also observed that if alcohol had been unavailable to the Soviet soldiers, half the rapes would not have happened. She argues that the soldiers had to "goad themselves on to such brazen acts" and alcohol helped to "drown their inhibitions," 173.

62. Niarchos, "Women," 665–66.

63. Anonymous, *A Woman in Berlin*, 52.

64. Ibid., 147, 150.

65. Ibid., 215.

66. Djilas, *Conversations*, 95.

67. Solzhenitsyn, *The Gulag Archipelago*, 16.

68. Brownmiller, *Against Our Will*, 71.

69. Ibid., 55.

70. Judgment of the International Military Tribunal for the Far East, Tokyo (1948) cited in Brownmiller, *Against Our Will*, 61.

71. Enloe, *Maneuvers*, 111.

72. Ibid., 111.

73. "Who Were the Comfort Women?" Also see Hicks, *The Comfort Women*.

74. "Okamura Yasuji taisho shiryo I: senjo kaisohen," Tokyo, 1970 quoted in "Who Were the Comfort Women?"

75. Timm, "Sex," 224.

76. Fall, *Street Without Joy*, 132–33.

77. Ibid., 133.

78. See Appendix A.

79. Report of the Commission on International Humanitarian Law (1974), 86 (ICRC-A).

80. "Official Records of the Diplomatic Conference on the Reaffirmation and Development of International Humanitarian Law Applicable in Armed Conflicts, Geneva (1974–1977)," v.7, 61.

81. Ibid., 87.

82. Ibid., v.10, 104.

83. Ibid., 49.

84. Ibid., v.15, 51.

85. Ibid., v.7, 89.

86. Ibid., 89.

87. Ibid., 90–91.

88. Bettauer, Report of the United States Delegation. The term "high threshold of application" refers to the definition of the parties who are supposed to apply the protocol. The insurgents in internal wars, for instance, should meet certain criteria (like being under responsible command or controlling a territory) in order to be in a position to apply the Protocol.

89. Aldrich, "Comments on the Geneva Protocols," 510.

90. This is when Brownmiller talks about the rape cases between the South and

North Vietnamese, not the rapes committed by American forces. Although rape cases committed by the South Vietnamese increased as the war progressed, Northern forces never resorted to rape. Brownmiller, *Against Our Will*, 88–90. Also, the civil wars with low rates of rape she talks about are not the ones with ethnic and religious divisions, which would be high-rape wars in the latter part of the twentieth century, such as the former Yugoslavia and Rwanda.

91. The rarity of rape during the American Civil War can also be tied to the fact that it was clearly prohibited by the Lieber Code and enforced as such.

92. Freidel, *Francis Lieber*, 325.

93. "Official Records of the Diplomatic Conference," V.15, 56.

94. Bothe et al., "New Rules," 469.

95. International Committee of the Red Cross, "Draft Additional Protocols," 401.

96. Bothe et al., "New Rules," 507.

97. See Appendix A.

98. Bothe et al., "New Rules," 512.

99. Ibid., 512.

100. Ibid., 514, 522.

101. "Official Records of the Diplomatic Conference," v.6, 280.

102. Ibid., 297.

103. Bothe et al., "New Rules," 522.

104. Ibid., 507.

105. "Official Records of the Diplomatic Conference," v.4, 126.

106. Ibid., 132.

107. Ibid., 128–29.

108. Walters, *Feminism*, 108.

109. Mitchell, *Woman's Estate*, 101–20.

110. Walters, *Feminism*, 112, 114.

111. Davis, *Violence against Women*, 6.

112. Bevacqua, *Rape*, 30, 35–36.

113. Ibid., 9.

114. Ibid., 9–10, 58–59, 63.

115. Brownmiller, *Against Our Will*.

116. Bevacqua, *Rape*, 63. The psychiatric profession is partly responsible for reinforcing the myth that uncontrollable sexual urges of men or some psychological problems related to them lead to rape. See Brownmiller, *Against Our Will*, 176–79.

117. Bevacqua, *Rape*, 106. Anti-crime sentiments and the conservative politicians who wanted to play into those sentiments through the law-and-order approach for political gain helped the anti-rape legal agenda, though it meant feminists had to compromise their struggle for reframing rape as a form of male domination. Instead, the lawmakers and society at large considered the new rape laws a chance to "protect women" from just another crime rather than as a step toward ending sexism by ending the violation of women's bodily integrity (121).

118. Ibid., 127–31, 135–36.

119. Ibid., 93.

120. Ibid., 105. Also see Matthews, *Confronting Rape*.

121. Patricia Smith regards the changes in rape laws as surprisingly few (especially in terms of the definition of rape), given that cultural attitude toward rape changed considerably since the 1970s. See Smith, "Social Revolution," 35. Alternatively, Susan Estrich considers the changes in law very comprehensive, but she thinks the law change did not bring about much change in the attitudes toward rape (by the 1980s), especially by the courts. Estrich, *Real Rape*, 80.

122. Besides the changes in all states in the United States (by 1996) and Canada (1983), 22 European countries changed their rape laws between 1980 and 2003; 21 of these changes happened before 1998. Regan and Kelly, "Rape."

123. Brownmiller, *Against Our Will*; Clark and Lewis, *The Price of Coercive Sexuality*; Rose, "Rape"; Groth, *Men Who Rape*; Schwendinger and Schwendinger, *Rape and Inequality*.

124. Bandura, "Social Learning Theory of Aggression"; Burt, *Attitudes*; Burt, "Cultural Myths"; Donnerstein, "Agressive Erotica"; Donnerstein and Berkowitz, "Victim Reactions"; Malamuth, "Rape Fantasies"; Malamuth and Check, "The Effects of Mass Media"; Malamuth et al., "Testing Hypotheses"; Malamuth and Donnerstein, "The Effects of Aggressive"; Zillmann, *Connections*.

125. Bandura, *Aggression*; Bandura, *Social Learning Theory*; Bandura and Walters, *Social Learning and Personality Development*. Although there had been others who proposed some type of a social learning theory, Bandura was the first to study modeling as a form of social learning and the idea that the time lapse between cause and effect during the learning process can be long. He also popularized the theory within the discipline of psychology.

126. Vito et al., *Criminology*, 285.

127. For example, scholars and activists like Catherine MacKinnon and Andrea Dworkin led the feminist anti-pornography movement starting in the late 1970s, singling out pornography as an important source of sexual violence against women. Gerhard, *Desiring Revolution*, 173–74.

128. Enloe, *Maneuvers*, 110.

129. MacKinnon, "Turning Rape"; Copelon, "Surfacing Gender"; Copelon, "Gender Crimes."

130. For a background on the establishment of the CSW, see *The United Nations and the Advancement of Women, 1945–1996*. Also for the contestations during its establishment see Joachim, *Agenda Setting*, 69–71.

131. Fraser, *The UN Decade*, 12; Pietila and Vickers, *Making Women*, 73.

132. See Tinker, "NGOs," on the activism of NGOs within the UN.

133. Fraser, *The UN Decade*, 14.

134. Antrobus, *The Global Women's Movement*, 43. She asks the same question without an answer.

135. Joachim, *Agenda Setting*, 92.

136. Ibid., 81. World Plan of Action is the document produced by the conference and it offered guidelines for governments and the international community to secure equal access to resources for women.

137. Joachim, "Shaping," 144–46. When, for instance, the Australian delegation proposed a definition of sexism to be used for a common action against discrimination, it was rejected because many delegations thought it would be "preoccupation with sex." Joachim, *Agenda Setting*, 78. Given this attitude, why violence issues, sexual violence in particular, could not be brought to the table becomes clearer.

138. Joachim, *Agenda Setting*, 105–12.

139. Later during the decade (1989), the Committee on the Elimination of Discrimination against Women, the UN body overseeing the implementation of CEDAW, adopted General Recommendation 12, which says that although CEDAW does not mention violence against women, Articles 2, 5, 11, 12, and 16 require protection of women against violence.

140. Interview with a leader, September 11, 2007.

141. Fraser, "The Convention," 77.

142. A reservation is defined as "a unilateral statement, however phrased or named, made by a State, when signing, ratifying, accepting, approving or acceding to a treaty, whereby it purports to exclude or to modify the legal effect of certain provisions of the treaty in their application to that State." See the Vienna Convention on the Law of Treaties (1969).

143. Fraser, "The Convention," 91.

144. Davis, *Violence Against Women*, 8.

145. Paglia (1992), cited in Bevacqua, *Rape*, 184.

146. Bevacqua, *Rape*, 131.

147. Estrich, *Real Rape*, 82.

148. Menen, July 23, 1972, cited in Brownmiller, *Against Our Will*, 85.

149. Brownmiller, *Against Our Will*, 104–5.

150. Ibid., 92–95.

151. Ibid., 96–99, 106–7.

152. Ibid., 91.

153. Ibid., 80.

154. Fried, December 27, 1971, cited in Brownmiller, *Against Our Will*, 79.

155. Brownmiller, *Against Our Will*, 113.

Chapter 5. The Prohibition of Rape in War: Success: The Rome Statute

1. The first ICTY indictment for rape was in June 1996 in the case of *Gagovic et al.* The first ICTR indictment for rape came in June 1997 in the *Akayesu* case.

2. See *The Prosecutor v. Akayesu*; *The Prosecutor v. Delalic and Delic* (Celebici case). It has been argued that the explicit language of the Rome Statute with respect to sexual crimes had an impact on the jurisprudence of the ICTY. See Oosterveld, "Sexual Slavery," 647.

3. Indeed, Abbott et al. (406) give the International Criminal Court as an example of an institution where all the elements of legalization, obligation, precision, and delegation are at the highest.

4. See Appendix A.

5. See Appendix A.

6. See Appendix B. The precedents set by the ICTR and the ICTY also gave more detailed definitions of what constitutes sexual violence.

7. See Appendix A. Although the ICC has one of the highest degrees of delegation among the existing body of international law (and the highest for international humanitarian law), we need to recognize that it does have some weaknesses caused by the principle of complementarity, which means the ICC cannot take a case if the state with the jurisdiction over the case is investigating, prosecuting, or has already investigated that case and decided not to prosecute. Article 17 says that in such cases, the ICC can only prosecute if the state is "unwilling or unable genuinely" to investigate and prosecute. See Schabas, *An Introduction*, 85–89.

8. "Rome Statute of the International Criminal Court: Overview."

9. See Keck and Sikkink, *Activists*.

10. For instance, during the 2350th meeting at the UN, the special rapporteur, Mr. Thiam (Senegal), brings up an earlier argument about the effect of the Second World War on international laws and the suggestion that the present draft has to be renamed according to the recent events in former Yugoslavia and Rwanda. "Summary Records," 1: 145.

11. Interview with a member of the CICC, July 27, 2007.

12. "Who We Are and What We Do: Our History."

13. Interview with a member of the CICC, July 27, 2007.

14. Benedetti and Washburn, "Drafting the International Criminal Court Treaty," 3.

15. *International Criminal Court MONITOR* 3, January 1997, 1–2 (CICC-A).

16. Kinkel, "The World's," 4.

17. De Vries, "President of EP Liberal Group," 5.

18. Interview with a member of the CICC, July 27, 2007. Also see Van Der Vyver, "Civil Society," 426–27.

19. Joachim, *Agenda Setting*, 25–26.

20. Van Der Vyver, "Civil Society," 426.

21. See Haas, *Saving the Mediterranean*; Keck and Sikkink, *Activists*; Joachim, *Agenda Setting*, for the centrality of expertise in the effectiveness of NGOs.

22. Interview with a member of the CICC, July 27, 2007.

23. *International Criminal Court MONITOR* 8, June 1998, 1 (CICC-A). Also see Van Der Vyver, "Civil Society," 428–29.

24. Interview with a member of the CICC, July 27, 2007.

25. *International Criminal Court MONITOR* 2, October 1996, 2 (CICC-A).

26. *International Criminal Court MONITOR* 10, November 1998, 11 (CICC-A).

27. *International Criminal Court MONITOR* 6, November 1997, 8 (CICC-A).

28. Broomhall, "An Overview," 15.

29. International Committee of the Red Cross War Crimes Working Paper prepared by ICRC for Preparatory Committee for the Establishment of an International Criminal Court, New York, February 13, 1997, 5 (CICC-A).

30. "Dakar Declaration for the Establishment of the International Criminal Court in 1998," February 6, 1998, 33–35. Also see International Commission of Jurists, The International Criminal Court, Third ICJ Position Paper, August 1995, 20; "Establishing An International Criminal Court Major Unresolved Issues In The Draft Statute," A Position Paper of the Lawyers Committee for Human Rights, August 1996, 16 (CICC-A).

31. Speech by Mr. Sane, observer for Amnesty International at the Rome Conference, in United Nations Diplomatic Conference of Plenipotentiaries on the Establishment of an International Criminal Court Rome, New York, 2002, vol. II, 80–81; 129 (CICC-A).

32. Human Rights Watch Recommendations (Excerpted from Human Rights Watch Action Alert February 1998), in *International Criminal Court MONITOR*, PrepCom Six Special Edition, April 1998, 7 (CICC-A).

33. Benjamin Ferencz, former Nuremberg prosecutor, in "Perspectives on the ICC and Rome," *International Criminal Court MONITOR* 8, June 1998, 8 (CICC-A).

34. See Schabas, *An Introduction*, 16.

35. Interview with a member of the CICC, July 27, 2007. The interviewee mentioned that though the like-minded group was very important in terms of furthering the NGO agenda, there were other states who were not members of the like-minded group but were nevertheless very sympathetic to their cause, such as Japan.

36. See Joachim, *Agenda Setting*, for the way influential allies help NGOs by providing institutional resources and access.

37. "United Nations Diplomatic Conference of Plenipotentiaries on the Establishment of an International Criminal Court Rome, 15 June–17 July 1998, Official Records," v.II.

38. Ibid.

39. Ibid., 160.

40. Ibid., 164.

41. Meron, "Rape as a Crime," 425. Also see Steains, "Gender Issues."

42. Women's organizations moved the issue of women's rights from the initial framework of discrimination (then development) prevalent through the 1960s and 1970s toward the "human rights" framework in the late 1980s and 1990s. See Keck and Sikkink, *Activists*, 180, 184.

43. Connors, "NGOs," 160.

44. Interview with a leader in the women's movement, September 11, 2007.

45. *Decade for Women: Equality, Development and Peace*, Chapter I, Section A.

46. Fraser, *The UN Decade*, 52.

47. For example, rape law reforms were passed in the 1970s in several states in the United States. Canada rape law reform passed in 1983. See Berger et al., "The Dimensions."

48. Fraser, *The UN Decade*, 10; Keck and Sikkink, *Activists*, 177–78.

49. Edwards, *Female Sexuality*, 157–58.

50. Skjelsbaek, *Gendered Battlefields*, 9; Gaer, "And Never," 14. But, still, there is the emphasis on violence as a major obstacle to peace. Gaer, "And Never," 62.

51. "Women 2000: Sexual Violence and Armed Conflict: United Nations Response," 5–6.

52. Joachim, *Agenda Setting*, 93–99.

53. Ibid., 116–22.

54. Gaer, "And Never," 23.

55. Joachim, *Agenda Setting*; Risse and Sikkink, "The Power of Principles."

56. Keck and Sikkink, *Activists*, 183, 186.

57. Although violations of the laws and customs of war were committed by all sides of the conflict, Serbian forces perpetrated the majority of them, including the ethnic-cleansing campaign against the Muslim population.

58. Stiglmayer, "The War," 25.

59. Connors, "NGOs," 169.

60. Vigarello, *A History of Rape*, 223. Also see Copelon, "Surfacing Gender," 198.

61. The estimated total number of German women raped by Allied soldiers in the Eastern Sector in 1945 is 1.9 million; see Sander (1992), cited in Engle, "Feminism and Its (Dis)contents," 811. The number of German women raped in Berlin when Soviet soldiers were capturing the city in 1945 is 110,000. For the rape of Italian women by Moroccan soldiers in the French army in 1943–1944, see Niarchos, "Women," 665–66. Also for the rapes in Asia by Japanese soldiers, see Chang, *The Rape of Nanking*.

62. Unlike Nuremberg, in Tokyo there were rape charges (for failing to prevent the crime at the command level) brought and prosecuted through the evidence introduced by affidavit and missionaries who remained in the city, although no victim had testified in person. Those charges were limited, however, by some of the cases in Nanking; the issue of "comfort women" was ignored, and those cases did not lead to rape's inclusion among the grave breaches in the Geneva Conventions. See Brownmiller, *Against Our Will*, 58.

63. *International Criminal Court MONITOR 2*, October 1996, 8 (CICC-A).

64. Kowert and Legro, "Norms," 473–74.

65. Florini, "The Evolution," 375.

66. Meron, *War Crimes*, 204.

67. See Rochon, *Culture Moves*.

68. Although the laws of war, international humanitarian law, non-combatant immunity, and the principle of not causing unnecessary suffering stand at the background as well (as in the case of land-mines, Price, "Reversing," 629), and in fact that the norms against genocide are built on them, these had not been sufficient to bring about reconceptualization of the use of rape as a horrible, unintelligible grave breach, which translates to a shock and change.

69. Speech of Ms. Sajor (Observer for the Asian Centre for Women's Human

Rights), United Nations Diplomatic Conference of Plenipotentiaries on the Establishment of an International Criminal Court Rome, New York, 2002, vol. II, 119 (CICC-A).
The reflection of women's activism on the cases in the ICTY is apparent as well. Of the
cases, 20 percent involved charges for sexual assault and three focused on rape in particular. Engle, "Feminism and Its (Dis)contents," 781. It is significant that the Statute of
the ICTY does not mention rape among war crimes, although it mentions it as a crime
against humanity. The threshold for "crimes against humanity" is higher, requiring the
crime to be systematic, which is very hard to prove in the case of rape. See Steains,
"Gender Issues," 361–62.

70. Joachim, *Agenda Setting*, 122–25.

71. Bunch and Reilly, *Demanding Accountability*, 100–101.

72. Gaer, "And Never," 35.

73. *Testimonies of the Global Tribunal*, 3. See Keck and Sikkink, *Activists*; Price,
"Reversing;" Joachim, *Agenda Setting*, for the way NGOs use testimonials in their
campaigns.

74. Gaer, "And Never," 33.

75. Ibid., 33; Keck and Sikkink, *Activists*, 187; Joachim, *Agenda Setting*, 129.

76. UNIFEM is the acronym of the French name of the UN Development Fund for
Women, Fonds de Développement des Nations Unies pour la Femme.

77. Gaer, "And Never," 35; Bunch and Reilly, *Demanding Accountability*, 102–3.

78. Interview with a leader in the women's movement, September 11, 2007.

79. Connors, "NGOs," 170–71. Also see Sullivan, "Women's Human Rights."

80. Vienna Declaration and Programme of Action, section 1/ article 28.

81. Ibid., section 2/ article 38.

82. "Special Rapporteur on Violence against Women, Its Causes and Consequences."

83. See Penn and Nardos, *Overcoming Violence*.

84. "Women and Violence."

85. Interview with a leader in the women's movement, September 11, 2007.

86. There was one indictment at the ICTY in 1996 for rape. See *The Prosecutor v.
Gagovic et al.* The judgment was not issued until 2001. The first indictment in the ICTR
for rape was in the Akayesu case, issued in June 1997. According to one of the judges
(1995–1999) and later the president of the ICTR (1999–2003), Judge Navanethem Pillay,
after two years and 21 indictments, there was not a single count of rape at the court, until
finally the judges picked up that several witnesses were testifying about rape and paved
the way for the amendment of the charges by the prosecutor. See *If Hope Were Enough*.

87. Gaer, "And Never," 63, 64, 529.

88. Gassoumis et al., "Women's Caucus," 5.

89. See *Ending Impunity for Gender Crimes*, 3; Gassoumis et al., "Women's Caucus,"
5.

90. Interview with a member of the CICC, July 27, 2007; interview with a former
member of the Women's Caucus, February 6, 2008.

91. Gassoumis et al., "Women's Caucus," 5.

92. Norris, "Work Still Needed," 9.

93. Steains, "Gender Issues," 364–65.

94. Facio, "A Word," 5.

95. Axel et al., "Women's Caucus," 8.

96. Women's Caucus for Gender Justice in the International Criminal Court "Recommendations and Commentary for December 1997 PrepCom on the Establishment of an International Criminal Court," United Nations Headquarters, December 1–12, 1997 (CICC-A).

97. Axel et al., "Women's Caucus," 8.

98. *International Criminal Court MONITOR* 7, February 1998, 8. (CICC-A)

99. Interview with an observer at the Rome (1998), Beijing (1995) and Vienna (1993) conferences, May 10, 2007.

100. The controversy over the "enforced pregnancy" provision started during the December 1997 PrepCom and continued during the March–April 1998 PrepCom, where the Holy See proposed to replace "enforced pregnancy" with "forcible impregnation." But it was not accepted on the basis of the fact that what happened in Bosnia-Herzegovina—forcible impregnations followed by detentions to force women to bear the babies of the rapists. The text forwarded to the Rome Conference contained "enforced pregnancy." See Steains, "Gender Issues," 365–66.

101. *Ending Impunity for Gender Crimes*, 10–11.

102. Steains, "Gender Issues," 367.

103. The states that argued against the use of "gender" due to their concern over the possibility of it including homosexuals were Guatemala, Venezuela, Syria, and Qatar. See Steains "Gender Issues," 372.

104. *International Criminal Court MONITOR* 10, November 1998, 4 (CICC-A).

105. Interview with an observer at the Rome (1998), Beijing (1995) and Vienna (1993) conferences, May 10, 2007.

106. Interview with a member of the CICC, July 27, 2007.

107. "War Crimes Treaty Stalls Over Inclusion of Rape."

108. Interview with an observer, May 10, 2007.

109. Interview with a member of the CICC, July 27, 2007.

110. Keck and Sikkink, *Activists*, 183.

111. *Excluding Crimes Sgainst Women from the ICC Is Not an Option*, 38.

112. Ibid., 39.

113. Joachim, *Agenda Setting*; Keck and Sikkink, *Activists*.

114. Schön and Rein (1994), cited in Joachim, *Agenda Setting*, 20.

115. Bedont and Martinez, "Ending Impunity," 77.

116. Vranic, *Breaking*, 234. She suggests that these violations were shocking reminders of the Second World War horrors, in which case the appeal to human rights became all the more powerful.

117. *Introduction*, 2.

118. Bedont and Martinez, "Ending Impunity," 65.

119. *International Criminal Court MONITOR* 5, August 1997, 6 (CICC-A).

120. Facio, "A Word," 10.

121. Bedont and Martinez, "Ending Impunity," 65.

122. Allen, "Whose Law?" 9.

123. Women's Caucus for Gender Justice in the International Criminal Court "Recommendations and Commentary for December 1997 PrepCom on the Establishment of an International Criminal Court," United Nations Headquarters December 1–12, 1997, 38–39 (CICC-A).

124. *The International Criminal Court MONITOR*, 4, May 1997, 8 (CICC-A).

125. *If Hope Were Enough* was produced by the Women's Caucus.

126. Coomaraswamy, "Reinventing International Law," 7; Keck and Sikkink, *Activists*, 166, 196. In discussing the way they had to deal with the strong opposition and challenges in the ICC negotiations, the Women's Caucus said that they were "emphasizing the need for all working on the issue of women's rights from a human rights perspective to evolve strategies to effectively deal with these challenges," in *Objective*, 1.

127. Bunch, "Women's Rights," 496.

128. *Clarification of the Term Gender*, 1.

129. Ibid., 1–2.

130. Ibid., 2.

131. *ICC Women News*, 3.

132. Interview with an observer, May 10, 2007.

133. Saland, "International," 216.

134. Interview with an observer, May 10, 2007.

135. The use of the concept "genocidal rape" by some feminists like Beverly Allen (see Allen, *Rape Warfare*) and Catherine MacKinnon (see MacKinnon, "Turning Rape") in the context of Bosnia and Herzegovina was contested by other feminists at the beginning of the feminist campaign. These critics argued that emphasizing rape as a tool for genocide downplays the other rapes in war perpetrated without any intention of genocide or ethnic cleansing. However, the contention subsided once the campaign started with the establishment of the ICTY. See Engle, "Feminism and Its (Dis)contents."

136. Engle, "Feminism and Its (Dis)contents," 787.

137. MacKinnon, "Rape," 190.

138. Meron, *War Crimes*, 210; MacKinnon, "Rape," 187.

139. Vranic, *Breaking*, 234.

140. See for example MacKinnon, "Comment," 89.

141. Meron mentions the role of media in this case as the distinguishing factor from the previous atrocities. Instant reporting was the key for sensitization of public opinion, thus making immediate response to the tragedy possible. See Meron, *War Crimes*, 204. Vranic also emphasizes the role of media, particularly American media, in stimulating public consciousness, in Vranic, *Breaking*, 28. Also see Keck and Sikkink, *Activists*, 180–81.

142. Stiglmayer, "The War," 26.

143. Ramos et al., "Shaping," 390, 401.

144. Vranic, *Breaking*, 235.

145. "NGO Activities in Rome," *International Criminal Court MONITOR* 10, November 1998, 11 (CICC-A).

146. *Ending Impunity for Gender Crimes*, 15.

147. The Vatican, Ireland, and a group of anti-choice organizations were against the forced pregnancy part. *Ending Impunity for Gender Crimes*, 10–11. There had also been a contest over the terms "gender" versus "sex" between them and women's groups; at the end, though "gender" was the term that has been used, a special definition was stated in the treaty: "For the purpose of this Statute, it is understood that the term "gender" refers to the two sexes, male and female, within the context of society. The term "gender" does not indicate any meaning different from the above" (Art. 7 (3)).

148. Bedont and Martinez, "Ending Impunity," 69.

149. "'Forced pregnancy' means the unlawful confinement, of a woman forcibly made pregnant, with the intent of affecting the ethnic composition of any population or carrying out other grave violations of international law. This definition shall not in any way be interpreted as affecting national laws relating to pregnancy" (Article 7 (2) f).

150. Madagascar, Syria, Qatar, Oman, Iran, Libya, United Arab Emirates, Kenya, Kuwait, Indonesia, Egypt, and Iraq were some of these states. See Steains, "Gender Issues," 381.

151. Appendix A.

152. Steains, "Gender Issues," 382–85, 387.

153. The Newsletter of the NGO Coalition on Women's Human Rights in Conflict Situations produced by the International Centre for Human Rights and Democratic Development (ICHRDD), May 1999 (CICC-A).

154. Women's Caucus for Gender Justice in the International Criminal Court, "Recommendations and Commentary for August 1997 PrepCom on the Establishment of an International Criminal Court," United Nations Headquarters August 4–15, 1997, 16 (CICC-A).

155. Women's Caucus for Gender Justice in the International Criminal Court "Recommendations and Commentary for December 1997 PrepCom on the Establishment Of An International Criminal Court," United Nations Headquarters December 1–12, 1997, 28. (CICC-A).

156. *The Prosecutor v. Akayesu*, 96–97.

157. Ibid., 132.

158. *The Prosecutor v. Delalic and Delic* (Celebici case).

159. *The Prosecutor v. Furundzija*.

160. Strumpen-Darrie, "Rape," 14.

161. Poolos, "Yugoslavia."

162. Organized by the International Centre for Migration Policy Development (ICMPD) within European Union Odysseus Project in cooperation with the governments of Austria and Sweden.

163. *Rape Is a War Crime: How to Support the Survivors*, 7.

164. Ibid., 15.

165. *The Prosecutor v. Kunarac, Kovac, and Vukovic.*

166. Amanpour, "Q&A: The Impact of the Ruling."

167. Mertus, "Judgment," 4–6.

168. Elements of Crimes is part of the Annex I to the Rome Statute prepared by a Preparatory Commission that met ten times between 1999 and 2002. It explains what each crime mentioned in Articles 6, 7, and 8 (genocide, crimes against humanity, and war crimes) of the Rome Statute includes in order to help the ICC with the interpretation and application of the Statute.

Rules of Procedure and Evidence is another part of the Annex I to the Rome Statute prepared by the same Preparatory Commission. It explains how the ICC will work to apply the Rome Statute—how investigations into the cases, prosecutions, trial proceedings, determination of the sentences, and appeals will be handled under the jurisdiction of the court, as well as the composition and the administration of the court.

169. Steains, "Gender Issues."

170. Some states that supported "gender balance" to ensure fair representation of women judges on the Court included Costa Rica, Bosnia-Herzegovina, Samoa, Italy, Australia, Botswana, Switzerland, New Zealand, Canada, Belgium, Slovenia, Singapore, Germany, France, Finland, India, Netherlands, Austria, United States, Mozambique, Thailand, South Africa, Philippines, Trinidad and Tobago, Slovakia, Colombia, Czech Republic, Senegal, Israel, Chile, Oman, Libya, Iraq, Burundi, Algeria, Ghana, Sweden, Namibia, and Swaziland. The countries opposed were Syria, United Arab Emirates, Madagascar, Iran, and Russia. See Steains, "Gender Issues," 378.

171. Frey, *A Fair Representation*, 11–13.

172. Spees, "Many Gender Issues," 4.

173. "Public Hearings on Crimes Against Women in Recent Wars and Conflicts," 1 (CICC-A).

174. *Crimes against Women are Crimes against Humanity*, 49.

175. *International Criminal Court MONITOR* 18, September 2001, 15 (CICC-A).

176. For examples see *International Criminal Court MONITOR*, 15, June 2000, 15; 17, May 2001, 8; 20, April 2002, 5 (CICC-A).

177. See *International Criminal Court MONITOR* 29, April 2005; 30, August 2005; 31, November 2005; 34, May–October 2007; *ICC-AFRICA*, Newsletter of the Coalition for the ICC, 4, January 2007; 5, April 2007 (CICC-A).

178. "Punishing Rape as a War Crime," 7–8.

179. *The Prosecutor v. Jean-Pierre Bemba Gombo; The Prosecutor v. Germain Katanga and Mathieu Ngudjolo Chui; The Prosecutor v. Omar Hassan Ahmad Al Bashir; The Prosecutor v. Ahmad Muhammad Harun ("Ahmad Harun") and Ali Muhammad Ali Abd-Al-Rahman ("Ali Kushayb").*

Chapter 6. Conclusion

1. Words attributed to General Andrew Jackson during the War of 1812, Brownmiller, *Against Our Will*, 35–36.

2. Morrow, "When Do States Follow," 560.

3. Reus-Smith explains the formation of international institutions in a similar way, arguing that political action that results in the formation of international law integrates four different types of reasoning: idiographic (identity), purposive (collective legitimate purposes), ethical (norms), and instrumental reasoning. Reus-Smith, "Introduction," 25–30.

4. Redlich, *De Praeda Militari*.

5. Nabulsi, *Traditions*.

6. This picture of non-state actors managing to push for the creation of international laws with the backing of certain states at a convenient historical moment, despite widespread opposition from important powerful states, is very similar to the picture we saw with the creation of the ICC.

7. The fact that pillage during the Napoleonic Wars was at its worst when the French Army was without food and clothing, and became less intensive after supply improved, indicates the feasibility of preventing pillage through appropriate measures. See Lynn, "Wave of Rape," 98.

8. Brownmiller, *Against Our Will*, 31.

9. Ibid., 32.

10. Vigarello, *A History of Rape*, 13.

11. Brownmiller, *Against Our Will*, 36 n.

12. Even Brownmiller's contention that "men rape because they can" is gendered in this respect.

13. For example see Yusuf, "Rape-Related," for the ways proverbs reflect this kind of thinking in popular culture.

14. Seifert, "War and Rape," 55.

15. Anonymous, *A Woman in Berlin*, xix.

16. The possibility of compensation in cases of violation is a major concern of states. The Hague Conventions' related regulations were accordingly designed to make sure that when illegal appropriation of property happens during wars, later compensations can be secured. See Kalshoven, "State Responsibility."

17. See Garbarino et al., *No Place*, for examples of this phenomenon with respect to children. Also see Forero, "Prosperous."

18. Brownmiller, *Against Our Will*, 37.

19. Caron, "War," 8.

20. Schlichtmann, "Japan," 381.

21. Broomhall, *International Justice*.

22. Johnson, "The Okinawan Rape."

23. Bedont and Martinez, "Ending Impunity."

244 Notes to Pages 175–181

24. See Fletcher, *In Hell*; Fremont-Barnes, *The Napoleonic Wars*.

25. Taylor, *Nuremberg*, 40.

26. Morrow, "When Do States Follow." Also see Chayes and Chayes, "On Compliance"; Simmons, "Capacity."

27. Kahler, "Legalization."

28. See Henkin, *How Nations Behave*; Kelley, "Who Keeps."

29. Reus-Smith, "Introduction," 3.

30. Abbott and Snidal, "Hard and Soft Law." Also see Simmons, "International Law," for the positive effect of legalization on compliance.

31. See Morrow, "When Do States Follow," for a comparison of cases where compliance to laws of war may vary according to their requirement of compliance by individuals versus compliance by states.

32. Ibid.

33. Mearsheimer, "The False Promise"; Strange, "Cave!"; Goldsmith and Posner, *The Limits*. The only exception to compliance with international law against one's national interests will be when it is enforced by a more powerful state on a weaker one.

34. Keohane, *After Hegemony*; Abbott et al., "The Concept of Legalization."

35. Henkin, *How Nations Behave*; Kratochwil and Ruggie, "International Organization"; Wendt, *Social Theory*; Franck, *The Power of Legitimacy*; Finnemore and Toope, "Alternatives to 'Legalization.'"

36. Franck, *The Power of Legitimacy*.

37. Morrow, "When Do States Follow," 561.

38. Ibid., 569.

39. This is all the more important in the case of rape in war, since research has shown that men never presume t they will be prosecuted for rape. See Mezey, "Rape in War."

40. Nainar, "Initiatives."

41. Hopkinson, "The Treatment."

42. Kalijarvi, "Settlements," 200.

43. Simpson, *Spoils of War*; Von Glahn, *The Occupation*, 189.

44. Price, "Emerging Customary Norms," 106.

45. Von Glahn, *The Occupation*, 229.

46. Downey, Jr., "Captured Enemy Property," 495.

47. *Karmatzucas v. Germany*, cited in ibid., 498.

48. "Inter-Allied Declaration."

49. Downey, Jr., "Captured Enemy Property," 502–4.

50. See "Nuremberg Trial Proceedings."

51. Graber, *The Development*, 257.

52. Woolsey, "The Forced Transfer," 283, 284. Also see Lew, "Manchurian."

53. "Netherlands Hails Return of Stolen Art," "Kandinsky Painting Row Settled," "Family Compensated for Tate's Nazi Art," "Nazi Loot Is Won Back." The protection of cultural property is further legalized by the 1954 Hague Convention for the Protection of Cultural Property in the Event of Armed Conflict.

54. Some example cases at the ICTY: Jelisić (IT-95–10) "Brčko," Judgment 14 December 1999; Blaškić (IT-95–14) "Lašva Valley," Judgment 29 July 2004; Kordić and Čerkez (IT-95–14/2) "Lašva Valley," Judgment 17 December 2004. The ICTR: Gatete (ICTR-2000–61–I), Indictment 14 December 2000.

55. The two major modern cases of wartime pillage of artwork and cultural property were the Napoleonic Wars and Nazi pillage during World War II.

56. "Troops 'Vandalise' Ancient City of Ur"; Warren, "War."

57. The legal obligation of the United States is actually unclear, since the legal document requiring occupying powers to prevent pillage is the Hague Convention of 1954, and the United States had not yet ratified it in 2003.

58. "U.S. Troops 'Encouraged' Iraqi Looters."

59. "Bush Panel Members Quit over Looting: Cultural Advisers Say U.S. Military Could Have Prevented Museum Losses."

60. Rothfield, *The Rape of Mesopotamia*, 82–83; Rumsfeld and Myers, Department of Defense News Briefing.

61. Several ICC cases include indictments for pillage: *The Prosecutor v. Bahar Idriss Abu Garda*; *The Prosecutor v. Germain Katanga and Mathieu Ngudjolo Chui*; *The Prosecutor v. Omar Hassan Ahmad Al Bashir*; *The Prosecutor v. Abdallah Banda Abakaer Nourain and Saleh Mohammed Jerbo Jamus*; *The Prosecutor v. Ahmad Muhammad Harun ("Ahmad Harun") and Ali Muhammad Ali Abd-Al-Rahman ("Ali Kushayb")*.

62. Watt et al., "Serbs Have Rape Camp," 1–3.

63. Eddy, "Rape as War Weapon," 2.

64. *Federal Republic of Yugoslavia. Kosovo: Rape as a Weapon of "Ethnic Cleansing."*

65. Mertus, "Yugoslavia," A19.

66. Bumiller, "Deny Rape."

67. A body of customary law under which the clans of Albania have lived since the fifteenth century, which says that a man who fails to exact blood revenge for the dishonor of one of his womenfolk brings shame on his entire family, which leads many to think that the rape victim has brought shame on her family. Igric, "Kosovo," 1.

68. See Bumiller, "Deny Rape," A1; U.S. Department of State, *Serbia-Montenegro Country Report*, 22; McDougall, *Contemporary Forms of Slavery*, 4 for how this social stigma worked in the face of rapes in Kosovo.

69. See Vranic, *Breaking*, 29; Skjelsbaek, *Gendered Battlefields*, 31; Susskind, "Demanding Justice," 2; Brownmiller, *Against Our Will*, 82 for a detailed explanation of the causes of not testifying, such as shame, fear of retaliation, ostracism by families or communities, or the lack of witness protection. Also, see Igric, "Kosovo," for how the social stigma works to push women not to testify.

70. Articles 43, 54, and 57 of Part IV and Articles 64, 68, and 69 of Part VI are about witness protection. The gist of these articles is that the prosecutor will take the appropriate measures for witness protection, but whether they will be effective in protecting the women from the social stigma in their own communities, and therefore convince them to testify, remains a question. See De Brouwer, *Supranational Criminal Prosecution*, for

the procedure the ICC can follow to make rape cases easier on the victims as well as the sentencing and the reparation regime.

71. Amnesty International, *Sudan: Darfur; Democratic Republic of Congo.*

72. *The Prosecutor v. Germain Katanga and Mathieu Ngudjolo Chui; The Prosecutor v. Omar Hassan Ahmad Al Bashir; The Prosecutor v. Ahmad Muhammad Harun ("Ahmad Harun") and Ali Muhammad Ali Abd-Al-Rahman ("Ali Kushayb").* The case before the ICC, of Côte d'Ivoire against former president Laurent Gbagbo, also includes rape charges.

73. Toeka, *Sexual Violence.*

74. *The Prosecutor v. Germain Katanga and Mathieu Ngudjolo Chui.*

75. *The Prosecutor v. Thomas Lubanga Dyilo.*

76. *Justice in the Democratic Republic of Congo.*

77. Even if we start the evolution process from the Middle Ages, where in some exceptional cases rape was prohibited by the kings, it was related to the just war doctrine, noncombatant immunity, and honor, rather than the illegitimacy of the act itself. Meron, *War Crimes.*

78. Philipose, "The Laws," 56–57.

79. Engle cited in Charlesworth and Chinkin, *The Boundaries,* 57.

80. Keck and Sikkink, *Activists*; Koh, "Why Do Nations Obey."

81. See Charlesworth and Chinkin, *The Boundaries,* 55–61, 322–24.

Bibliography

". . . And the First on Rape and Sexual Assault Charges Since Tokyo." *ICTY Bulletin* 110, 15/16 (1997).

Abbott, K.W., R. O. Keohane, A. Moravcsik, A. Slaughter, and D. Snidal. "The Concept of Legalization." *International Organization* 54, 3 (2000): 401–19.

Abbott, K.W., and D. Snidal. "Hard and Soft Law in International Governance." *International Organization* 54, 3 (2000): 421–56.

Actes de la Conférence de Bruxelles 1874. Bruxelles: Société Belge de Librairie, 1899.

Adler, E., and P. M. Haas. "Epistemic Communities, World Order, and the Creation of a Reflective Research Program." In *International Policy Coordination*, Special Issue, *International Organization* 46, 1 (1992): 367–90.

Aldrich, G. H. "Comments on the Geneva Protocols." *International Review of the Red Cross* 320 (1997): 508–10.

Allen, B. *Rape Warfare: The Hidden Genocide in Bosnia-Herzegovina and Croatia.* Minneapolis: University of Minnesota Press, 1996.

———. "Whose Law?" *International Criminal Court MONITOR* 1 (July–August 1996).

Amanpour, C. "Q&A: The Impact of the Ruling." CNN, February 22, 2001. http://www.cnn.com.

Amnesty International. *Democratic Republic of Congo: Mass Rape—Time for Remedies.* October 25, 2004. http://www.amnesty.org/en/library/info/AFR62/018/2004.

———. *Sudan: Darfur: Rape as a Weapon of War: Sexual Violence and Its Consequences.* July 18, 2004. http://www.amnesty.org/en/library/info/AFR54/076/2004.

Anderson, B. S. "The Lid Comes Off: International Radical Feminism and the Revolutions of 1848." *NWSA Journal* 10, 2 (1998).

Anonymous. *A Woman in Berlin: Eight Weeks in the Conquered City: A Diary.* New York: Metropolitan Books, 2005.

Antrobus, P. *The Global Women's Movement: Origins, Issues, and Strategies.* London: Zed, 2004.

Ashley, R. K. "The Poverty of Neorealism." *International Organization* 38, 2 (1984): 225–86.

Askin, K. D. *War Crimes Against Women: Prosecution in International War Crimes Tribunals.* The Hague: Nijhoff, 1997.

Askin, K. D., and D. M. Koenig, eds. *Women and International Human Rights Law*. Vol. 1. Ardsley, N.Y.: Transnational, 1999.

Axel, D. K., M. Marrow, and K. Martinez. "Women's Caucus on International Cooperation." *International Criminal Court MONITOR*, Special Edition, 52nd General Assembly (December 1997).

Axelrod, R., and R. O. Keohane. "Achieving Cooperation under Anarchy: Strategies and Institutions." In *Cooperation Under Anarchy*, ed. K. A. Oye. Princeton, N.J.: Princeton University Press, 1986.

Balthazar, S. "Gender Crimes and the International Criminal Tribunals." *Gonzaga Journal of International Law* 10, 1 (2006): 43–48.

Bandura, A. *Aggression: A Social Learning Analysis*. Englewood Cliffs, N.J.: Prentice-Hall, 1973.

———. *Social Learning Theory*. New York: General Learning Press, 1977.

———. "Social Learning Theory of Aggression." *Journal of Communication* 28, 3 (1978): 12–29.

Bandura, A., and R. Walters. *Social Learning and Personality Development*. New York: Holt, Rinehart, 1963.

Barkan, J. "As Old as War Itself: Rape in Foca." *Dissent* 49, 1 (2002): 60–66.

Bedont, B., and K. Martinez. "Ending Impunity for Gender Crimes Under the International Criminal Court." *Brown Journal of World Affairs* 6, 1 (1999): 65–85.

Benedetti, F., and J. L. Washburn. "Drafting the International Criminal Court Treaty: Two Years to Rome and an Afterword on the Rome Diplomatic Conference." *Global Governance* 5 (1999): 1–37.

Bentwich, N. *The Law of Private Property in War*. London: Sweet and Maxwell, 1907.

Berger, R. J., P. Searles, and W. L. Neuman. "The Dimensions of Rape Reform Legislation." *Law & Society Review* 22, 2 (1988): 329–57.

Berger, T. U. "Norms, Identity, and National Security in Germany and Japan." In *The Culture of National Security*, ed. P. J. Katzenstein. New York: Columbia University Press, 1996.

Best, G. "Peace Conferences and the Century of Total War: The 1899 Hague Conference and What Came After." *International Affairs* 75, 3 (1999): 619–34.

Bettauer, R. J. *Report of the United States Delegation to the Diplomatic Conference on the Reaffirmation of International Humanitarian Law Applicable in Armed Conflicts*. Second Session, Geneva, February 3–April 18, 1975.

Bevacqua, M. *Rape on the Public Agenda: Feminism and the Politics of Sexual Assault*. Boston: Northeastern University Press, 2000.

Blanning, T. C. W. *The French Revolution in Germany: Occupation and Resistance in the Rhineland 1792–1802*. Oxford: Clarendon, 1983.

Bolt, C. *The Women's Movements in the United States and Britain from the 1790s to the 1920s*. Amherst: University of Massachusetts Press, 1993.

Bothe, M., K. J. Partsch, and W. A. Solf. *New Rules for Victims of Armed Conflicts: Commentary on the Two 1977 Protocols Additional to the Geneva Conventions of 1949*. The Hague: Nijhoff, 1982.

Broomhall, B. "An Overview of NGO Positions on Key ICC Issues." *International Criminal Court MONITOR* 8 (June 1998).

———. *International Justice and the International Criminal Court: Between Sovereignty and the Rule of Law.* New York: Oxford University Press, 2003.

Brownmiller, S. *Against Our Will: Men, Women, and Rape.* New York: Simon and Schuster, 1975.

Bugnion, F. "The Arrival of Bourbaki's Army at Les Verrières: The Internment of the First French Army in Switzerland on 1 February 1871." *International Review of the Red Cross* 311 (1996): 181–93.

Bull, H. *The Anarchical Society: A Study of Order in World Politics.* Basingstoke: Macmillan, 1977.

Bumiller, E. "Deny Rape or Be Hated: Kosovo Victims' Choice." *New York Times,* June 22, 1999.

Bunch, C. "Women's Rights as Human Rights: Toward a Re-Vision of Human Rights." *Human Rights Quarterly* 12, 4 (1990): 486–98.

Bunch, C., and N. Reilly. *Demanding Accountability: The Global Campaign and Vienna Tribunal for Women's Human Rights.* New Brunswick, N.J.: Center for Women's Global Leadership, Rutgers University, 1994.

Burgess-Jackson, K. "A History of Rape Law." In *A Most Detestable Crime: New Philosophical Essays on Rape,* ed. K. Burgess-Jackson. New York: Oxford University Press, 1999.

———. *Rape: A Philosophical Investigation.* Aldershot: Dartmouth, 1996.

Burt, M. R. *Attitudes Supportive of Rape in American Culture.* House Committee on Science and Technology, Subcommittee on Domestic and International Scientific Planning, Analysis and Cooperation, Research into Violent Behavior: Sexual Assaults. Washington, D.C.: U.S. GPO, January 10, 1978.

———. "Cultural Myths and Supports for Rape." *Journal of Personality and Social Psychology* 38, 2 (1980): 217–30.

Bury, J. B. *The Idea of Progress: An Inquiry into Its Origin and Growth.* Westport, Conn.: Greenwood, 1982.

"Bush Panel Members Quit over Looting: Cultural Advisers Say U.S. Military Could Have Prevented Museum Losses." *Washington Post,* April 17, 2003.

Card, C. "Rape as a Weapon of War." *Hypatia* 11, 4 (1996): 5–18.

Carnahan, B. M. "Lincoln, Lieber, and the Laws of War: The Origins and Limits of the Principle of Military Necessity." *American Journal of International Law* 92, 2 (1998): 213–31.

Caron, D. D. "War and International Adjudication: Reflections on the 1899 Peace Conference." *American Journal of International Law* 94, 1 (2000): 4–30.

Chang, I. *The Rape of Nanking.* New York: Penguin, 1997.

Charlesworth, H., and C. Chinkin. *The Boundaries of International Law: A Feminist Analysis.* Manchester: Manchester University Press, 2000.

Chayes, A., and A. Handler Chayes. "On Compliance." *International Organization* 47, 2 (1993): 175–205.

Clarification of the Term Gender. Women's Caucus for Gender Justice Publications, 1999.

Clark, A. "Rape or Seduction? A Controversy over Sexual Violence in the Nineteenth Century." In *The Sexual Dynamics of History: Men's Power, Women's Resistance.* London Feminist History Group. London: Pluto Press, 1983.

———. *Women's Silence, Men's Violence: Sexual Assault in England 1770–1845.* London: Pandora, 1987.

Clark, L., and D. J. Lewis. *The Price of Coercive Sexuality.* Toronto: Women's Press, 1977.

Connors, J. "NGOs and the Human Rights of Women at the United Nations." In *The Conscience of the World: The Influence of Non-Governmental Organizations in the UN System,* ed. P. Willetts. Washington, D.C.: Brookings Institution, 1996.

Coomaraswamy, R. "Reinventing International Law: Women's Rights as Human Rights in the International Community." Human Rights Program, Harvard Law School, 1997. http://www.law.harvard.edu/programs/HRP/Publications/radhika.html.

Cooper, S. *Patriotic Pacifism: Waging War on War in Europe 1815–1914.* Oxford: Oxford University Press, 1991.

Copelon, R. "Gender Crimes as War Crimes: Integrating War Crimes Against Women into International Criminal Law." *McGill Law Journal* 46 (2000): 217–40.

———. "Surfacing Gender: Reconceptualizing Crimes Against Women in Time of War." In *Mass Rape: The War Against Women in Bosnia-Herzegovina,* ed. A. Stiglmayer. Lincoln: University of Nebraska Press, 1994.

Crimes Against Women Are Crimes Against Humanity. Long Island City, N.Y.: Women's Caucus for Gender Justice, 1999.

Davis, A. *Violence Against Women and the Ongoing Challenge to Racism.* Latham, N.Y.: Kitchen Table Press, 1987.

Davis, C. D. *The United States and the First Hague Peace Conference.* Ithaca, N.Y.: Cornell University Press, 1962.

———. *The United States and the Second Hague Peace Conference.* Durham, N.C.: Duke University Press, 1976.

De Brouwer, A. M. L. M. *Supranational Criminal Prosecution of Sexual Violence: The ICC and the Practice of the ICTY and the ICTR.* Antwerp: Intersentia, 2005.

De Vries, G. "President of EP Liberal Group Outlines Needed Improvements to Statute." *International Criminal Court MONITOR* 7 (February 1998).

Decade for Women: Equality, Development, and Peace. Copenhagen: Final Report of the World Conference of the UN. New York: United Nationa, July 14, 1980.

Desan, S. *The Family on Trial in Revolutionary France.* Berkeley: University of California Press, 2004.

Djilas, M. *Conversations with Stalin.* New York: Harcourt, Brace, 1962.

Donat, P. L. N., and J. D'Emilio. "A Feminist Redefinition of Rape and Sexual Assault: Historical Foundations and Change." In *Confronting Rape and Sexual Assault,* ed. M. E. Odem and J. Clay-Warner. Lanham, Md.: Scholarly Resources, 1998.

Donnerstein, E. "Aggressive Erotica and Violence Against Women." *Journal of Personality and Social Psychology* 39, 2 (1980): 269–77.

Donnerstein, E., and L. Berkowitz. "Victim Reactions in Aggressive Erotic Films as a Factor in Violence Against Women." *Journal of Personality and Social Psychology* 41, 4 (1981): 710–24.

Downey, W. G., Jr. "Captured Enemy Property: Booty of War and Seized Enemy Property." *American Journal of International Law* 44, 3 (1950): 488–504.

Downs, G. W., D. M. Rocke, and P. N. Barsoom. "Is the Good News About Compliance Good News About Cooperation?" *International Organization* 50, 3 (1996): 379–406.

Duffy, C. *The Military Experience in the Age of Reason.* New York: Atheneum, 1988.

Eddy, M. "Rape as War Weapon." *Associated Press,* March 21, 2000. http://www.abcnews.go.com/sections/world/DailyNews/rape000321.html.

Edwards, S. M. *Female Sexuality and the Law.* Oxford: Martin Robertson, 1981.

Ellis, L. *Theories of Rape: Inquiries into the Causes of Sexual Aggression.* New York: Hemisphere, 1989.

Elshtain, J. B. *Public Man, Private Woman: Women in Social and Political Thought.* Princeton, N.J.: Princeton University Press, 1981.

———. *Women and War.* New York: Basic Books, 1987.

Engels, F. *The Origin of the Family, Private Property, and the State.* New York: International, 1972.

Engle, K. "Feminism and Its (Dis)contents: Criminalizing Wartime Rape in Bosnia and Herzegovina." *American Journal of International Law* 99, 4 (2005): 778–816.

Enloe, C. "Afterword: Have the Bosnian Rapes Opened a New Era of Feminist Consciousness?" In *Mass Rape: The War Against Women in Bosnia-Herzegovina,* ed. A. Stiglmayer. Lincoln: University of Nebraska Press, 1994.

———. *Bananas, Beaches, and Bases: Making Feminist Sense of International Politics.* Berkeley: University of California Press, 1990.

———. *Maneuvers: The International Politics of Militarizing Women's Lives.* Berkeley: University of California Press, 2000.

———. *The Morning After: Sexual Politics at the End of the Cold War.* Berkeley: University of California Press, 1993.

Estrich, S. *Real Rape.* Cambridge, Mass.: Harvard University Press, 1987.

Excluding Crimes Against Women from the ICC Is Not an Option. New York: Women's Caucus for Gender Justice Publications, 2000.

Facio, A. "A Word (or Two) About Gender." *International Criminal Court MONITOR* 6 (November 1997).

Fall, B. B. *Street Without Joy: The French Debacle in Indochina.* Harrisburg, Pa.: Stackpole, 2005.

"Family Compensated for Tate's Nazi Art." *BBC News,* January 18, 2001.

Federal Republic of Yugoslavia. Kosovo: Rape as a Weapon of "Ethnic Cleansing." Human Rights Watch Report, March 21, 2000. http://www.hrw.org/hrw/reports/2000/fry/index.htm.

Feilchenfeld, E. H. *The International Economic Law of Belligerent Occupation.* Washington, D.C.: Carnegie Endowment for International Peace, 1942.

Finnemore, M. *National Interest in International Society*. Ithaca, N.Y.: Cornell University Press, 1996.

Finnemore, M., and K. Sikkink. "International Norm Dynamics and Political Change." *International Organization* 52, 4 (1998): 887–917.

Finnemore, M., and S. J. Toope. "Alternatives to 'Legalization': Richer Views of Law and Politics." *International Organization* 55, 3 (2001): 743–58.

Fletcher, I. *In Hell Before Daylight: The Siege and Storming of the Fortress of Badajoz, 1812*. Tunbridge Wells: Howel, 1998.

Florini, A. "The Evolution of International Norms." *International Studies Quarterly* 40, 3 (1996): 363–89.

Forero, J. "Prosperous Colombians Flee, Many to U.S., to Escape War." *New York Times*, April 10, 2001.

Franck, T. M. *The Power of Legitimacy Among Nations*. New York: Oxford University Press, 1990.

Fraser, A. S. "The Convention on the Elimination of All Forms of Discrimination Against Women (The Women's Convention)." In *Women, Politics, and the United Nations*, ed. A. Winslow. Westport, Conn.: Greenwood, 1995.

———. *The UN Decade for Women: Documents and Dialogue*. Boulder, Colo.: Westview, 1987.

Freidel, F. *Francis Lieber: Nineteenth-Century Liberal*. Baton Rouge: Louisiana State University Press, 1947.

Fremont-Barnes, G. *The Napoleonic Wars: The Peninsular War 1807–1814*. Oxford: Osprey, 2002.

Frey, B. A. *A Fair Representation: Advocating for Women's Rights in the International Criminal Court*. Case. Center on Women and Public Policy, University of Minnesota, 2004.

Fukumura, Y., and M. Matsuoka. "Redefining Security: Okinawa Women's Resistance to U.S. Militarism." In *Women's Activism and Globalization: Linking Local Struggles and Transnational Politics*, ed. N. A. Naples and M. Desai. New York: Routledge, 2002.

Gaer, F. D. "And Never the Twain Shall Meet? The Struggle to Establish Women's Rights as International Human Rights." In *The International Human Rights of Women: Instruments of Change*, ed. C. E. Lockwood, D. B. Magraw, M. F. Spring, and S. I. Strong. Washington, D.C.: American Bar Association, 1998.

Garbarino, J., K. Kostelny, and N. Dubrow. *No Place to Be a Child: Growing up in a War Zone*. Lexington, Mass.: Lexington Books, 1991.

Gardam, J. "Women and Law of Armed Conflict: Why the Silence?" *International and Comparative Law Quarterly* 46, 1 (1997): 55–80.

———. "The Law of Armed Conflict: A Gendered Regime?" In *Reconceiving Reality: Women and International Law*, ed. D. G. Dallmeyer. Washington, D.C.: American Society of International Law, 1993.

Gassoumis, A., G. Lerner, and M. Marrow. "Women's Caucus Brings Crimes Against Women to Forefront of Debate." *International Criminal Court MONITOR* 4 (May 1997).

Gerhard, J. F. *Desiring Revolution: Second-Wave Feminism and the Rewriting of American Sexual Thought 1920 to 1982*. New York: Columbia University Press, 2001.

Glazier, D. W. "Ignorance Is Not Bliss: The Law of Belligerent Occupation and the U.S. Invasion of Iraq." *Rutgers Law Review* 58, 1 (2005): 121–94.

Goldsmith, J. L., and E. A. Posner. *The Limits of International Law*. New York: Oxford University Press, 2005.

Goldstein, J., and R. O. Keohane, eds. *Ideas and Foreign Policy: Beliefs, Institutions, and Political Change*. Ithaca, N.Y.: Cornell University Press, 1993.

Goldstein, J., M. Kahler, R. O. Keohane, and A. Slaughter. "Introduction: Legalization and World Politics." *International Organization* 54, 3 (2000): 385–99.

Gourevitch, P. *Politics in Hard Times*. Ithaca, N.Y.: Cornell University Press, 1986.

Grabar, V. E. *The History of International Law in Russia, 1647–1917*. Oxford: Clarendon, 1990.

Graber, D. A. *The Development of the Law of Belligerent Occupation 1863–1914*. New York: Columbia University Press, 1949.

Grant, R., and K. Newland. *Gender and International Relations*. Bloomington: Indiana University Press, 1991.

Griffith, P. *The Art of War of Revolutionary France 1789–1802*. London: Greenhill, 1998.

Groth, A. N. *Men who Rape: The Psychology of the Offender*. New York: Plenum, 1979.

Grotius, H. *The Rights of War and Peace*. Ed. R. Tuck. 3 vols. Indianapolis: Liberty Fund, 2005.

Haas, P. M. "Epistemic Communities and the Dynamics of International Environmental Cooperation." In *Regime Theory and International Relations*, ed. V. Rittberger. Oxford: Clarendon, 1993.

———. "Introduction: Epistemic Communities and International Policy Coordination." *International Organization* 46, 1 (1992): 1–35.

———. *Saving the Mediterranean: The Politics of International Environmental Cooperation*. New York: Columbia University Press, 1990.

Hasenclever, A., P. Mayer, and V. Rittberger. *Theories of International Regimes*. Cambridge: Cambridge University Press, 1997.

Hecker, E. A. *A Short History of Women's Rights: From the Days of Augustus to the Present Time*. Westport, Conn.: Greenwood, 1971.

Henkin, L. *How Nations Behave: Law and Foreign Policy*. New York: Praeger, 1968.

Herschberger, R. *Adam's Rib*. New York: Harper and Row, 1948.

Hicks, G. L. *The Comfort Women: Japan's Brutal Regime of Enforced Prostitution in the Second World War*. New York: Norton, 1995.

Higgins, A. P. *The Hague Peace Conferences and Other International Conferences Concerning the Laws and Usages of War: Texts of Conventions with Commentaries*. Cambridge: Cambridge University Press, 1909.

———. *War and the Private Citizen*. London: P.S. King, 1912.

Hillis, N. D. *German Atrocities, Their Nature and Philosophy: Studies in Belgium and France During July and August of 1917*. New York: Revell, 1918.

Hirschon, R. *Women and Property—Women as Property.* New York: St. Martin's, 1984.

Hogue, L. L. "Lieber's Military Code and Its Legacy." In *Francis Lieber and the Culture of the Mind,* ed. C. R. Mack and H. H. Lesesne. Columbia: University of South Carolina Press, 2005.

Holcombe, L. *Wives and Property: Reform of the Married Women's Property Law in Nineteenth-Century England.* Toronto: University of Toronto Press, 1983.

Hopkinson, A. "The Treatment of Civilians in Occupied Territories." In *Problems of the War 2, The Grotius Society.* London: Sweet and Maxwell, 1916–1918.

Hull, W. I. *The Two Hague Conferences and Their Contributions to International Law.* Boston: For International School of Peace, Ginn, 1908.

Hurrell, A. "International Society and the Study of Regimes." In *Regime Theory and International Relations,* ed. V. Rittberger. Oxford: Clarendon, 1993.

ICC Women News: September 2000. Women's Caucus for Gender Justice Publications, 2000.

Women's Caucus for Gender Justice. *If Hope Were Enough.* Video, Women's Caucus for Gender Justice/WITNESS, 2000.

Igric, G. "Kosovo Rape Victims Suffer Twice." *Institute for War and Peace Reporting,* June 18, 1999.

Ikenberry, J. G. "Creating Yesterday's New World Order: Keynesian 'New Thinking' and the Anglo-American Postwar Settlement." In *Ideas and Foreign Policy: Beliefs, Institutions, and Political Change,* ed. J. Goldstein and R. O. Keohane. Ithaca, N.Y.: Cornell University Press, 1993.

Ilkkaracan, P. "Doğu Anadolu'da Kadın ve Aile." In *75 Yılda Kadın ve Erkekler.* Istanbul: Tarih Vakfı Yayınları, 1998.

Inge, W. R. *Outspoken Essays.* London: Longmans, Green, 1927.

Inter-Allied Declaration Against Acts of Dispossession Committed in Territories Under Enemy Occupation and Control." 1943. http://www.lootedartcommission.com/inter-allied-declaration.

International Committee of the Red Cross. "Draft Additional Protocols to the Geneva Conventions of August 12, 1949, Commentary." October 1973.

Introduction. Women's Caucus for Gender Justice Pamphlet. New York: Women's Caucus for Gender Justice Publications, 1999.

Jeffreys, S. " 'Free from All Uninvited Touch of Men': Women's Campaigns Around Sexuality, 1880–1914." *Women's Studies International Forum* 5, 6 (1982): 629–45.

Jervis, R. "Ideas and Foreign Policy: Beliefs, Institutions, and Political Change (book reviews)." *Political Science Quarterly* 109, 5 (1994): 907–9.

Joachim, J. M. *Agenda Setting, the UN, and NGOs: Gender Violence and Reproductive Rights.* Washington, D.C.: Georgetown University Press, 2007.

———. "Shaping the Human Rights Agenda: The Case of Violence Against Women." In *Gender Politics in Global Governance,* ed. M. K. Meyer and E. Prügl. Lanham, Md.: Rowman and Littlefield, 1999.

Johnson, C. "The Okinawan Rape Incident and the End of the Cold War in East Asia." JPRI Working Paper 16. Japan Policy Research Institute, University of San Francisco Center for the Pacific Rim, 1996. http://www.jpri.org/publications/workingpapers/wp16.html.

Johnson, J. T. "Lieber and the Theory of War." In *Francis Lieber and the Culture of the Mind*, ed. C. R. Mack and H. H. Lesesne. Columbia: University of South Carolina Press, 2005.

Justice in the Democratic Republic of Congo: A Background. The Hague Justice Portal, December 17, 2009. http://www.haguejusticeportal.net/eCache/DEF/11/284.html.

Kahler, M. "Legalization as Strategy: The Asia-Pacific Case." *International Organization* 54, 3 (2000): 549–71.

Kalijarvi, T.V. "Settlements of World War I and II Compared." *Annals of the American Academy of Political and Social Science* 257, 1 (1948): 194–202.

Kalshoven, F. "State Responsibility for Warlike Acts of the Armed Forces: From Article 3 of Hague Convention IV of 1907 to Article 91 of Additional Protocol I of 1977 and Beyond." *International and Comparative Law Quarterly* 40, 4 (1991): 827–58.

"Kandinsky Painting Row Settled." *BBC News*, July 3, 2002.

Katzenstein, P. J., ed. *The Culture of National Security*. New York: Columbia University Press, 1996.

Keck, M. E., and K. Sikkink. *Activists Beyond Borders*. Ithaca, N.Y.: Cornell University Press, 1998.

Kelley, J. "Who Keeps International Commitments and Why? The International Criminal Court and Bilateral Nonsurrender Agreements." *American Political Science Review* 101, 3 (2007): 573–89.

Kenney, S.J. "New Research on Gendered Political Institutions." *Political Research Quarterly* 49, 2 (1996): 445–66.

Keohane, R. O. *After Hegemony: Cooperation and Discord in the World Political Economy*. Princeton, N.J.: Princeton University Press, 1984.

Kinkel, K. "The World's Hope for Justice." *International Criminal Court MONITOR*, Special Edition, 52nd General Assembly (December 1997).

Koh, H. H. "Why Do Nations Obey International Law? Review Essay." *Yale Law Journal* 106, 8 (1997): 2599–2659.

Kowert, P., and J. Legro. "Norms, Identity, and Their Limits: A Theoretical Reprise." In *The Culture of National Security*, ed. P. J. Katzenstein. New York: Columbia University Press, 1996.

Krasner, S., ed. *International Regimes*. Ithaca, N.Y.: Cornell University Press, 1983.

Kratochwil, F. V. *Rules, Norms, and Decisions: On the Conditions of Practical and Legal Reasoning in International Relations and Domestic Affairs*. Cambridge: Cambridge University Press, 1989.

Kratochwil, F. V., and J. G. Ruggie. "International Organization: A State of the Art on the Art of the State." *International Organization* 40, 4 (1986): 753–75.

"The League of Nations and the Laws of War." *Michigan Law Review* 19, 8 (1921): 835–48.

Legro, J. *Rethinking the World: Great Power Strategies and International Order.* Ithaca, N.Y.: Cornell University Press, 2005.

Lew, D. H. "Manchurian Booty and International Law." *American Journal of International Law* 40, 3 (1946): 584–91.

Lynn, J. A. *The Bayonets of the Republic: Motivation and Tactics in the Army of Revolutionary France, 1791–1794.* Urbana: University of Illinois Press, 1984.

MacKinnon, C. A. Comment: "Theory Is Not a Luxury." In *Reconceiving Reality: Women and International Law,* ed. D. G. Dallmeyer. Washington, D.C.: American Society of International Law, 1993.

——. "Rape, Genocide, and Women's Human Rights." In *Mass Rape: The War Against Women in Bosnia-Herzegovina,* ed. A. Stiglmayer. Lincoln: University of Nebraska Press, 1994.

——. "Turning Rape into Pornography: Postmodern Genocide." In *Mass Rape: The War Against Women in Bosnia-Herzegovina,* ed. A. Stiglmayer. Lincoln: University of Nebraska Press, 1994.

Mainardi, P. *Husbands, Wives, and Lovers: Marriage and Its Discontents in Nineteenth-Century France.* New Haven, Conn.: Yale University Press, 2003.

Malamuth, N. M. "Rape Fantasies as a Function of Exposure to Violent Sexual Stimuli." *Archives of Sexual Behavior* 10, 1 (1981): 33–47.

Malamuth, N. M., and J. Check. "The Effects of Mass Media Exposure on Acceptance of Violence Against Women: A Field Experiment." *Journal of Research in Personality* 75 (1981): 436–46.

Malamuth, N. M., and E. Donnerstein. "The Effects of Aggressive Pornographic Mass Media Stimuli." In *Advances in Experimental Social Psychology,* vol. 15, ed. L. Berkowitz. New York: Academic Press, 1982.

Malamuth, N. M., S. Haber, and S. Feshbach. "Testing Hypotheses Regarding Rape: Exposure to Sexual Violence, Sex Differences and the 'Normality' of Rape." *Journal of Research in Personality* 74 (1980): 121–37.

Mallock, W. H. *Aristocracy and Evolution.* New York: Macmillan, 1901.

March, J. G., and J. P. Olsen. *Rediscovering Institutions: The Organizational Basis of Politics.* New York: Free Press, 1989.

——. "The Institutional Dynamics of International Political Orders." *International Organization* 52, 4 (1998): 943–69.

Matthews, N. *Confronting Rape: The Feminist Anti-Rape Movement and the State.* London: Routledge, 1994.

McBride, T. "Public Authority and Private Lives: Divorce after the French Revolution." *French Historical Studies* 17, 3 (1992): 747–68.

McDougall, G. J. *Contemporary Forms of Slavery: Systematic Rape, Sexual Slavery and Slavery-like Practices During Armed Conflict.* UN Sub-Commission on the Promotion and Protection of Human Rights, 1999.

McNamara, K. R. *The Currency of Ideas: Monetary Politics in the European Union.* Ithaca, N.Y.: Cornell University Press, 1998.

Mearsheimer, J. J. "The False Promise of International Institutions." *International Security* 19, 3 (1995): 5–49.

Meron, T. "Rape as a Crime Under International Humanitarian Law." *American Journal of International Law* 87, 3 (1993): 424–28.

———. *War Crimes Law Comes of Age.* Oxford: Clarendon, 1998.

Mertus, J. "Judgment of Trial Chamber II in Kunarac, Kovac, and Vukovic Case." ASIL Insight, 2001. http://www.asil.org/insigh65.cfm.

———. "Yugoslavia Has Become an Outlaw Nation." *Chicago Tribune*, January 21, 1999.

———. Mezey, G. "Rape in War." *Journal of Forensic Psychiatry* 5, 3 (1994): 583–97.

Mill, H. T. "Enfranchisement of Women." In *Essays on Sex Equality*, ed. A. S. Rossi. Chicago: University of Chicago Press, 1970.

Mill, J. S. *The Subjection of Women.* London: Longmans, Green, 1878.

Mitchell, J. *Woman's Estate.* New York: Vintage, 1973.

Morris, M. "By Force of Arms: Rape, War, and Military Culture." *Duke Law Journal* 45, 4 (1996): 651–781.

Morrow, J. D. "When Do States Follow the Laws of War?" *American Political Science Review* 101, 3 (2007): 559–72.

Moses, C. G. *French Feminism in the Nineteenth Century.* Albany: State University of New York Press, 1984.

Müller, H. "Arguing, Bargaining, and All That: Communicative Action, Rationalist Theory, and the Logic of Appropriateness in International Relations." *European Journal of International Relations* 10, 3 (2004): 395–435.

Nabulsi, K. *Traditions of War: Occupation, Resistance, and the Law.* Oxford: Oxford University Press, 1999.

Nadelmann, E. A. "Global Prohibition Regimes: The Evolution of Norms in International Society." *International Organization* 44, 4 (1990): 479–526.

Nainar, V. "Initiatives to Influence the International Criminal Court Continue!" 2004. http://www.hrea.org/lists/women-rights/markup/msg00250.html.

"Nazi Loot Is Won Back." *BBC News*, October 21, 2000. http://news.bbc.co.uk/2/hi/europe/982698.stm.

"Netherlands Hails Return of Stolen Art." *BBC News*, April 20, 2004. http://news.bbc .co.uk/2/hi/entertainment/3640951.stm.

Niarchos, C. N. "Women, War, and Rape: Challenges Facing the International Tribunal for the Former Yugoslavia." *Human Rights Quarterly* 17, 4 (1995): 649–90.

Nietzsche, F. W. *Thus Spake Zarathustra: A Book for All and None.* New York: Algora, 2003.

Norris, P. "Work Still Needed on Crimes Against Humanity Text." *International Criminal Court MONITOR* 4 (May 1997).

"Nuremberg Trial Proceedings." Avalon Project at Yale Law School. http://www.yale .edu/lawweb/avalon/imt/imt.htm.

Objective. Women's Caucus for Gender Justice Pamphlet. New York: Women's Caucus for Gender Justice Publications, 1999.

Odell, J. S. *U.S. International Monetary Policy: Markets, Power, and Ideas as Sources of Change*. Princeton, N.J.: Princeton University Press, 1982.

Offen, K. "The Theory and Practice of Feminism in Nineteenth-Century Europe." In *Becoming Visible: Women in European History*, ed. R. Bridenthal, C. Koonz, and S. Stuard. Boston: Houghton Mifflin, 1987.

Official Records of the Diplomatic Conference on the Reaffirmation and Development of International Humanitarian Law Applicable in Armed Conflicts, Geneva (1974–1977), Volumes I-XVII. Bern: Federal Political Department, 1978.

Okin, S. M. *Women in Western Political Thought*. Princeton, N.J.: Princeton University Press, 1979.

Oldfield, S. *International Woman Suffrage: Ius Suffragii, 1913–1920*. London: Routledge, 2003.

Oosterveld, V. "Sexual Slavery and the International Criminal Court: Advancing International Law." *Michigan Journal of International Law* 25 (2004): 605–52.

Pateman, C. *The Sexual Contract*. Stanford, Calif.: Stanford University Press, 1988.

Patton, G. S., and P. D. Harkins. *War as I Knew It*. Boston: Houghton Mifflin, 1995.

"Peace Conference at The Hague 1899: Russian Circular January 11, 1899," December 30, 1898. http://www.yale.edu/lawweb/avalon/lawofwar/hague99/hag99–02.htm.

Penn, M. L., and R. Nardos. *Overcoming Violence Against Women and Girls: The International Campaign to Eradicate a Worldwide Problem*. Lanham, Md.: Rowman and Littlefield, 2003.

Perkin, J. *Women and Marriage in Nineteenth-Century England*. Chicago: Lyceum, 1989.

Perrin, N. *Dr. Bowdler's Legacy: A History of Expurgated Books in England and America*. New York: Atheneum, 1969.

Peterson, S. V. *Gendered States: Feminist (Re)Visions of International Relations Theory*. Boulder, Colo.: Lynne Rienner, 1992.

Philipose, L. "The Laws of War and Women's Human Rights." *Hypatia* 11, 4 (1996): 46–61.

Pietila, H., and J. Vickers. *Making Women Matter: The Role of the United Nations*. London: Zed, 1990.

Polian, P. *Against Their Will: The History and Geography of Forced Migrations in the USSR*. Budapest: Central European University Press, 2004.

Poolos, A. "Yugoslavia: Human Rights Advocates Say Rape Is War Crime." May 24, 1999. http://www.ess.uwe.ac.uk/Kosovo/Kosovo-Current_News189.htm.

Porter, R. "Does It Have a Historical Meaning?." In *Rape*, ed. S. Tomaselli and R. Porter. Oxford: Blackwell, 1986.

Price, R. M. "Emerging Customary Norms and Anti-Personnel Landmines." In *The Politics of International Law*, ed. C. Reus-Smith. Cambridge: Cambridge University Press, 2004.

———. "Reversing the Gun Sights: Transnational Civil Society Targets Land Mines." *International Organization* 52, 3 (1998): 613–44.

———. *The Chemical Weapons Taboo.* Ithaca, N.Y.: Cornell University Press, 1997.

Proceedings at the Laying of a Wreath on the Tomb of Hugo Grotius in the Nieuwe Kerk in the City of Delft. The Hague: Nijhoff, 1899.

McDonald, James."Punishing Rape as a War Crime. Letter to the Editor. *San Francisco Chronicle*, 27 February 2001." *ICC Update*, March 15, 2001.

Pustogarov, V. "Fyodor Fyodorovich Martens (1845–1909): A Humanist of Modern Times." *International Review of the Red Cross* 312 (1996): 300–314.

Quynn, D. M. "The Art Confiscations of the Napoleonic Wars." *American Historical Review* 50, 3 (1945): 437–60.

Ramos, H., J. Ron, and O. N. T. Thoms. "Shaping the Northern Media's Human Rights Coverage, 1986–2000." *Journal of Peace Research* 44, 4 (2007): 385–406.

Rape Is a War Crime: How to Support the Survivors. Vienna Conference Report, International Centre for Migration Policy Development, June 20, 1999.

Raymond, G. A. "Lieber and the International Laws of War." In *Francis Lieber and the Culture of the Mind*, ed. C. R. Mack and H. H. Lesesne. Columbia: University of South Carolina Press, 2005.

———. "Problems and Prospects in the Study of International Norms." *Mershon International Studies Review* 41, 2 (1997): 205–45.

Redlich, F. *De Praeda Militari, Pillage and Booty 1500–1815.* Wiesbaden: Franz Steiner, 1956.

Regan, L., and L. Kelly. "Rape: Still a Forgotten Issue (Briefing Document for Strengthening the Linkages: Consolidating the European Network Project)." London Metropolitan University, 2003.

Reiss, E. *Rights and Duties of Englishwomen: A Study in Law and Public Opinion.* Manchester: Sherrat and Hughes, 1934.

Renault, L. (1908). "The Work at The Hague in 1899 and in 1907, Nobel Lecture." In *Peace, 1901–1925*, ed. F. W. Haberman, 1901–1925. Amsterdam: Elsevier, 1972.

Reus-Smith, C. "Introduction." In *The Politics of International Law*, ed. C. Reus-Smith. Cambridge: Cambridge University Press, 2004.

Risse, T., and K. Sikkink. "The Power of Principles: The Socialization of Human Rights Norms into Domestic Practices." In *The Power of Human Rights: International Norms and Domestic Change*, ed. T. Risse, S. C. Ropp, and K. Sikkink. Cambridge: Cambridge University Press, 1999.

Rochon, T. R. *Culture Moves: Ideas, Activism, and Changing Values.* Princeton, N.J.: Princeton University Press, 1998.

Rome Statute of the International Criminal Court: Overview." http://untreaty.un.org/cod/icc/general/overview.htm.

Rose, V. M. "Rape as a Social Problem: A Byproduct of the Feminist Movement." *Social Problems* 25, 1 (1977): 75–89.

Rosenne, S. *The Hague Peace Conferences of 1899 and 1907 and International Arbitration: Reports and Documents.* The Hague: TMC Asser Press, 2001.

Rothfield, L. *The Rape of Mesopotamia.* Chicago: University of Chicago Press, 2009.

Rousseau, J. J. *Discourse on the Origin and Foundations of Inequality Among Men*, 1754.
———. *The Social Contract*, 1762.
Rumsfeld, D. H., and R. B. Myers. Department of Defense News Briefing, April 11, 2003. http://www.defense.gov/transcripts/transcript.aspx?transcriptid=2367.
Rupp, L. J. "Constructing Internationalism: The Case of Transnational Women's Organizations, 1888–1945." *American Historical Review* 99, 5 (1994): 1571–1600.
———. *Worlds of Women: The Making of an International Women's Movement*. Princeton, N.J.: Princeton University Press, 1997.
Ryan, A. *Property*. Minneapolis: University of Minnesota Press, 1987.
Saland, P. "International Criminal Law Principles." In *The International Criminal Court: The Making of the Rome Statute: Issues, Negotiations, Results*, ed. R. S. Lee. The Hague: Kluwer Law, 1999.
Sanday, P. R. "Rape-Free Versus Rape-Prone." In *Evolution, Gender, and Rape*, ed. C. Brown-Travis. Cambridge, Mass.: MIT Press, 2003.
Schabas, W. A. *An Introduction to the International Criminal Court*. Cambridge: Cambridge University Press, 2004.
Scheffer, D. "Rape as War Crime." October 29, 1999. http://www.flora.org/flora.mai-not/17296.
Schlichtmann, K. "Japan, Germany, and the Idea of The Hague Peace Conferences." *Journal of Peace Research* 40, 4 (2003): 377–94.
Schwendinger, J. R., and H. Schwendinger. *Rape and Inequality*. Beverly Hills, Calif.: Sage, 1983.
Scott, J. B., ed. *The Hague Conventions and Declarations of 1899 and 1907*. Oxford: Oxford University Press, 1915.
———. *The Proceedings of The Hague Peace Conferences: Translation of the Official Texts. The Conference of 1899*. New York: Oxford University Press, 1920.
———. *The Proceedings of The Hague Peace Conferences: Translation of the Official Texts. The Conference of 1907, Volumes I, II and III*. New York: Oxford University Press, 1920.
Scully, P. *Liberating the Family? Gender and British Slave Emancipation in the Rural Western Cape, South Africa, 1823–1853*. Portsmouth: Heinemann, 1997.
Seifert, R. "War and Rape: A Preliminary Analysis." In *Mass Rape: The War Against Women in Bosnia-Herzegovina*, ed. A. Stiglmayer. Lincoln: University of Nebraska Press, 1994.
Shanley, M. L. *Feminism, Marriage, and the Law in Victorian England, 1850–1895*. Princeton, N.J.: Princeton University Press, 1989.
Simmons, B. A. "Capacity, Commitment, and Compliance: International Institutions and Territorial Disputes." *Journal of Conflict Resolution* 46, 6 (2002): 829–56.
———. "International Law and State Behavior: Commitment and Compliance in International Monetary Affairs." *American Political Science Review* 94, 4 (2000): 819–35.
Simpson, E., ed. *Spoils of War*. New York: Harry Abrams, 1997.
Skelley, A. R. *The Victorian Army at Home: The Recruitment and the Terms and Conditions of the British Regular, 1859–1899*. London: Croom Helm, 1977.

Skjelsbæk, I. *Gendered Battlefields: A Gender Analysis of Peace and Conflict*. Oslo: Peace Research Institute Oslo (PRIO), 1997.

Smart, C. "Disruptive Bodies and Unruly Sex: The Regulation of Reproduction and Sexuality in the Nineteenth Century." In *Regulating Womanhood: Historical Essays on Marriage, Motherhood, and Sexuality*, ed. C. Smart. London: Routledge, 1992.

Smith, A. *An Inquiry into the Nature and Causes of the Wealth of Nations (1776)*. Ed. R. H. Campbell and A. S. Skinner. Indianapolis: Liberty Fund, 1981.

Smith, P. "Social Revolution and the Persistence of Rape." In *A Most Detestable Crime: New Philosophical Essays on Rape*, ed. K. Burgess-Jackson. New York: Oxford University Press, 1999.

Solzhenitsyn, A. I. *The Gulag Archipelago 1918–1956*. New York: HarperCollins, 2002.

Spadafora, D. *The Idea of Progress in Eighteenth-Century Britain*. New Haven, Conn.: Yale University Press, 1990.

"Special Rapporteur on Violence Against Women, Its Causes and Consequences." Office of the United Nations High Commissioner for Human Rights. http://www2.ohchr .org/english/issues/women/rapporteur/.

Spees, P. "Many Gender Issues Remain to be Resolved at the June Prepcom." *International Criminal Court MONITOR* 15 (June 2000).

Steains, C. "Gender Issues." In *The International Criminal Court: The Making of the Rome Statute: Issues, Negotiations, Results*, ed. R. S. Lee. The Hague: Kluwer Law, 1999.

Stein, A. A. *Why Nations Cooperate: Circumstances and Choice in International Relations*. Ithaca, N.Y.: Cornell University Press, 1990.

Stiglmayer, A. "The War in the Former Yugoslavia." In *Mass Rape: The War Against Women in Bosnia-Herzegovina*, ed. A. Stiglmayer. Lincoln: University of Nebraska Press, 1994.

Strange, S. "Cave! Hic Dragones: A Critique of Regime Analysis." *International Organization* 36, 2 (1982): 479–96.

Strumpen-Darrie, C. "Rape: A Survey of Current International Jurisprudence." *Human Rights Brief* 7, 3 (2000): 12–14, 17.

Sullivan, D. J. "Women's Human Rights and the 1993 World Conference on Human Rights." *American Journal of International Law* 88, 1 (1994): 152–67.

"Summary Records of the Meetings of the Forty-Sixth Session, 2 May–22 July 1994, 2350th meeting, 7 June 1994, Twelfth Report of the Special Rapporteur." In *Yearbook of the International Law Commission, 1994*. New York: United Nations, 1996.

Sunstein, C. R. *Free Markets and Social Justice*. New York: Oxford University Press, 1997.

Susskind, Y. "Demanding Justice: Rape and Reconciliation in Rwanda." *MADRE Newsletter*, Winter 1997/98.

Taylor, T. *Nuremberg and Vietnam: An American Tragedy*. New York: Bantam, 1970.

Testimonies of the Global Tribunal on Violations of Women's Human Rights. Highland Park, Ill.: Center for Women's Global Leadership, 1994.

The Hague Appeal for Peace. "When did the Conference Take Place?" http://www .haguepeace.org/index.php?action=history&subAction=conf&selection=when.

The Prosecutor v. Akayesu (ICTR-96-4-I) (Judgment of ICTR-96-4-T).

The Prosecutor v. Delalic and Delic (Celebici case) (Judgment of ICTY-96-21-T).

The Prosecutor v. Furundzija (Judgment of ICTY-95-17/1).

The Prosecutor v. Gagovic et al. (ICTY-96-23).

The Prosecutor v. Germain Katanga and Mathieu Ngudjolo Chui (ICC-01/04-01/07).

The Prosecutor v. Kunarac, Kovac, and Vukovic (Trio case) (Judgment of ICTY-IT-96-23 and IT-96-23/1).

The Prosecutor v. Thomas Lubanga Dyilo (ICC-01/04-01/06)

Thornhill, R., and C. T. Palmer. *A Natural History of Rape: Biological Bases of Sexual Coercion.* Cambridge, Mass.: MIT Press, 2000.

Tickner, A. J. *Gender in International Relations: Feminist Perspectives on Achieving Global Security.* New York: Columbia University Press, 1992.

Timm, A. F. "Sex with a Purpose: Prostitution, Venereal Disease, and Militarized Masculinity in the Third Reich." In *Sexuality and German Fascism*, ed. D. Herzog. New York: Berghahn, 2005.

Tinker, I. "NGOs: An Alternative Power Base for Women." In *Gender Politics in Global Governance*, ed. M. K. Meyer and E. Prügl. Lanham, Md.: Rowman and Littlefield, 1999.

Toeka, T. *Sexual Violence Charges for DRC Cases Scrapped: Human Rights Groups Warn Controversial Move Could Lead to a Culture of Impunity.* Institute for War and Peace Reporting, June 3, 2008. http://iwpr.net/report-news/sexual-violence-charges-drc-cases-scrapped.

Tomaselli, S., and R. Porter, eds. *Rape: An Historical and Cultural Enquiry.* Oxford: Blackwell, 1986.

"Troops 'Vandalise' Ancient City of Ur." *The Observer*, May 18, 2003.

Trustram, M. "Distasteful and Derogatory? Examining Victorian Soldiers for Venereal Disease." In *The Sexual Dynamics of History: Men's Power, Women's Resistance*. London Feminist History Group. London: Pluto Press, 1983.

United Nations Diplomatic Conference of Plenipotentiaries on the Establishment of an International Criminal Court Rome, 15 June–17 July 1998, Official Records, Volumes I–III. New York: United Nations, 2002.

The United Nations and the Advancement of Women, 1945–1996. Intro. Boutros Boutros-Ghali. UN Blue Book Series. New York: United Nations, rev. ed. 1996.

U.S. Department of State. *Serbia-Montenegro Country Report on Human Rights Practices for 1998.* Bureau of Democracy, Human Rights, and Labor, February 26, 1999. http://www.state.gov/www/global/human_rights/1998_hrp_report/serbiamo.html.

"U.S. Troops 'Encouraged' Iraqi Looters." *BBC News*, May 6, 2003.

Van Der Vyver, D. "Civil Society and the International Criminal Court." *Journal of Human Rights* 2, 3 (2003): 425–39.

Vienna Declaration and Programme of Action. Adopted by World Conference on Human Rights, 25 June 1993.

Vigarello, G. *A History of Rape: Sexual Violence in France from the 16th Century to the 20th Century.* Cambridge: Polity Press, 2001.

Vito, G. F., J. R. Maahs, and R. M. Holmes. *Criminology: Theory, Research, and Policy.* Sudbury: Jones and Bartlett, 2007.

Vogel, U. "Whose Property? The Double Standard of Adultery in Nineteenth-Century Law." In *Regulating Womanhood: Historical Essays on Marriage, Motherhood, and Sexuality,* ed. C. Smart. London: Routledge, 1992.

Von Glahn, G. *The Occupation of Enemy Territory.* Minneapolis: University of Minnesota Press, 1957.

Von Müffling, C. *The Memoirs of Baron von Müffling: A Prussian Officer in the Napoleonic Wars.* London: Greenhill, 1997.

Vranic, S. *Breaking the Wall of Silence.* Zagreb: Izdanja Antibarbarus, 1996.

Wagar, W. W. *Good Tidings: The Belief in Progress from Darwin to Marcuse.* Bloomington: Indiana University Press, 1972.

———. "Modern Views of the Origins of the Idea of Progress." *Journal of the History of Ideas* 28, 1 (1967): 55–70.

Walters, M. *Feminism: A Very Short Introduction.* Oxford: Oxford University Press, 2005.

"War Crimes Treaty Stalls over Inclusion of Rape." *International Herald Tribune,* July 10, 1998.

Warren, J. "War and the Cultural Heritage of Iraq: A Sadly Mismanaged Affair." *Third World Quarterly* 26, 4 (2005): 815–30.

Watt, N., I. Traynor, and M. O'Kane. "Serbs Have Rape Camp, Says Cook." *Guardian,* April 14, 1999.

Wendt, A. *Social Theory of International Politics.* Cambridge: Cambridge University Press, 1999.

Wendt, A., and R. Duvall. "Institutions and International Order." In *Global Changes and Theoretical Challenges: Approaches to the World Politics for the 1990s,* ed. E. O. Czempiel and J. N. Rosenau. Lexington, Mass.: Lexington Books, 1989.

White, A. D. *The Hague Peace Conference.* Boston: World Peace Foundation, 1912.

Whittick, A. *Woman into Citizen.* London: Athenaeum with Frederick Muller, 1979.

"Who We Are and What We Do: Our History." Coalition for the International Criminal Court. http://www.iccnow.org/?mod=cicchistory.

"Who Were the Comfort Women? The Establishment of Comfort Stations." Digital Museum—The Comfort Women Issue and the Asian Women's Fund. http://www.awf.or.jp/e1/facts-01.html, accessed May 16, 2008.

Willetts, P. "Consultative Status for NGOs at the United Nations." In *The Conscience of the World: The Influence of Non-Governmental Organizations in the UN System,* ed. P. Willetts. Washington, D.C: Brookings Institution, 1996.

Woloch, I. *Eighteenth-Century Europe, Tradition and Progress: 1715–1789.* New York: Norton, 1982.

"Women 2000—Sexual Violence and Armed Conflict: United Nations Response." UN Division for the Advancement of Women Department of Economic and Social Affairs Publication, April 1998.

"Women and Violence." UN Department of Public Information, February 1996. http://www.un.org/rights/dpi1772e.htm

Woolsey, L. H. "The Forced Transfer of Property in Enemy Occupied Territories." *American Journal of International Law* 37, 2 (1943): 282–86.

Young, O. R. "The Effectiveness of International Governance Systems." In *International Governance, Protecting the Environment in a Stateless Society*, ed. O. R. Young. Ithaca, N.Y.: Cornell University Press, 1994.

———. "The Politics of International Regime Formation: Managing Natural Resources and the Environment." *International Organization* 43, 3 (1989): 349–75.

Yusuf, Y. K. "Rape-Related English and Yoruba Proverbs." *Women and Language* 21, 2 (1998): 39–42.

Zillmann, D. *Connections Between Sex and Aggression*. Hillsdale, N.J.: Erlbaum, 1984.

Archives

(SFA) Swiss Federal Archives, Bern.

(ICRC-A) International Committee of the Red Cross Archives, Geneva.

(SSC) Sophia Smith Collection, Smith College Library, Northampton, Massachusetts.

(CICC-A) Archives of the Coalition for the International Criminal Court, http://www.iccnow.org/?mod=documents.

Interviews

Interview with observer at Rome (1998), Beijing (1995), and Vienna (1993), May 10, 2007.

Interview with member of the CICC, July 27, 2007.

Interview with leader in women's movement, September 11, 2007.

Interview with former member of Women's Caucus, February 6, 2008.

Acknowledgments

Writing this book was the longest journey of my life and I would like to take this opportunity to thank the people who were there throughout; without their support, encouragement and guidance, I could not have done this.

Professor Kathryn Sikkink's knowledge, vision, and personal support made this project possible. She guided me in so many ways that I cannot imagine how this book (or myself) would be without her light. I would also like to thank Professor Mary Dietz for her invaluable mentorship, never letting my brain get numb, and listening to my never-ending worries. I am thankful to Professor Sally Kenney for believing in me through the ups and downs of the last thirteen years. Without her encouragement and guidance I would not have found my interest in women's movements or known how to write about them.

Professor Colin Kahl, my friends at the University of Minnesota, and Peter Agree at the University of Pennsylvania Press helped me enormously.

Many thanks to my husband, Hakan Inal, for his love and support. I also thank my babies, Alim and Beka, for being the joys of my life.

I dedicate this book to my parents, Sule and Latif Cilingiroglu, who have gone beyond believing in me and beyond being behind me. No parent can be as devoted as they are and I wish I could dedicate to them more than a book.

The writing of this book was supported by a Peace Scholar award from the United States Institute of Peace. The views expressed in this book are those of the author and do not necessarily reflect the views of the United States Institute of Peace. My fieldwork in Geneva and Bern was supported by the MacArthur Interdisciplinary Program on Global Change, Sustainability and Justice.

CPSIA information can be obtained at www.ICGtesting.com
Printed in the USA
BVOW01s1951240716

456334BV00002B/5/P